THEM OR US

Patrick Lucanio

THEM
OR
US

Archetypal
Interpretations of
Fifties Alien
Invasion Films

Indiana University Press

BLOOMINGTON AND INDIANAPOLIS

MANUFACTURED IN THE UNITED STATES OF AMERICA

Library of Congress Cataloging-in-Publication Data

Lucanio, Patrick.
  Them or us.

  Filmography: p.
  Bibliography: p.
  Includes index.
  1. Science fiction films—History and criticism.
2. Horror films—History and criticism. 3. Monsters
in motion pictures. I. Title.
PN1995.9.S26L8 1987   791.43'09'09356   86-43049
ISBN 0-253-35871-X
ISBN 0-253-20435-6 (pbk.)
1 2 3 4 5 91 90 89 88 87

To my parents, and especially to Barbara,
who taught me the true meaning of Love

To the man who loves art for its own sake, it is frequently in its least important and lowliest manifestations that the keenest pleasure is to be derived.

Sherlock Holmes, in
The Copper Beeches

CONTENTS

Preface

Can films with such titles as *The Crawling Eye, Attack of the Fifty Foot Woman, Gog,* and *The Blob* transcend their presumed exploitative absurdity to genuinely express true meaning and value to their audiences? That is the question I intend to answer in this study, which is an investigation into a film genre that has been ignored at best and despised at worst: the "monster movie," or what I prefer to call the alien invasion film.

As a work of critical film history, this study has a twofold purpose. First, I intend to show that there exists a specific body of films, separate from the horror film, that is best described as the alien invasion film and best understood as a distinct part of the science fiction genre. Moreover, I will show that C. G. Jung's analytical psychology is the proper methodology for the interpretation of meaning and value in the science fiction genre and hence in the alien invasion film as well. Second, and in a much narrower and more circumscribed sense, I offer Jungian psychology as a practical and meaningful methodology for the study of films which, like the alien invasion film, have too often been excluded from critical assessment for vague and arbitrary reasons, foremost of which is their ostentatious rejection because the titles alone imply some kind of irresponsible, tasteless, and inconsequential formula. I make this offer not to debase Jung, as his sycophants might contend, but rather to elevate these forgotten films to at least a level of understanding from which true aesthetic value may arise. As a contribution to film criticism, my study, I trust, will further verify the importance of the aesthetic principles derived from Jungian psychology.

Since my first purpose is to show that the alien invasion film (including all the films about space invaders, giant insects, and revived prehistoric monsters) is a distinct subgenre of the science fiction genre and, as a corollary, that the science fiction genre itself is independent of the horror genre, I first reexamine the tradition of genre criticism as it relates to the horror film and the science fiction film. I believe that the qualities of both the horror film and the science fiction film are best appreciated in the psychological context, because each genre relies upon the projection of psychic material from the unconscious to elicit its meaning and value. Genre criticism has maintained that the monsters and aliens in both horror and science fiction genres are best seen as projections from the repressed unconscious described by Sigmund Freud. I contend, however, that these creatures in the alien invasion film are rather projections from the collective unconscious described by Jung. As such, alien invasion films are rich, in the Jungian sense, with universal symbols of transformation that evoke shared symbolic qualities in their audiences. Such mythic concepts as hero and contest, death and rebirth hold fascinating truths for the films and for the audiences who watch them.

My emphasis is on the components that make up the alien invasion genre. I have examined these films fully, and I have elicited the particular myths, motifs, iconography, and conventions, in terms of Jungian aesthetics and myth criticism, that coalesce to define and shape the genre. We will discover that two basic narrative patterns, or myths, comprise the alien invasion film, and that these patterns of delineation join with the visual imagery and thematic constructs to define the genre. I also examine the often censured "ridiculousness" of many of the films, concluding, however, that the films' own exploitative absurdity is part of the value in these films. What may be described as ridiculous in these films actually becomes profound. In addition, we will discover how the alien invasion film works to elicit true meaning and value by comprehensively analyzing two representative films, *Fiend without a Face*, a 1958 British production directed by Arthur Crabtree, and *Invaders from Mars*, a 1953 American color production directed by William Cameron Menzies.

I have allowed the films to speak for themselves, as it were, by avoiding the use of publicity stills as illustrations whenever possible and using frame enlargements. My intention is to document textual assertions by offering direct and best evidence from the films themselves.

A task of this nature is seldom the product of a single effort. I owe much to many who have through the years supplied me with prints for screening, access to memorabilia collections, notes and monographs, and moral support. Special thanks are due the following: All my friends at the University of Oregon, particularly Ron Sherriffs, Ellen Seiter, and Sharon Sherman for their valuable comments on and support for the project; Bill Willingham, who got me started and organized on the project; and my good friend Bill Cadbury for his patience, perseverence, and invaluable comments on and criticisms of the manuscript. Also, thanks are due Don Fredericksen of Cornell University for sharing his priceless insights into Jung and film; my good friend Gary W. Coville for access to his massive collection of radio and television works and to his monograph on the detective story in film, radio, and television; Ken Eilers and Gene Lanz for their assistance with producing the frame enlargements, a task made all the more difficult by scratched, grainy, and poor contrast prints; and Richard Gordon of Gordon Films for sharing last-minute production data for his wonderful alien invasion film, *Fiend without a Face*, and for permission to reproduce the poster art from the film. And finally, a simple thank you to Dave Henry, Bob Rolfe-Redding, Denise Houser, Glen Moore, Margaret Kelley, and Bob Schiopen, who aided and supported this project in their own special ways.

THEM OR US

Science Fiction
and Horror

The proliferation of science fiction films is one of the most interesting developments in post–World War II film history. An estimated 500 film features and shorts made between 1948 and 1962 can be indexed under the broad heading of science fiction. One might argue convincingly that never in the history of motion pictures has any other genre developed and multiplied so rapidly in so brief a period. And, as Paul Michael comments, "On a sheer statistical basis, the number of fantasy and horror films [and he includes science fiction here] of the 1950s . . . has not been equaled in any country before or since."[1] Moreover, Alan Frank observes that the 1950s "saw science fiction at its peak in terms of sheer output and diversity of theme and diversification into various subgenres, notably the monster picture."[2]

It is the "monster picture" that is the chief concern of this study. Whereas both science fiction and horror films have a long and distinguished history in terms of theory and critical assessment, dating back to Georges Méliès and the very origins of film,[3] the monster movie, or what I prefer to call the alien invasion film, is a product, in terms of development and output, of one particular decade, the fifties. Moreover, the alien invasion film, unlike the horror film and various other science fiction subgenres (including the films of the future and of space exploration), has been the subject of scant and supercilious attention. Vivian Sobchack, in *The Limits of Infinity: The American Science Fiction Film*, succinctly states the typical critic's attitude when she describes monster movies as "embarrassments" that "come under the most critical fire and are—in fact—often hated, usually for the least objective of reasons."[4]

In light of this contemptuous attitude toward the alien invasion film, this study intends to show that alien invasion films are properly a subgenre of science fiction separate from the horror genre and that C. G. Jung's analytical psychology is the proper methodology to use in seeking the meaning inherent in these films. As a first step, I will examine the history of science fiction and horror criticism with regard to its treatment of the characteristics of the genre and will look at the tradition of genre criticism itself with regard to its treatment of questions of meaning and value in films. My goal at this point is to show that no rationally grounded consensus exists on the differences between science fiction and horror films, though there should be one. Genre critics have not made a clear distinction between science fiction and horror, either in terms of the meaning inherent in the genres as such or in terms of the aesthetic value characteristic of works in these genres.

The tradition of science fiction and horror criticism as it relates specifically to the characteristics of each genre is rooted deeply in the acceptance of science fiction and horror as synonymous. At best, science fiction is considered an offshoot of the broad notion of horror (Fig. I.1). William Johnson summarizes this point: "When applied to films, the term [science fiction] may be used so loosely that it becomes meaningless. . . . There is no clearly recognized border between SF and such genres as fantasy and horror."[5] Philip Strick laments that "the range [of definitions] is indicative of indecision rather than of a wish to encompass all preferences and make everybody happy."[6] And Jeff Rovin writes that "*Science fiction* is, at best, a very subjective label. . . . It is, therefore, best that people build their own definitions."[7]

Perhaps most indicative of the reluctance of writers and critics to distinguish horror and science fiction is the inclusion of science fiction in studies that purport to deal exclusively with the horror genre. In *The Illustrated History of the Horror Film*, which was one of the first books to take a serious approach to its subject, Carlos Clarens devotes an entire chapter ("Keep Watching the Skies") to the science fiction film. Frank Manchel's *Terrors of the Screen* discusses, in the context of the "terror film," such diverse works as Hitchcock's *Psycho*, George Pal and Irving Pichel's *Destination Moon*, and Jack Arnold's *Tarantula*. Alan Frank's *Horror Movies* and *Horror Films* and Denis Gifford's *A Pictorial History of the Horror Movies* discuss alien invasion films. William K. Everson's *Classics of the Horror Film* includes discussions of James Whale's *Frankenstein*, Rouben Mamoulian's *Dr. Jekyll and Mr. Hyde*, and Ernest B. Schoedsack's *Dr. Cyclops*—all of which are best seen as alien invasion films. And S. S. Prawer's *Caligari's Children: The Film as Tale of Terror*, in discussing the evolution of the horror film, includes "five thematic categories" of science fiction films. What makes this listing all the more revealing is that recent works on science fiction, including those by

Fig. I.1. Advertisement for one of many science fiction and horror midnight shows of the fifties. In this rare instance, the two genres are considered distinct and are pitted against each other, presumably for designation as the more frightening of the two.

Strick, Rovin, and Johnson and John Baxter's *Science Fiction in the Cinema,* do not respond in kind. Few works dealing with science fiction ever discuss the traditional horror film, and no work calling itself an investigation into science fiction ever discusses films like *Dracula, The Mummy, The Wolf Man,* and *The Exorcist.* Clearly, the proper inference is that most critics simply see science fiction as a branch of the horror film (Fig. I.2).

That is not to say that distinctions are never made.[8] When a distinction is attempted, however, it often appears in the context of treatments of the horror genre. Critics, after having identified crucial characteristics of the horror genre, often describe certain traits of science fiction as variations of the general characteristics of horror. That is particularly so when they describe the alien invasion theme as nothing more than a variation on the theme of the horror genre proper. They seem to think that a monster is just a monster no matter what its form or motivation

Fig. I.2. If scholars and critics have trouble pigeonholing the alien invasion film, the films themselves have little trouble identifying with science fiction, as these title cards from coming attractions trailers show: above, a) *Invasion of the Body Snatchers,* b) *Attack of the Fifty Foot Woman;* below, c) *Killers from Space,* d) *Tarantula.*

and no matter what the general purport of the film in which it appears. Clarens has such a view when he claims that science fiction became outmoded and "a new element added itself to science fiction: horror."[9] This traditional view is narrow, for it fails to consider the most significant aspect of the alien invasion film: The monsters do not just add to science fiction; they make it different.

The tradition of criticism that seeks to discover meaning and value in the horror and science fiction genres through an application of the principles of Freudian psychoanalysis has a long history. Most critics point to the horror genre as a manifestation of libidinal repression.[10] "The cinema of horror concretizes this nightmare world—our abstract fears of destruction and death," as Stanley Solomon argues.[11] And, as Stuart Kaminsky believes, horror films "are overwhelmingly concerned with the fear of death and the loss of identity in modern society."[12] Although neither of these writers specifically cites Freud as his source, the correlation nonetheless becomes clear when their notions are expounded in the context of Freudian theories about the fear of death. Harvey B. Greenberg, in *The Movies on Your Mind*, argues that the horror film "often lays the blame for blowing the lid off the Id within the unquiet spirit of the candidate for monsterdom, and/or upon malignant outside spirits."[13] Hence, to the horror film critic, repressed fears and desires are crucial to a proper understanding of the genre.

With respect to science fiction, criticism also emphasizes a strain of repression. Solomon argues that there is no actual difference between science fiction and horror, but just a variation of the theme of fear; moreover, this fear derives "from suppressed fears within every individual and differs for each of us, at least in its details."[14] Kaminsky remarks that science fiction extols the "fear of life and future,"[15] the opposite of the "fear of death" notion common to the horror film.

Freud's theory about repressed fears has been clearly linked to the science fiction film by Margaret Tarratt in her essay "Monsters from the Id." She writes that science fiction is not so much social comment as it is "the dramatization of the individual's anxiety about his own repressed sexual desires, which are incompatible with the morals of civilized life."[16]

Finally, Susan Sontag, in her essay on science fiction, "The Imagination of Disaster," argues that the dominant theme in science fiction films, which she links to the dominant theme of horror films, is that of impending disaster, what she describes as "the aesthetics of destruction."[17] Sontag, then, sees the science fiction film as a perverse celebration of the conquest of the fear of death, what Greenberg describes as "blowing the lid off the Id" or, simply put, overcoming repression.

The gist is that the tradition of horror and science fiction criticism, a tradition that ignores the difference between them, is based on a Freudian dogma concerning the depiction of our repressed fears and desires. When the alien invasion film is discussed (which is rare, since most critics, for one reason or another, dismiss the genre as a "juvenile exercise in special effects"[18]), it is discussed in terms of the horror genre. Solomon exemplifies such an approach:

> Science fiction films differ from true horror films, though they both frequently employ monsters, in that the implicit danger in the former is supposed to originate in the outer world and to be dealt with accordingly, whereas the dangers in the world of the horror film are symbols of our nightmares, projections of our own inner reality—even though the necessity of the cinematic form requires, in most cases, some overtly corporeal menace. The horror film aims at psychological effects, the science fiction film at logical possibilities.[19]

The emphasis is on Freud's ideas about libidinal anxiety. Anxiety, or fear, is the foundation on which both the horror film and the science fiction film are, to these critics and many others, meaningfully based; fear, to these critics, elicits meaning and value in these heretofore overlapping genres. To differentiate horror from science fiction is not to distinguish the two as separate genres; rather, it is to recognize, as Solomon has done, the separate but equal *projections* of fear. Thus, the horror film relies on the presentation within an irrational milieu of symbols that easily bear a Freudian interpretation and thus delineate the psychological workings of repressed fears. The expressionistic designs and exaggerated characterizations found in such films as Robert Wiene's *The Cabinet of Dr. Caligari* (1919) and Edgar G. Ulmer's *The Black Cat* (1934) become metaphors for material within the id. Likewise, the science fiction film relies, according to this scheme, on the presentation of naturalistic images within an easily recognized milieu, such as a major city, to delineate comparable psychological workings of repressed fears. Realistic designs, like those found in George Pal's pseudo documentaries on space travel, *Destination Moon* (1950) and *Conquest of Space* (1955), and naturalistic characterizations become similes for material within the id. As interesting and basically sound as these descriptions are, we must remember that such a distinction is merely an assessment of each film's unique projection of libidinal anxiety.

Horror: The Alternate World

The horror film can be differentiated from the science fiction film by looking at the presentational qualities of each. Horror exists within what I call the alternate world, while science fiction, as Solomon has implied, exists within the continuous world.

The most important characteristic of the horror film[20] is its emphasis on an alternate state of the actual world. In the horror films produced over the past fifty years one finds an exotic, often European setting and equally exotic characters, which coalesce to form an alternate world. Moreover, the monster/villain of the horror film represents what the film presumes to be absolute evil: an incarnation, as it were, of the devil. Set against this evil is the hero/protagonist, who represents what the film's value system insists upon as absolute good; the hero, if not a representation of Christ, is at least an angel sent to combat evil through an apocalyptic confrontation.

Any examination of the traditional horror film will reveal its exotic settings and characters, presentational qualities that encourage a sense of estrangement from the real world. Each quality complements the other; the use of one without the other does not produce the horror film.

Transylvania is perhaps the quintessential setting of the horror film. Although Transylvania is an actual geographic area of Romania, its reality is negligible. As Elizabeth MacAndrew notes in *The Gothic Tradition in Fiction*, what is essential to the horror story is an isolated environment derived from literature or painting and not from nature: a "dream landscape of a closed world separated from that of everyday; a symbolic landscape within the ordinary 'world' [whose purpose is to] convey mood, tone, and emotions."[21] Transylvania emerges from the cinema as a representational idea rather than a naturalistic reproduction. The creation of just such a setting is indeed one of the most obvious and appealing aspects of the horror film produced during the thirties and forties (Fig. I.3). Such films as Tod Browning's *Dracula* (1931), Lambert Hillyer's *Dracula's Daughter* (1936), George Waggner's *The Wolf Man* (1941), Robert Siodmak's *Son of Dracula* (1943), and Lew Landers's *The Return of the Vampire* (1944) provide imaginative and exotic settings: twisted trees with moss hanging ominously from other-

Fig. I.3. Studio-bound set in George Waggner's *The Wolf Man* (1941) reveals strange, eerie landscape of the alternate world of horror films as werewolf emerges from the fog.

wise barren branches, low-lying mist whirling about ancient gravestones and forgotten crypts, jagged crags rising menacingly toward
dark clouds against a black sky—and all accentuated by the sharp
contrasts of chiaroscuro lighting.

The modern horror film, exemplified by Roger Corman's color
adaptations of Poe's stories and Hammer Films's color remakes (particularly those directed by Terence Fisher) of classic horror films (*Horror
of Dracula*, 1958, *The Mummy*, 1959, *The Phantom of the Opera*, 1962) is
not to be denied similar landscape designs. Indeed, art directors, notably Daniel Haller for Corman and Bernard Robinson for Hammer, used
colored filters in lieu of black and white chiaroscuro lighting to accent
their highly stylized settings. The low-lying mist now drifted in and out
of red, green, yellow, and blue pastel backgrounds, as in the cemetery
sequence in Fisher's *Horror of Dracula* and the village square in Corman's *The Haunted Palace* (1963), adding color as a new distinguishing
feature to the established image of the horror film.

Situated within these strange and eerie landscapes are the
ubiquitous old, dark houses and medieval castles, an imagery that
complements the overall Gothic setting (Fig. I.4). MacAndrew writes:

> The omnipresent old house or castle is one of the most stable characteristics
> of the Gothic. A dire and threatening place, it remains more than a dwell-
> ing. It starts out as a stone representation of the dark, tortured windings in
> the mind of those eminently civilized, and, therefore, "unnatural" vices,
> ambition and cruelty; it bears the whole weight of the ages of man's drift
> away from an ideal state; and it becomes a lasting representation of the
> torments of the subconscious pressing upon the conscious mind and making
> a prison of the Self.[22]

The allegorical implications here bring us to the second presentational quality of the horror film, the depiction of exotic characters.
Generally, the horror film offers two extremes of characterization, the
embodiment of pure good and the embodiment of pure evil, the virtuous
and the villainous. And traditionally, these extremes have been manifested, quite naturally, in the protagonist, or hero, and the monster/
villain.[23] Any examination of the horror film reveals such characters;
notable are Dr. Van Helsing and Count Dracula in Fisher's *Horror of
Dracula* (Figs. I.5 and I.6). It is important to note, moreover, that the
heroes are not the youthful heroes of myth. They are often men of
knowledge and experience; as David Pirie observed in the films of
Terence Fisher, they are "Renaissance scholars, scientists and
doctors."[24] Consequently, the heroes and their nemeses approach the
conflict as equals. The confrontation is often one of "wills"—the will of
good against the will of evil—and not one that leads to growth and

Fig. I.4. Highly stylized old house or castle, a principal image of the horror film, has a varied history, as evidenced by these matte paintings for a) above, Tod Browning's *Dracula* (1931), b) Michael Curtiz's *Doctor X* (1932); c) below, Roger Corman's *The Raven* (1963), d) Terence Fisher's *The Gorgon* (1964).

understanding in the hero. Hence, the hero of the horror film emerges as the opposite (good/Christ) of the villain (evil/Satan). In Fisher's *The Brides of Dracula* (1960), for example, the villain, Baron Meinster, a disciple of the obscene cult of vampirism, as the narrator explains, is set against his opposite, Dr. Van Helsing, a "Doctor of Philosophy, Doctor of Theology, and Professor of Metaphysics," who, when confronted by the evil of the vampires, shows no fear, though saying confidently that "only God has no fear." Such a depiction of the hero is not simply part of the *oeuvre* of Fisher; similar depictions, albeit not quite as blatant or stylish, run the course of film history: Dr. Muller against Im-Ho-Tep in Karl Freund's *The Mummy* (1932); Dr. Garth against Sandor, the evil servant of Dracula, in *Dracula's Daughter* (1936); Lady Jane Ainsley, a physician, against Armand Tessla in *The Return of the Vampire* (1944); and Father Karas against the devil himself in William Friedkin's *The Exorcist* (1973).

Fig. I.5. Peter Cushing as Dr. Van Helsing in Terence Fisher's masterpiece, *Horror of Dracula* (1958), personifies horror film hero: a man of knowledge and experience who emerges as an equal of the villain.

Fig. I.6. Villain of the horror film is an incarnation of absolute evil, and Christopher Lee as Count Dracula offers a nightmarish image of this evil in Fisher's *Horror of Dracula.*

These characters exhibit one outstanding distinction, their blatant unreality. As MacAndrew writes, "The characters are more nearly representations of the general human state than depictions of individual human beings."[25] Moreover, these characters simply *exist*. There is seldom an attempt by any secondary or background characters in the horror story to question the existence of the villain, for to do so would be to destroy their own sense of value and worth in the symbolic story itself. To the inhabitants of these dream landscapes, the villain is merely *another* vampire, werewolf, demon, or whatever. These images exist unto themselves on an alternate plane where such irrational things (to our minds) as vampires, werewolves, and ghosts are accepted inhabitants and "nuisances" of a strange world.

If the horror film is to present itself as such, this sense of an alternate world must be preserved. It is essential that the depictions of exotic settings and exotic characters blend in harmony to form a gestalt that denotes the horror film. A vampire prowling the streets of contemporary Los Angeles, as in Bob Kelljan's *Count Yorga-Vampire* (1970), or Dracula himself stalking London's "miniskirt girls" in Alan Gibson's Hammer production, *Dracula A.D. 1972*, strains to the point of farce or satire the willing suspension of disbelief so crucial to the traditional horror tale. This sense of parody is painfully evident in *Count Yorga-Vampire;* as Alain Silver and James Ursini note in *The Vampire Film,* "this vacillation between seriousness and satire . . . reduces its integrity both as drama and as genre piece to the point where it loses its interior reality."[26] The same can be said for Al Adamson's *Blood of Dracula's Castle* (1969), William Caine's *Blacula* (1972), and Dan Curtis's *House of Dark Shadows* (1970).

The depiction of an alternate world preserves the integrity of the horror film. The exaggerated characterizations and settings complement one another to coalesce into a unified whole, or what Maurice Beebe describes in the works of Poe as "the initial unity of singleness, . . . the unity of mutual relationship . . . [where], like the universe, everything is related and nothing is irrelevant."[27] The world of the horror film is a world unto itself that is very much unlike our world. Indeed, the horror film's artificial design is the very thing that imparts its meaning and value. Its obvious difference from the real world invites an examination of its highly symbolic quality. One must remember that "realistic" standards do not apply. Such a view would dilute if not lose altogether the meaning and value of the genre. Rather, one must view and interpret the meaning and value of the horror film on *its* terms; we will discover its true meaning and value only by fathoming its charged symbolism. We must learn to speak its language. The genre thus unites its two presentational qualities to form a singleness of effect: horror. By presenting this effect in terms of an alternate reality—a self-contained world with an inner logic—the entire tale, as evidenced by its images, becomes symbolic and therefore asks us at the outset to discover its meaning.

Science Fiction: The Continuous World

The science fiction film, by contrast, has as its major characteristic an emphasis on the depiction of a continuous, or historical, world. The value systems of these films do not ground themselves in the presumption of such absolutes as good and evil; their physical world exists as a milieu in which to present events that could very well be factual. Vivian Sobchack sees this point when she distinguishes science fiction from horror by claiming that the distinction is "how much we know about the process and the product, how much we are told about the cause and effect."[28]

The monsters of the science fiction film come from the outer (physical) world either by means of scientific experimentation or by invasion from a "real" extraterrestrial world. They are not magical or supernatural, or at least they do not have that air about them. Rather, they are presented as living beings from a disjunctive reality, be it another planet or a scientific laboratory. To see clearly the major difference between the monsters of the horror film and those of the science fiction film, take a look at the characters of Dracula and the Frankenstein monster. Both bring about destruction, but Dracula, as already noted, is the manifestation of an absolute, omnipotent evil, whereas the Frankenstein monster is the result of a scientific experiment rooted in the manipulation of physical reality. The horror film offers a supernatural force grounded in a theological, closed world; the science fiction film offers a natural force grounded in a physical, historical context.

My example raises an important question: Why can't the characters' manipulation of physical reality in science fiction films be a manifestation of absolute evil? Obviously, it can and in certain films it is; the difference lies in character *intent* in the two types of film. If the scientist depicted in a particular film conducts his experiments with the explicit desire to gain power and influence, then, I maintain, the film is in the horror genre; the evil of the scientist's motives overrides the innocence of intellectual curiosity to a point where the film resonates with questions of good and evil as absolute forces. The "mad doctor/scientist" film is indicative of this quality. In these films the doctor/scientist is motivated by a desire to control the world or enslave mankind or to actuate a heinous plan of retribution against those who have mocked him. Dr. Praetorius (Fig. I.7), in James Whale's *The Bride of Frankenstein* (1935), for example, is motivated by a desire to "usurp the rights of God" by creating a living being; moreover, we learn that Praetorius was "booted" by the faculty of Goldstadt University for his unorthodox experiments. His character is made even more complex by Whale's juxtaposition of two scenes: Initially, we see Henry Frankenstein telling Elizabeth that perhaps it is all part of God's plan that he discover the secrets of life; Elizabeth retorts, "It is the *devil* that prompts you!" Whale then cuts to Dr. Praetorius making his way

Fig I.7. Role of Dr. Praetorius makes James Whale's *The Bride of Frankenstein* (1935) a horror film. Here he displays his homunculus, a devil he says resembles himself.

toward the Frankenstein home. This juxtaposition, coupled with Praetorius's known "magical" powers (his unexplained creation of homunculi), raises the suspicion that Praetorius is not merely a doctor but something else, perhaps the devil himself. Later, he heightens the suspicion by comparing himself to the miniature devil he has created: "There's a certain resemblance, don't you think, or do I flatter myself?" Similar characters are found in Michael Curtiz's *Doctor X* (1932), Charles Brabin and Charles Vidor's *The Mask of Fu Manchu* (1932), Erle C. Kenton's *The Island of Lost Souls* (1932), Karl Freund's *Mad Love* (1935), George Sherman's *The Lady and the Monster* (1944), and a trilogy featuring Boris Karloff and directed by Nick Grindé: *The Man They Could Not Hang* (1940), *The Man with Nine Lives* (1941), and *Before I Hang* (1941).[29]

Yet another quality distinguishes the two types of film: the horror film's emphasis on characterization and the science fiction film's emphasis on plot. Character articulation in the horror film is not identical to character development in mainstream fiction. Horror film characters represent ideas and hence come close to the "flat character" described by E. M. Forster in *Aspects of the Novel*—striking and intriguing but nonetheless lacking in depth.[30] They are not real people with real problems; rather, they are centerpieces for the articulation of questions of good and evil. As a result, the horror film's events reveal meaning and value much less than do the symbolic functions of its characters. The audience, with a sort of perverse enjoyment, identifies with the monster/villain "blowing the lid off the Id," as Greenberg puts it, and vicariously lives out heretofore repressed passions. It is no wonder, then, that the titles of most horror films highlight the monster/villain (Fig. I.8): *Dracula, The Phantom of the Opera, The Wolf Man, Cat People, Captive Wild Woman, The Leopard Man, Doctor X, The Cat Man of Paris, The Mummy's Ghost, She-Wolf of London, The Mad Doctor of Market Street, Voodoo Man, Bluebeard.*

The science fiction film, by contrast, emphasizes plot to such a degree that, as John Baxter writes, "characters have no function except as symbols in the writer's chessboard development of his premise."[31] Baxter cites Kingsley Amis's observation that "in sf the 'hero' is often the plot itself."[32] The narrative action investigates and explicates a scientific notion or concept. Often this concept appears as a thesis within a fictional work. George Pal's previously mentioned pseudo documentaries (*Destination Moon* and *Conquest of Space*), for example, base their speculative narratives on state-of-the-art scientific knowledge, extrapolating from it to formulate a working "hypothesis." Character development is rather negligible.

Fig. I.8. Titles of most horror films use character as the dominant motif, as evidenced by frame enlargements from four films.

The emphasis on plot is not confined to the pseudo documentaries.[33] Science fiction film as a genre eschews characterization for the development of strong, cohesive narrative action. Accordingly, the titles of science fiction films emphasize action devoid of personality (Fig. I.9): *Destination Moon, Conquest of Space, Flight to Mars, The Day the World Ended, Earth vs. the Flying Saucers, From the Earth to the Moon, Twelve to the Moon, War of the Worlds, Things to Come, 2001: A Space Odyssey, Twenty Million Miles to Earth, Five Million Years to Earth, Star Wars, Close Encounters of the Third Kind.*

This emphasis on narrative action—specifically on a scientific idea or concept but literally on the course of events itself (including cause-and-effect relationships)—gives meaning and value to the science fiction film. To investigate the meaning and value in this genre, it is necessary to turn our attention not to Freud and psychoanalysis but to Jung and analytical psychology. The science fiction film is concerned with what Rollo May describes as man's inherent sense of wonder, and this concern echoes Jung's perception of the human condition.[34] This

Fig. I.9. Titles of many science fiction films emphasize action rather than character, as evidenced by frame enlargements from four science fiction films.

sense of wonder is persuasively unveiled by putting the emphasis on plot rather than character exposition.

Jungian principles state, first, that everything is made up of opposites and second, that the psyche is an autonomous complex motivated by psychic energy to reconcile these opposites and thereby reach a higher state of consciousness. Jung called this process individuation. The science fiction film's narrative action (and all it represents and signifies) functions in the Jungian perspective as a teleological gradient, avoiding questions of good and evil as such and inspiring in the viewer wonder and hope, aspiration and ideals. This gradient is a path toward rebirth, "not another natural birth, but a spiritual birth into any one individual's true 'self.' "[35] Herein lies the strength of the science fiction film: Using ideas and events extrapolated from the natural (physical/historical) world as its milieu, it affirms human potential and aspiration.

This connection between the notion of wonder and mystery and the

science fiction film is most pronounced in films that take their audiences to other worlds. In Stanley Kubrick's *2001: A Space Odyssey*
(1968), for example, the depiction of rebirth is literal: Bowman passes
through the mystical "star-gate" to confront his maturing "self" only to
reemerge as the "star-child." George Lucas's *Star Wars* trilogy centers
its action on the mystical, pseudo-religious Force, concluding in *Return
of the Jedi* (1983) with the figurative rebirth of youthful Luke Skywalker
into manhood (and with actor Mark Hamill literally growing up).

Although such matters as aspiration and wonder may be obscure
when exploring the alien invasion film, this type of film nevertheless is
rich with similar insights into the human condition. Thus it is perhaps
possible now to see how the alien invasion film is a subgenre of science
fiction, wholly separate from the horror genre. The alien invasion film
depicts humanity at the mercy of either malevolent or benign rational
(albeit alien) forces. These forces can be of extraterrestrial or terrestrial
origin (Fig. I.10). The term *extraterrestrial* refers to forces, humanoid or
otherwise, whose origins and essences are unknown yet are rationally

Fig. I.10. Classic theme of alien invasion is outlined in frame enlargements from trailer for Edward L. Cahn's *Invisible Invaders*
(1959).

understood (Fig. I.11). For example, the alien marauders in George Pal and Byron Haskin's *War of the Worlds* (1953) remain mysteries to humanity even though they are scientifically explained away in the narration as merely beings from the planet Mars. *Terrestrial* refers to forces, again either humanoid or otherwise, whose essences are known to be of earthly origin but whose raison d'être is explained away in rational terms (Fig. I.12). Jack Arnold's *Tarantula* (1955) depicts a giant spider wreaking havoc in an Arizona desert. The tarantula itself is an understood known quanity, an earthly life form; its enormous size, however, is alien to man's knowledge and experience. Hence, the hugeness, the unknown quanity, is rationalized through scientific means and explained away to the satisfaction of all concerned.

The terrestrial force is marked by an emphasis on its reason for being. The monster usually appears through the manipulation of physical reality—scientific experimentation, atomic testing—that went awry. The means by which the monster appears may be one of the following:

Genesis. The monster is an entirely new organism spawned by scientific experimentation; for example, the "mental vampires" in Arthur Crabtree's *Fiend without a Face* (1958) and the "silicates" in Terence Fisher's *Island of Terror* (1966).

Fig. I.11. Alien warriors in Fred F. Sears's *Earth vs. the Flying Saucers* (1956), like aliens in countless other films, remain mysteries to humanity but are nonetheless explained away as simply beings from another planet.

Fig. I.12. The invader of the terrestrial invasion story is a known quantity, but its reason for existence becomes the center of scientific inquiry. In Jack Arnold's *Tarantula* (1955), Professor Deemer examines the large tarantula— what the ads proclaim as Deemer's "deadly accident of science."

Mutation. A creature is changed into a prowling monster; for example, the spate of giant insect films of which Arnold's *Tarantula* and Gordon Douglas's *Them!* (1954) are exemplary.

Metamorphosis. A creature completely changes its form and structure; for example, Andre Delambre-into-insect in Kurt Neumann's *The Fly* (1958) and Victor Carroon-into-space-creature in Val Guest's *The Creeping Unknown* (1956) (Fig. I.13).

Resurrection. An extinct creature is revived, usually by means of atomic bomb testing; for example, the rhedosaur in Eugene Lourié's *The Beast from 20,000 Fathoms* (1953) and the huge Conquistador in Richard E. Cunha's *Giant from the Unknown* (1958).

Terrestrial, then, covers those films that are referred to as "monster movies," whereas extraterrestrial refers to those films that are often described as merely "science fiction movies." With these distinctions in mind, one can see why and how the alien invasion film is distinctly a subgenre of science fiction: The alien invasion film is rooted in the manipulation of physical reality as a milieu for presenting insights into the human condition; however, this manipulation of physical reality is not proof of an underlying evil (Fig. I.14).

Freud and Jung

Vivian Sobchack has done much groundwork in differentiating horror from science fiction, but one can go further. Her thesis, somewhat akin to the notions of critics who preceded her, sees science fiction and horror as merely "shadings on a spectrum of need, moving from one end to the other and back, shifting emphasis from magic to religion to science or resting in the middle in a type of stasis between two poles."[36] Thus they are distinguished only by thematic and presentational degrees, or "shadings," and the total effect of each is but a complementary opposite of the other. Such a scheme, to my thinking, allows far too many variables to enter; in the long run we will have no distinction at all. Placing the alien invasion film in the middle of a spectrum is not the

Fig. I.13. In Val Guest's *The Creeping Unknown* (1956), astronaut Victor Carroon is slowly and agonizingly metamorphosed into a slinking, squidlike space monster.

Fig. I.14. Insect-o-thon means alien invasion in advertisement for midnight show in the mid-sixties (notice the mention of Beatles photo). Accompanying news article identified the three films as *The Spider, Beast with a Million Eyes,* and *Night of the Blood Beast,* all alien invasion features of the fifties.

answer; it is not a hybrid, as Sobchack suggests, of the horror film and the science fiction film. Rather, the alien invasion film is a wholly integrated subgenre of the science fiction film replete with all the meaning and value inherently alive in the science fiction genre itself. And to discover and appreciate this meaning, we need the tenets of analytical psychology.

This study, in addition to distinguishing the presentational qualities of the horror film from those of the science fiction film, will show that the prevailing tradition of horror and science fiction criticism is not germane to a proper understanding of the meaning and value inherent in the science fiction film and consequently in the alien invasion film. Freudian psychoanalysis, though well suited to probing the fears and nightmare representations of the horror film, is improperly applied to the science fiction film. Even though the science fiction milieu is distinctly physical—that is, continuous or historical—the thrust of the science fiction film is not sociological, as many believe, but, like the thrust of the horror film, psychical. The psychic situation projected, however, is not a Freudian confrontation of fears and repressed desires, but rather the celebration of human aspiration toward an absolute, higher state of existence. Accordingly, the monsters and aliens of the alien invasion film are best seen not as projections of the repressed unconscious but rather as projections of the collective unconscious. They serve, in the films and for their audiences, as symbols of transformation in the process of individuation outlined by Jung. The qualities of the films are most easily appreciated and described when their characteristic elements are understood in this psychological context. That is why I find Jung's analytical psychology to be the proper methodology for interpreting the alien invasion film.

Myths and Motifs
of the Monster Movie

Before applying Jung's principles to the inner workings of the alien invasion film, let us consider the components and characteristics of the genre itself. First, the alien invasion film is defined by its particular patterns of expression, its myth. Narrative that is concerned with invasion from outer space or inner earth I call the classical text. Narrative concerned with scientific experimentation and its results I consider to be a variation of that pattern, and I call it the Prometheus variation. Second, the alien invasion film as a whole is dominated by particular motifs that help shape and fuse these narrative patterns. Both the classical text and the Prometheus variation possess two significant motifs: the contest and death and rebirth. Peculiar to the classical text is the character motif best described as the intellectual hero, and peculiar to the Prometheus variation is the narrative motif of taboo and the character motif of the intuitive hero. These myths and motifs define the alien invasion genre.

By the term *myth* I mean two things. First, it refers to the components that constitute the narrative, the simple pattern of plot. In analytical psychology it is called a mythologem, the pattern of continuous action.[1] As we shall note, the narrative components of the alien invasion film were firmly established at the very beginning of the genre and seldom varied from film to film. Second, myth refers to the deeper and more complex meanings behind the narrative—a living myth whose meanings serve as continual "models of human behavior and, by that very fact, [give] meaning and value to life."[2] The living myth is a "symbolic expression of the inner unconscious by way of projection," and projection is the key to interpreting and appreciating the mythologem itself; that is, the images and events that make up the mythologem are the manifestations of unconscious material.[3] The precise meaning of these manifestations is discussed in the next two chapters. The purpose here is to offer a descriptive analysis of the components of the alien invasion film.

Before examining these contextual definitions, I need to examine the "functioning quality" of each narrative, its appeal, that is, to a particular psychological function. Jung's psychology of consciousness is essential to understanding this notion. Jung describes psychological function as "a particular form of psychic activity that remains the same principle under varying conditions."[4] What that means, according to Jolande Jacobi, is that "we are concerned primarily with a mode of apprehending and assimilating psychic data regardless of their content."[5] Thus psychological function is an activity and not an object; it is the action that creates thought.

For Jung, the conscious psyche is composed of four basic functions that are constitutionally present in every individual: thinking and feeling, which are the rational processes, and intuition and sensation, which are the irrational processes.[6] Jung calls thinking and feeling rational since they both work within judgment and evaluation. For example, deciding upon an answer to a "true/false" question is "thinking," and responding to an odor as pleasant or unpleasant is "feeling."[7] On the other hand, intuition and sensation are considered irrational since they discover meaning and value in events and images through perceptions of things and not through any cognitive or decision-making process. Unfortunately, by their very obscurity, intuition and sensation remain aloof and difficult to comprehend (and hence irrational), but, simply put, the irrational functions find meaning and value in things through "not knowing why." That is not to say that the irrational processes are inferior qualities of consciousness, for both intuition and sensation perceive things as they are and not otherwise. Rather, intuition and sensation are as much a part of consciousness as are the rational processes of thinking and feeling.

Our next step is to examine the rational and irrational in the context of the alien invasion story. We are now dealing with easily recognized story elements that can be labeled and discussed. But to better appreciate this fact we need to turn our attention to another genre, the detective story, whose narrative patterns are similar to the narrative patterns of the alien invasion genre.[8]

The alien invasion genre is like the detective story in that much of the narrative is taken up by the hero's pursuit of a solution to a perplexing problem. The difference is that the alien invasion genre concentrates not so much on finding the who or what as on finding the means to overcome the who or what. For the classical text, the emphasis in characterization is almost always centered on analytical thinking, or precise, calculated, cause-and-effect analysis. Like his counterpart in the "whodunit" detective story, the hero of the classical text arrives at his conclusions not through intuition but through methodical evaluation and judgment. He does not act impulsively but thoughtfully; his solution to the problem works because logic and reason affirm its reliability. Likewise, the scenarios themselves are structured in a sensible, organized way: This leads to this and that leads to that. Moreover, the look, or mise-en-scène, of the classical text is straightforward, offering a visual reference to the historical or rational world. The classical text eschews the artifice of, say, chiaroscuro lighting and the forced perspective of expressionism for the documentary qualities of natural lighting and natural settings. Many of these films were produced in actual locations or in skillfully reproduced locations in Hollywood studios (Fig. II.1). Robert Gordon's *It Came from Beneath the Sea* (1955) and Fred F. Sears's *Earth vs. the Flying Saucers* (1956), for example, are set quite obviously in San Francisco and Washington, D.C., respectively. Other such films include Nathan Juran's *Twenty Million Miles to Earth* (1957), which is set in Rome, and Eugene Lourié's *The Giant Behemoth* (1959) and *Gorgo* (1961), which are set in London.

For the Prometheus variation, characterization is centered less on analytical thinking than on intuition. Like his counterpart, the "hard-boiled detective/gumshoe," the hero (often a layman) of the Prometheus variation arrives at his understanding of the situation through inspired wisdom. He follows hunches, and his solution to the problem often comes as an intuitive idea at the film's climax. The solution works not so much because of rational, cause-and-effect thinking but because it is morally right when set against the "evil" of some Promethean scientist's experimentation. The look of these films is often strange; some actually resemble horror films—for example, Edgar G. Ulmer's *The Daughter of*

Fig II.1. A) Flying saucers in Sears's *Earth vs. the Flying Saucers* land in front of Capitol building, and b) prehistoric beast in Eugene Lourié's *Gorgo* (1961) approaches London's Big Ben, both easily recognizable settings for historical, or continuous, world of the classical text narrative.

Dr. Jekyll (1957) and Henry Cass's *Blood of the Vampire* (1958)—while others vacillate between scenes of expressionistic design resembling horror films (Fig. II.2) and scenes of natural design. Jack Arnold's *Monster on the Campus* (1958), for example, shifts focus from the natural settings of the university to the shadows and forced perspective of the monster prowling the countryside at night. Robert Day's *First Man into Space* (1959) shifts focus from the documentary quality of the rocket launch and space flight in the first half of the film to the shadowy dark of the astronaut-turned-monster prowling the New Mexico countryside in the second half. These films are not horror films; rather, they are "irrational," shunning the natural look for an artificial one and conveying images that work against the natural look but nonetheless retain a certain natural air about them.

With these distinctions between the rational processes and the irrational processes in mind, it is possible to see that the classical text can be associated with the rational function and the Prometheus variation with the irrational function.

Fig. II.2. Expressionism in (a & b) Jack Arnold's *Monster on the Campus* (1958), above; c) Robert Day's *First Man into Space* (1959), below left; and d) Edward L. Cahn's *It! The Terror from Beyond Space* (United Artists 1958). It is a stylistic device that often clouds the distinction between the horror film and the science fiction film.

The Classical Text: The Rational Function

I call the first narrative pattern classical[9] because it defines the genre. H. G. Wells's *War of the Worlds*, written in 1898, is the prototype: Martians bent on enslaving the earth arrive en masse in cylinders and begin ravaging the world with their monstrous tripod machines and heat rays. It is not Wells's superior use of narrative resonance, what Scholes and Rabkin have described as his journalism,[10] that brings Wells to the fore with regard to the alien invasion genre. Rather, it is his idea, his simple theme of an invasion from another world, that serves as the impetus for the alien invasion genre. The cinema picked up this basic notion of an invasion from outer space or inner earth but quickly established its own strict and rigid pattern of delineation that owes little to Wells's narrative form. True to the Hollywood tradition of melodrama, the alien invasion film shunned the complexities of characterization and the journalistic form of the novel (although George Pal's adaptation of *War of the Worlds* basically followed the novel's structure) for the unconstrained luxury of simple melodramatic conflict, setting innocence against adversity.

The classical text tells of a sighting, usually by the hero (though in many instances the observer is a secondary character), of an unusual occurrence, either a spacecraft landing or a mysterious thing of unknown origin prowling the countryside. This sighting leads to the observer's humiliation when those he tells refuse to believe him; Dennis Saleh describes it as the observer's "instant but thoroughgoing cultural debunking."[11] Society, however, bears the consequences when the alien invader makes its presence known by waging war—in most cases, against society. Society then seeks the help of a strong leader, usually a scientist of great intellectual abilities, although society in many of the monster-on-the-loose films elects a strong, intuitive military commander. A battle is fought and society eventually emerges victorious.

I have outlined this pattern of exposition as follows: (1) Someone, usually the scientist hero, sees the invader appear on earth. (2) The observer is not believed by those he tells; in many instances, he is mocked and scorned. (3) Unexplained happenings occur, such as bizarre killings, people disappearing, and/or large-scale destruction. (4) Society searches for rational explanations for the strange occurrences, but the observer's explanations are rejected as unreasonable. (5) The scientist hero begins a lonely battle against the invader and the mocking society. The scientist is determined to save society in spite of itself. (6) The invader makes its presence known, usually by ravaging a highly populated area. (7) Society desperately turns to the scientist hero for leadership even though it may still be suspicious of his abilities. (8) The scientist hero offers a rational explanation for the invader's presence as well as a plan to repel the invader; society rallies in a common cause. (9) The battle, or contest, is waged; the invader is repelled (usually destroyed). (10) Humanity acknowledges that it has been arrogant in presuming upon its role in the cosmos.

The classical text is divided with regard to the source from which the invasion springs: terrestrial and extraterrestrial. The former is often referred to as the monster movie since the invader is usually a resurrected dinosaur or a giant insect—definitely of earthly origin. The extraterrestrial invader comes, as its name implies, from worlds beyond the earth. This division does not alter the basic pattern of exposition just outlined, but some variations do exist. Not all films can be conveniently classified according to each point in the outline. Howard Hawks and Christian Nyby's *The Thing from Another World* (1951), for example, is unique in that it eschews much of the first part of the outline to concentrate almost entirely on "the contest."

It is ironic that the most famous alien invasion story, Wells's *War of the Worlds*, deviates from the basic structure of the classical text. This deviation may be understood by recognizing that the two major-budgeted, big-studio productions of the era, *War of the Worlds* (Paramount 1953) and *The Day the Earth Stood Still* (20th-Fox 1951), neither of which follows the basic pattern, were attempts at uniqueness. These films shunned the usual structure followed by their low-budget brethren in favor of examinations by two prominent filmmakers, George Pal and Robert Wise, of the coexistence of religion and science in a changing culture. *War of the Worlds*, despite its emphasis on spectacle, retains the linear narrative of Wells's novel but with added allusions to mankind's relationship with God—something that undoubtedly would have caused Wells to writhe in intellectual agony. *The Day the Earth Stood Still* has a similar theme, but it avoids spectacle and prefers characterization; it offers allusions to the apocalypse, and its hero's plight to save mankind in spite of itself owes much of its structure to the New Testament. Perhaps it is because of their efforts to deviate from the norm that these films were revered by their contemporary critics as well as by modern scholarship; the films are considered gems in the rock pile, standing out for no other reason than their uniqueness. The rock pile, of course, refers to the collective works that form and shape the alien invasion narrative in general. Unlike the films just discussed, the alien invasion film, for the most part, was the product of minor studios and nearly always the result of low budgets; its intent was to please the masses and avoid the critics. As such, it relied heavily on a proven (and profitable) formula of delineation.

To show the classical text in action, I have chosen for analysis one representative film from each category, extraterrestrial and terrestrial: Jack Arnold's *It Came from Outer Space* and Eugene Lourié's *The Beast from 20,000 Fathoms.*

It Came from Outer Space, with a cast including Richard Carlson, Barbara Rush, and Charles Drake, is based on an original screen treatment by Ray Bradbury. Produced by Universal-International in 1953 in 3-Dimension (Fig. II.3), it has received much praise for its restraint and understatement and for Arnold's relaxed style.[12] The story is pure science fiction, telling of an alien spacecraft that crash-lands in the Arizona desert and the ensuing confusion and panic caused by the alien visitors before a scientist aids them in repairing their ship and returning to outer space. *Time* magazine called the film "a crisp combination of shocker and social commentary"; it lauded Carlson's performance as "mystically inclined,"[13] thereby recognizing the mold from which most of the intellectual scientist heroes of the classical text emerge.

The Beast from 20,000 Fathoms, with Paul Christian, Paula Raymond, Cecil Kellaway, and Kenneth Tobey, is also based on a story by Ray Bradbury.[14] The film was produced by Mutual Pictures of California, a small independent company headed by former Monogram Pictures producers Jack Dietz and Hal E. Chester; however, Warner Brothers purchased the film outright and released it in 1953. Early release prints are said to have been tinted sepia, but the main attraction of the film remains Ray Harryhausen's first-rate special effects. The film is often referred to as the prototype of the monster movie.

To fully appreciate these films in the context of the classical text, I will review each film's narrative structure as it corresponds to each point in the pattern of exposition already outlined.

1. Someone, usually the scientist hero, sees the invader appear on earth. In nearly every film of the classical text, the story opens on a rather serene setting. Nothing indicates that anything is out of the

Fig. II.3. Exciting title sequence in Jack Arnold's *It Came from Outer Space* (1953) uses 3-Dimension to great advantage as meteorite crashes "into the audience."

ordinary; life seems under control if not carefree and joyous. We are introduced to the principal characters, frequently the hero and his girl friend. We find that the hero's life is about to take a new turn; he has been offered a new job, or his book has been accepted for publication, or his attitude toward life is taking on a more positive meaning. Suddenly, this complacency is shattered by the sighting of an unidentified flying object or, in the terrestrial invasion story, of some kind of threatening creature or strong evidence to indicate that a threatening creature is running amok.

It Came from Outer Space opens on such a serene and complacent setting: Amateur astronomer and writer John Putnam (Richard Carlson) is entertaining his fiancée, schoolteacher Ellen Fields (Barbara Rush), at his mountaintop home in the Arizona desert. As they sit before a cozy fire, John tells Ellen that he has just placed another article in a scientific journal; he suggests that they consult the stars for a glimpse into their future. They go out into the desert and look up to the heavens. They are about to kiss when a fireball streaks across the sky (Fig. II.4). A meteorite crashes to earth and John, with the aid of his telescope, sees that it has struck the old Excelsior mine. He persuades helicopter pilot Pete Davis (Dave Willock) to fly them to the site, believing the meteorite to be "the biggest thing that's happened in our time." As Pete and Ellen wait at the crater's edge, John descends into the crater and discovers that the fireball was not a meteorite but a spacecraft and its occupant (Fig. II.5). Before he can make contact, an avalanche buries the ship.

In *The Beast from 20,000 Fathoms*, the opening is typical for the terrestrial invasion film of the fifties, in which a narrator (often William Woodson) explains a military exercise while stock footage shows military personnel preparing for action. In this case, the narrator (Woodson) explains that we are in the last few minutes of Operation Experiment,

Fig. II.4. Crash of meteorite interrupts a romantic interlude between amateur astronomer John Putnam and his fiancee, Ellen Fields. Tape across the top of this lobby card hides "3-Dimension" catchline; presumably, this card was used in a theatre showing the flat version.

Fig. II.5. John alone sees the craft and its occupant.

an exercise in nuclear fission conducted in the frigid air of the Arctic. As the clock ticks away the seconds, the military personnel and the government scientists prepare for the blast. Suddenly, the screen bleaches out and then dissolves into the familiar 1950s footage of a nuclear blast. Minutes later, Dr. Nesbitt and his associates are taking instrument readings in the blast area. A blizzard is approaching and the group is ordered back to the base, but as Nesbitt makes one final reading a huge and dark shape crosses his path. As he stands in the snow flurry, staring in awe at the figure, a thunderous roar shakes loose the ice, burying him. His associates dig him out, and as they prepare to rush him to medical aid, he cries out that he saw "a monster, a monster!"

2. *The observer is not believed by those he tells; in many instances, he is mocked and scorned.* Following the sighting, the observer is usually quick to report the occurrence to the authorities, but few if any of them believe him. The sighting is often dismissed as merely an illusion, "the mind playing tricks on people," and nothing more. Of particular note is the treatment of the teenage observer in the spate of "teenage monster movies" of the late fifties. In Irvin S. Yeaworth, Jr.'s *The Blob* (1958) and Edward L. Cahn's *Invasion of the Saucer Men* (1957), for example, the teenage witnesses are dismissed by the establishment as crazy kids. Age and credibility go hand in hand in these films, but the teenagers do get the last laugh, as it were, when the invaders march on the city and the establishment turns to the kids for help (Fig. II.6).

In *It Came from Outer Space*, John escapes to the ridge, where he is met by Pete. John explains that "there was something down there," and Pete emphatically replies, "You're not kidding—a couple of tons of earth that almost hit you!" John, however, muses that "some kind of ship . . . like nothing we've ever seen before" is buried in the rock and sand. Pete shakes his head and the first of several confrontations questioning John's veracity begins between John and members of the community:

PETE: Oh brother . . . something must have hit this guy in the head.

JOHN: I know it sounds crazy but I tell you it was there. Part of it was still showing.

PETE: Look, boy, you've been up in the stars too long!

JOHN: A huge ball rammed there inside the crater. . . . All right, all right, I'm not imagining; I tell you I saw this thing.

PETE: Oh brother!

JOHN: I saw an open portway.

PETE: What was inside?

JOHN: Something—and then the door slammed shut and started the landslide.

PETE: That figures. . . .

JOHN: Pete, will you listen to me?

PETE: I did. I let maniacs drag me off in the middle of the night and then I get rocketships thrown at me. You're not going to tell those people you saw Martians running around down there?

JOHN: What would you say if I had found a Martian down there?

PETE: I'd say hold them for a circus.

John Putnam is not believed by those he tells, and he is mocked and scorned by reporters, who refer to him as a stargazer. The press, indeed, is usually vitriolic in its descriptions of the observers in these films. Often, as in Fred F. Sears's *The Giant Claw* (1957) and even in *The Beast from 20,000 Fathoms*, the secondary observers—those who see the invader after the initial sighting—are forced into seclusion by the press attack on their credibility.

The primary observer, Nesbitt, is literally sent to a psychiatric ward in *The Beast from 20,000 Fathoms*. He awakens from his stupor, claiming that he saw a prehistoric beast prowling on an ice plateau near the blast area. He is placated by the medical staff until he is sent to New York for psychiatric interrogation; there, he is diagnosed as suffering from "traumatic hallucinations." Compounding Nesbitt's dilemma, Colonel Jack Evans (Kenneth Tobey) tells him that the official report Evans

Fig. II.6. Steve McQueen, known then as Steven, in Irvin S. Yeaworth, Jr.'s *The Blob* (1958), calms panic-stricken crowd that only moments earlier had censured him for being a crazy kid.

made out does not mention Nesbitt's claim to have seen something on the plateau.

At this stage of the narrative, the observer accepts one of two options with respect to the sighting. Either he remains adamant, like John Putnam, refusing to admit to anything other than what he saw; or, like Tom Nesbitt, he accepts his diagnosis with mild reservations, agreeing that he may have suffered an hallucination in the stress and excitement of the moment. Stylistically, these options are played out by the use of continuous action and parallel action, respectively.

In continuous action, the narrative remains fixed on the hero, following his plight from clue to clue as he desperately attempts to gather enough convincing evidence to prove to society that he was not hallucinating and that he is not crazy. In *It Came from Outer Space*, John tells Ellen that the people have talked about him before, and he considers them "fools" for their narrow-mindedness. He stresses that he did see something; he "even saw some kind of tracks—I can't be just imagining it!" John is determined not to turn his will over to the skeptics, and he begins a campaign to prove himself right and to convince society that alien invaders have landed on earth.

The action stays with John as he seeks counsel from his friend and mentor, Dr. Snell (George Eldredge) of the university. At the crater, Snell concludes that a meteorite struck the earth; when John pleads with Snell to believe him, Snell coldly wants "facts, John, facts." Nevertheless, John will not be denied:

> JOHN: I expected you to be more open to the idea than the others—you're a man of science.
> SNELL: And therefore less inclined to witchcraft, John.
> JOHN: Not witchcraft, Dr. Snell, imagination. Willingness to believe that there are lots of things that we don't know anything about. Look, there was a time when people thought the earth was a level plane between two mountains that were set there to hold up the sky and that the stars were lamps hung from the sky. A better idea came along and people were ready to listen.

Snell apologizes for not being able to corroborate John's sighting. As John leaves the site, Snell's assistant (Brad Johnson) describes John as an "odd man," to which Snell replies, "Not odd . . . individual and lonely; he's a man who thinks for himself."

John is then confronted by Sheriff Matt Warren (Charles Drake), a rival for Ellen's affections, who tells him that the town doesn't understand his "poking around in the desert and squinting up at the stars." "Putnam," he says, "you frighten them and what frightens them they're against." Undaunted, John pushes on to find the aliens.

In films in which the observer accepts his diagnosis, agreeing that his sighting may have been the result of a traumatic experience, the action crosscuts; that is, it cuts from its focus on the observer attempting to prove himself right to some acausal parallel action. Unlike the continuous action narrative, it changes its focus to the invader itself. In *The Beast from 20,000 Fathoms,* Tom Nesbitt accepts the explanation of his sighting; he does not pursue the object, nor does he even want to be reminded of the experience. At this stage of the narrative, the issue is closed for an observer like Nesbitt; life goes on and he returns to his work.

3. *Unexplained happenings occur, such as bizarre killings, people disappearing, and/or large-scale destruction.* At this point, the focus shifts altogether from the observer to the invader itself. The invader's substance and power are revealed to the spectator, who becomes aware of the invader's intentions as well as its ferocious or "parahuman" power. Although a minority of films depict the invader as having benign intentions—Wise's *The Day the Earth Stood Still* and Herbert Greene's *The Cosmic Man* (1959), for example—the vast majority depict the intentions as malevolent. And they are played out on a grand scale. The invader causes major disasters. In Sears's *The Giant Claw,* for example, the giant extraterrestrial bird wrecks a freight train, and in Lourié's *Gorgo* the prehistoric beast rises from the sea to demolish a quaint fishing village.

In *The Beast from 20,000 Fathoms,* the action cuts from Nesbitt's recuperation to a small tugboat making its way along the fogbound Newfoundland coast. It is dark, and the crew is having great difficulty sighting land. Suddenly the Beast rises out of the sea and with tremendous ferocity attacks and demolishes the tiny boat. Only one member of the crew survives, and the news media are quick to report that the tugboat's captain attributes the disaster to a "sea serpent." We then return to Nesbitt, who sees the newspaper account of the incident. Nesbitt is no longer willing to accept the official "reasonable" explanation for his sighting but is eager to prove himself right and to prove to society that an alien invader is indeed running amok. The focus now returns to the plight of the observer.

In many films, major disasters do not occur. Evidence of the presence of invaders is found in the subtle details of everyday life (Fig. II.7). Things just aren't as they should be; people are acting strangely, animals refuse to venture into certain areas, mysterious sounds are heard and lights seen, or mysterious power drains begin to affect everyday living. In Don Siegel's *Invasion of the Body Snatchers* (1956), physician Miles Bennell (Kevin McCarthy) is called back from a medical convention by his frantic nurse, concerned about the large number of patients who desperately need to see him. When he returns, he finds his office empty. He then stands at his window watching the people going about their daily routines, and he muses that everything is apparently normal. Later, he discovers that a friend is convinced that her uncle has become an imposter, that he is no longer her Uncle Ira but someone else. A young boy is convinced that his mother is not really his mother. Mind control, soul possession, or the loss of identity and individuality is a frequent theme in science fiction and is used to great advantage in several alien invasion films, including Gene Fowler, Jr.'s *I Married a Monster from Outer Space* (1958) and Nathan Hertz's *The Brain from Planet Arous* (1958).

In rather poetic fashion, *It Came from Outer Space* also emphasizes the commonplace. Following Snell's rejection, John and Ellen come across two friends, George (Russell Johnson) and Frank (Joe Sawyer), telephone linemen. John asks them to be on the alert for anything out of the ordinary, anything strange and unusual. Frank says he hasn't seen anything unusual but has been hearing things on the line. John climbs the ladder and, as he listens to the eerie hum emanating from the wires, Frank recites voice-over the following Bradbury passage as the director, Arnold, cuts to long shots of the telephone poles strung across the desert:

> After you've been working out on the desert fifteen years like I have, you hear a lot of things, see a lot of things, too: The sun in the sky, the heat, and all that sand out there with the rivers and lakes that aren't real at all. And sometimes you think the wind gets into the wires and hums and sings and talks just like what we're hearing now.

Fig. II.7. Dr. Hastings and others examine unexplained remains of slaughtered cattle in *Tarantula,* left; and Major Jeff Cummings and others examine curious corpse with missing brain and spinal cord in Arthur Crabtree's *Fiend without a Face* (1958).

The eerie sound vanishes from the line, and John once again asks them to be watchful.

The theme of loss of identity and individuality is prominent in *It Came from Outer Space*. John and Ellen find George and Frank's abandoned truck parked on the highway shoulder. Finding blood on the door, they search for their friends, believing they may have been injured in an accident. Suddenly George appears, but he is different—cold and aloof, with an uncanny ability to stare into the sun without blinking. He coldly tells John and Ellen that everything is all right; there is nothing to worry about. They nervously agree and leave. John tells Ellen that he believes Frank is dead. The couple race into town; they tell Warren that Frank is dead and George may be responsible. Warren reluctantly agrees to investigate, but at the scene they find nothing—no truck, no George, no Frank. Warren, however, finds blood, the blood of a dead animal. As they return to town, they see both Frank and George walking along the street; disgusted with Putnam and his crazy claims, Warren returns to his office.

Later, we learn that more strange events have occurred. Frank's wife reports to Warren that Frank came home and took his clothes, saying he would be gone for a long time but refusing to say where he was going. We also learn that large quantities of electrical equipment have been stolen since the meteorite fell; moreover, Warren reports that Dr. Snell is missing.

Even now the observers, both primary and secondary, are still not believed by society. The connection between the unexplained events and the invader is not made by society until the invader literally marches on a heavily populated area.

4. Society searches for rational explanations for the strange occurrences, but the observer's explanations are rejected as unreasonable. The significance is that society searches for a rational explanation for the strange occurrences at any cost; it unequivocally rejects the observer's explanation as unreasonable, if not nonsensical, and prefers the most "reasonable" explanation, even if that explanation leads to nescience. Often, society accepts the strange occurrence as precisely that, "a strange occurrence."

In John Putnam's case, this point is only implied at first, since John alone has encountered the strange occurrences. Later, after Warren reports the theft of the electrical equipment and Dr. Snell's disappearance, he listens to John's explanations but argues that the whole story is just too preposterous for his sanity's sake. Warren prefers to believe that the strange events are just the desert heat affecting everyone's behavior.

In Nesbitt's case, the rebuff is explicit. Intrigued by the report of the "sea serpent," he attempts to make contact with the tugboat captain, but the captain refuses to speak with anyone. He is fed up, his housekeeper says, with the mocking public and press. Nesbitt then visits Professor Thurgood Elson (Cecil Kellaway), a renowned paleontologist. But Elson rejects Nesbitt's theory that a prehistoric beast had been trapped inside a frozen tomb, hybernating until the nuclear blast freed it. "Just not so," Elson argues, adding that the creature would be well over 100 million years old. Such an idea, he claims, is simply too irrational and implausible.

5. *The scientist hero begins a lonely battle against the invader and the mocking society.*[15] Herein lies the basic thrust of the classical text: The scientist hero, often aided by his girl friend, launches his own investigation into the true reasons behind the strange occurrences. This investigation leads to what he knew all along, that he was not hallucinating when he saw the alien invader appear on earth. Because of society's disapproval, the hero becomes an outsider who must battle not only against the invader but also against the mocking, rejecting society. Hence, the hero's mission is to save society in spite of itself, and as such the hero functions as a redeemer, a heroic figure whose heritage is linked to biblical typology.

Such a description fits John Putnam and his plight. We have already mentioned the severe mocking and scorning he receives from public and press alike. We also know that he is considered somewhat of an outsider—a stargazer, as newspaper editor Dave Loring (Alan Dexter) calls him. In addition, Snell describes him as lonely and individual because he thinks for himself. His only support comes from Ellen, whose blind faith bolsters his drive to find the truth. As already noted, he adamantly refuses to turn his will over to the skeptical society. As the annoyed Sheriff Warren returns to his office, John cries out to Frank and George, who immediately duck into an alley. John follows and confronts them. They tell him that the real Frank and George are safe but the aliens need time to repair their ship. They also warn John not to interfere or "terrible things will happen." *It Came from Outer Space* then focuses more on John Putnam's need to calm the confused, frustrated society than on his intent to repel the invader.

Nesbitt's plight in *The Beast from 20,000 Fathoms* is more traditional. His foremost task is to repel the invader and make society safe and secure. During Nesbitt's visit with Professor Elson, they are overheard by Elson's assistant, Dr. Lee Hunter (Paula Raymond). She is interested not only in Nesbitt's theory but also in Nesbitt himself, and she decides to help him. Following another disaster at sea attributed to a sea serpent (yet another odd occurrence), Lee offers Nesbitt a chance to find his monster by having him choose it from among a group of drawings of prehistoric animals. She tells Nesbitt that if the drawing he chooses is also the drawing chosen by the survivors of the sea disasters, then Elson will be forced to listen and to act if necessary. After poring over hundreds of illustrations, Nesbitt finally finds the drawing of the creature he saw that day on the ridge of ice in the Arctic, a creature called the rhedosaur. Days later, Lee and Nesbitt locate the survivors of the second lost ship and they, too, pore over hundreds of drawings of prehistoric beasts until they both choose the identical drawing, the rhedosaur. Jacob Bowman (Jack Pennick), one of the survivors, returns with Lee and Nesbitt to New York with his testimony, and now Elson listens, but the military will not.

6. *The invader makes its presence known, usually by ravaging a highly populated area.* Special effects cinematography is a significant part of the narrative at this stage, since the invader literally marches against society on a vast scale (Fig. II.8). In Sears's *Earth vs. the Flying Saucers,*

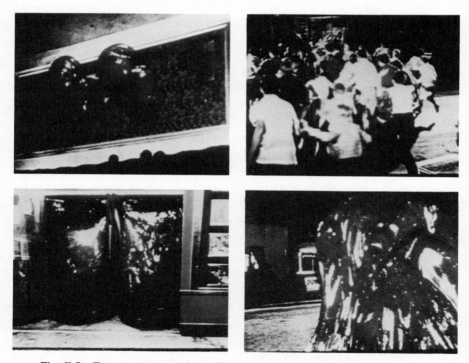

Fig. II.8. Frame sequence from *The Blob* shows alien making its presence known. A) The blob first oozes through projector portals in a theatre, b) sending the audience into the streets, and c) then oozes out the doors of the theatre to finally d) attack a diner.

for example, the aliens launch an all-out offensive with their war-saucers against Washington, D.C., destroying such landmarks as the Supreme Court building, the Washington Monument, and the Capitol dome, accomplished with outstanding model work and stop-motion photography by Ray Harryhausen. Harryhausen is also responsible for the special photography in *The Beast from 20,000 Fathoms*. When the Beast rises out of the Hudson River to terrorize the streets of New York City, Harryhausen's skill displays the Beast trampling people, smashing cars and trucks, and demolishing buildings before it returns to the river.

In some films, the presence of the invader is subtle; no one scene reveals the invader's presence to society, but a particular scene seems to confirm the suspicion that an alien has been present all along. In *It Came from Outer Space*, Frank's wife (Virginia Mullen) is upset over her missing husband and Warren suggests that Ellen drive her home. As Ellen is returning to the sheriff's office she is confronted by Frank on the highway. She stops the car and Frank gets in; cold and aloof, he orders her to drive to the mine. Ellen hesitates, watching Frank closely; his appearance suddenly changes into that of the true countenance of the alien. Here, Arnold, with Hitchcockian flair, dissolves from a medium close shot of Ellen screaming to a close shot of the telephone ringing in Warren's office (Fig. II.9). Warren answers and turns it over to John; John learns that the aliens now have Ellen. Warren is furious, finally admitting what he sensed all along, that the aliens are indeed real. Warren tells John: "I'd give anything if things were back the way things were this morning with me calling you a fool."

7. *Society desperately turns to the scientist hero for leadership even though it may still be suspicious of his abilities.* With the invader's presence now obvious to everyone, society has no other choice but to acknowledge its predicament. It also needs a knowledgeable and stalwart leader to guide it, if necessary, into battle against the invader. It now turns to the man it had spurned earlier, the one man who possesses the knowledge to repel the invader: the scientist hero. However, society is often suspicious of the hero, for, considering his knowledge of the invader's power and substance, he may not be who he claims to be but a part of the invasion itself.

In *It Came from Outer Space*, John persuades Warren to play along with the aliens' demands, but Warren remains suspicious of John. After a long meeting with the aliens at which John agrees to help them repair their ship and return to outer space, Warren becomes even more suspicious. As the desert heat rises, Warren grows progressively unstable; he is overly concerned about the aliens' truthfulness, and when he sees one of them walking freely about the town he becomes incensed, believing

Fig. II.9. Imitating Hitchcock's famous cut from landlady's scream to train whistle in *The 39 Steps*, Jack Arnold dissolves from a close shot (seen from alien's point of view) of Ellen (a, b, & c) reacting to Frank's transformation to (d & e) a close shot of telephone ringing in Warren's office; f) John then learns that the aliens hold Ellen hostage.

they are taking over the town. Furious at John for siding with them, he decides to do something about it, but John interferes and they scuffle. The alien notices the fight and flees from town. John follows to warn the aliens that the town has turned against them. Warren then organizes an angry posse that heads for the mine.

In the terrestrial invasion story, society usually places its total trust in the hero. Nesbitt, in *The Beast from 20,000 Fathoms*, is sought by the military authorities for guidance in dealing with the Beast in spite of the fact that Nesbitt is a nuclear scientist and not a paleontologist.

8. The scientist hero offers a rational explanation for the invader's presence as well as a plan to repel the invader; society rallies in a common cause. Once society accepts the scientist hero, he offers what amounts to a rational explanation for the invader's presence. This explanation is accepted as rational at this stage, since it makes sense in the context of the invader's presence and is often accompanied by a plan to repel the invader. Although many remain skeptical, the plan is accepted because it is the only viable alternative for the desperate society. As it turns out, the skeptics are proved wrong and the hero is unconditionally accepted by the society.

Leslie Norman's *X–The Unknown* (1957) is exemplary of this concern for the rational (Fig. II.10). Screenwriter Jimmy Sangster offers a preposterous account of the radioactive mud from the earth's core that menaces Scotland, and yet the explanation as given by Dr. Adam Royston (Dean Jagger) is quite reasonable and logical under the circumstances:

> I suggested this meeting because I think I have an idea about what we may be dealing with. Perhaps one of you may have a solution, then again one of you may think that I'm talking a lot of nonsense and can offer a more logical conclusion . . . [this is] partly fact, mostly theory . . . [and] I would like to resurrect for just a moment if I may a treatise I did when I was a student which has to do with the cooling of the earth's surface. Hundreds of millions of years ago the earth was like the sun; no form, no solidity to it, it was just a blazing mass of energy; and then the earth started cooling and as it cooled an outer crust was formed. The energy was still there but it was being compressed beneath this crust. As time went by the crust grew deeper, and the compression became greater as this vast energy was being squeezed into an ever decreasing space. . . . Well, then in a comparative short space of time, a matter of a hundred thousand years, man has evolved. Man has

Fig. II.10. Dr. Adam Royston explains his theory about strange events in Scotland to fellow scientists John and Peter Elliott in Leslie Norman's atmospheric *X–The Unknown* (1957).

evolved from nothing to become the most intelligent creature on the surface of this planet. Now, considering the far greater span of time involved, isn't it reasonable to assume that the forces contained in the center of this earth have developed an intelligence of their own? If we accept this we must then consider what these forces would think. Their world is slowly being compressed out of existence; therefore, survival must be uppermost in their thoughts. What's more natural in their search for survival than that they should return to the face of the planet where once they lived? Now, if you check you will find that every fifty years by virtue of the position of the earth and the solar system, a greater pull is exerted on the surface of this planet than at other times. Quite unnoticeable to us. But two thousand miles down, who knows? And during this short period of time that this pull is at its most powerful you will find that there's always been a freak tremor, and that in each of these cases a fissure has opened on the surface of the earth. Now, what if on these occasions some of the vast energy trapped below has caused the eruptions or tremors in an attempt to reach the surface, in fact it did reach the surface; it looked around for a means to sustain its existence, for to live one must have nourishment, and these forces are almost pure energy. Now what does energy live on? . . . Energy can only be fed with more energy, or radiation if you like. Fifty, hundred, a hundred and fifty years ago these forces found themselves without any means of sustenance and their mass became unstable and they disintegrated. Now, we come to this fifty year cycle; this time there's radiation. There was radiation in the hospital, there was radiation in my workshop. As long as this thing feeds it will live, and the more it lives the more it will grow.

Although the thought of "intelligent mud" is absurd to most of us, it nonetheless makes sense in the context of the film, since the mud itself is literally alive and preying on society. And no matter how absurd or even profound the explanation may be to the spectator, it is wrapped in the language of "scientism," and hence it "sounds" like an extrapolation of known scientific understanding. Often, substance is lacking and the entire explanation is nothing but jibberish, but the majority of alien invasion films present explanations that are understandable as scientific jargon though not as science itself. Thus the films remain linked to the historical world with its penchant for jargon.

In *The Beast from 20,000 Fathoms*, the explanation offered by Nesbitt was rejected at first by Elson as implausible. As the Beast marches against society, however, the explanation apparently is accepted, and what matters most is the plan to repel the invader. During the Beast's rampage through the streets of New York, a bazooka team manages to wound the creature's neck, but the spilt blood adds yet another threat to society: One by one the soldiers in pursuit of the Beast drop in their tracks, the victims of a potent, primordial plague. Nesbitt warns that while ordinary firepower would kill the Beast, it would also unleash a dangerous plague of unknown proportions. Cremation, he adds, would only exacerbate the problem by causing the infected ashes to be carried by the winds to all parts of the globe. The answer, he argues, is to destroy the Beast with radiation; he suggests that an army sharpshooter fire an isotope into the neck wound. The radioactivity, he claims, will poison the creature and destroy the diseased tissues. Without hesitation, Colonel Evans agrees.

Traditionally, the scientist hero explains the invader's presence to society, but in *It Came from Outer Space* the aliens themselves explain their situation to the scientist hero (Fig. II.11). Following Ellen's abduction by the aliens, John is summoned to the crater. At the entrance to the Excelsior mine, he confronts one of the aliens, demanding to know their secret. The alien, hidden in the shadows, replies:

> We are repairing our ship to leave your world. We need your help . . . [for] we have a long way to go. By nightfall we will have left your earth. You will not see us until it is time . . . [but] we have souls and minds and we are good . . . [and] we are not yet ready to meet in friendship . . . because you would be horrified at the sight of us. Had you fallen on our world it might have been different. We understand more. . . . We hold her hostage as well as the others; keep your people away or we will destroy them. . . . Our mission was to another world, you must believe me; only an error dragged us toward earth. . . . Let us stay apart, the people of your world and ours, for if we come together there will be only destruction.

The narrative in this instance does not call for a plan to repel the invader; rather, the aliens themselves seek John's help in preventing the townspeople from interfering with their plans to repair their ship and return to space. John agrees to help them; but, when he is unable to prevent Warren and the posse from attacking and killing one of them, it

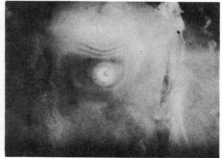

Fig. II.11. After John agrees to aid aliens, a) their leader, who has taken on John's appearance, b) changes into his true form, confirming his own words that "you would be horrified at the sight of us." Audience gets only a glimpse of the alien.

is nonetheless John who offers the final plan to assist them. With the posse closing in, John persuades the aliens to release the hostages as a good-will gesture. The aliens do so, and John dynamites the entrance to the mine, preventing the posse from entering and interfering.

It is at this point in the classical text that societal solidarity is avowed. In perhaps no other film genre is communal solidarity so richly displayed as in the alien invasion film. In film after film, absolutely no signs of dissension, rancor, or discontent are shown by any individual or group. The country is absolutely unified; as Brian Murphy writes, "Americans respond nobly: they do precisely as they are told."[16] That has led many critics, including Murphy, to suggest that the alien invasion film is a celebration of militarism. The potential for such an interpretation is readily apparent; indeed, many scenes show the military marching through American cities and taking complete authority. But we must accept these films in the context of their time as well as in the context of their own value system.[17] True, the army represents a solution for everything, but such a notion is not surprising when one considers the ideology of the time—as one must, since films often relate to specific historical and social events. During the fifties, the threat of communism—the "red menace"—was uppermost in the concerns of western society. Many critics even suggest that the aliens and monsters of the alien invasion film were surrogates for the Sino-Soviet menace.[18] We can accept, then, a view of these films such as Murphy's; evidence in the films themselves affirms this position. Nevertheless, we can see its limitations, for to us this military imagery suggests something more significant: a vision of social unity rather than the authoritarian reason for it. Far from being arbitrarily imposed, the authoritarian control in these films is actively sought and willingly accepted by society.

Even in films in which there is no military command—*It Came from Outer Space*, for example—society still seeks a unifying force or spirit. Initially, society rallies behind Warren. But once the true nature of the aliens is revealed, society rallies behind John. That is exemplified in the closing scene, in which the townspeople—including Warren—gather around John.

What matters in the value system of these films is the *idea* of a unifying force, or the power to unify and bind humanity into a moral whole. As such, the military and police are symbolic representations of the notion of unity. The military control of the population is not to be taken in a literal sense; rather, like everything else in the alien invasion film, it is to be taken on a symbolic level. Thus we can discover a meaning behind the image that may or may not be a reflection of that image—a process Jung calls amplification.[19]

These films are likeable even though they have foolish aspects. One can gain intensity and symbolic force from the reducing of life to such crude components as single-minded, logic-machine scientists, inhuman monsters, intuitive and valiant men of action, and armies of national unity. On the other hand, one can lose contact with social and ideological reality and run the risk of seeming to be talking about reality when one is actually talking about symbolic value. What is certain is that it does no good to ignore one very real aspect of alien invasion films: their ridiculousness (Fig. II.12). But one proper way of reading these films reduces their ridiculousness to a manageable level by bringing out another set of valuable aspects. By viewing these films in the context of symbolic value in the sense of Jungian aesthetics, what may seem ridiculous at the outset often becomes complex and meaningful—even profound—at the end.

9. *The battle, or contest, is waged; the invader is repelled (usually destroyed)*. The climactic duel between society and the invader is fought at this stage of the narrative, and special effects cinematography is again a significant part of the film form. Spectacular visual effects highlight the climactic confrontations in many films, including Sears's *Earth vs. the Flying Saucers*, Inoshira Honda's *The Mysterians* (1959) and *Battle in Outer Space* (1960), Edward Ludwig's *The Black Scorpion* (1957), Juran's *Twenty Million Miles to Earth* and Pal and Haskin's *War of the Worlds*.

In *The Beast from 20,000 Fathoms*, the Beast has once again emerged from the river; this time it takes refuge near the roller coaster ride at Coney Island. Nesbitt and the sharpshooter, Corporal Stone (Lee Van Cleef), take their positions atop the amusement ride. The Beast rears up and Stone fires. The Beast screams, and the roller coaster plunges off the broken track, igniting the structure into flames. Once again Harryhausen's amazing skill at stop-motion photography and optical printing is evident as the Beast writhes in the flaming structure and finally collapses, dead from the poisonous isotope.

Fig. II.12. Huge hypodermic syringe in Bert I. Gordon's *The Amazing Colossal Man* (1957) seems ridiculous; but in a figurative sense it expresses infantile fears.

Often the confrontation is less spectacular and more mundane, if not subdued. It is best described as a contest in the sense that the hero often struggles against both society and the invaders in an attempt to bring peace and harmony to each side. In this case, it is not so much a violent battle—no armies against invaders—as it is ordinary citizens of small communities struggling against the alien invaders. A few films use the alien invasion motif to investigate social issues, predominantly xenophobia, or the fear of strangers. Lee Sholem's *Superman and the Mole Men* (1951) deals more with hate-monger Luke Benson (Jeff Corey) and the frightened and confused citizens of Silsby than with any threat from the mole men. So frightened are these citizens that they even defy Superman (George Reeves).[20]

In *It Came from Outer Space,* which also has allusions to xenophobia, the contest involves John's efforts to mediate between the hostile townspeople and the frightened and desperate aliens. The crucial point that demonstrates John's success is the scene in which he dynamites the mine entrance, in effect placing a wall between the mob and the aliens. This act allows Warren and his posse a chance at introspection as the aliens finally return to outer space with the promise to return to earth when the time is right.

10. Humanity acknowledges that it has been arrogant in presuming upon its role in the cosmos. If a message can be extracted from the alien invasion film, it is one of humility. The genre presents a vision of humanity no longer alone in the cosmos. Though humanity defeats the invader, life can never be the same after the experience; that which humanity has understood as real is amended to include things heretofore understood as unreal.

For the most part this element of the narrative is implicit. The closing images of the films reveal triumph mixed with loss; the invader has been repelled but at the same time man's perception of himself and his world has been altered. In Norman's *X–The Unknown*, for example, Doctor Royston succeeds in destroying the deadly mud only to have an unexpected explosion shatter his confidence. "What happened, Adam?" asks Inspector McGill (Leo McKern), and the puzzled Royston replies, "I don't know but it shouldn't have happened." The camera remains fixed on a long shot of the diminutive, pathetic figure of Royston standing alone at the fissure, knowing all too well that he and his science have not mastered the mysteries of existence. The closing image of *The Beast from 20,000 Fathoms* is similar. Nesbitt and Lee survey the shambles of their earthly world, knowing, like Royston, that science has not solved the vast complexities of life.

Occasionally, films explicitly note the humbling of mankind. Wise's *The Day the Earth Stood Still* is the most overt and profound of these films (Fig. II.13). In a farewell speech, Klaatu (Michael Rennie) not only chides humanity for its arrogance but places the burden of survival squarely on humanity's shoulders:

> I am leaving soon and you will forgive me if I speak bluntly. The universe grows smaller every day, and the threats of aggression by any group anywhere can no longer be tolerated. . . . For our policemen we created a race of robots. Their function is to patrol the planets in spaceships like this one and preserve the peace. In matters of aggression we have given them absolute power over us. This power cannot be revoked. At the first signs of violence they act automatically against the aggressor. The penalty for provoking their action is too terrible to risk. The result is we live in peace without arms or armies, secure in the knowledge that we are free from aggression and war, free to pursue more profitable enterprises. Now, we do not pretend to have achieved perfection, but we do have a system, and it works. I came here to give these facts. It is no concern of ours how you run your own planet, but if you threaten to extend your violence, this earth of yours will be reduced to a burned-out cinder. Your choice is simple: join us and live in peace or pursue your present course and face obliteration. We shall be waiting for your answer. The decision rests with you.

Certainly, Klaatu's words, backed up by the prowess of his giant robot, Gort, signal the closing of a way of life and the emergence of a new life for humanity. They also reveal the power of the alien invasion film; the humbling of humanity is not to be taken as a defeat but rather as a victory. Humanity is now free to discover its true self with respect to the powers and forces that run through the cosmos. This awareness, this discovery of a more profound level of consciousness, is precisely the meaning and value inherent in the alien invasion genre, which is filled with wonder and hope for all humanity. The closing image of *It Came from Outer Space* epitomizes such wonder (Fig. II.14). In an image

Fig. II.13. Benevolent but misunderstood Klaatu with his robot Gort rebukes humanity for its arrogance in Robert Wise's *The Day the Earth Stood Still* (1951).

Fig. II.14. Once-hostile townspeople gather around John, a) watching the alien ship take off, b) then listening to John as he expresses hope that "they'll be back."

suggestive of the disciples gathering around Christ, Ellen and the townspeople gather around John as the alien spacecraft leaves the earth for outer space. As Arnold's camera slowly tracks toward a closeup of John, he tells us all that "it wasn't the right time for us to meet, but there'll be other nights, other stars for us to watch; they'll be back."

The Prometheus Variation: The Irrational Function

The narrative pattern of most alien invasion films follows the basic outline of the classical text, but a close investigation reveals a structure in some of these films that is a variation on the classical text. Although these films deal with an invader unleashed against society, the invader's presence is the direct result of man's intervention in the natural order of the cosmos. Unlike the classical text, this variation does not have an invader that comes to earth from outer space or inner earth but one that is "created" by what the films declare to be an inherent flaw in man, nature, or science. As such, these films center much of their narrative structure on the characterization of the reclusive scientist responsible for the invader's existence, a man who experiments with unknown forces in hope of improving the quality of life. Since the message of these films is similar to the message of the myth of Prometheus—that man should not meddle with the natural order of things—I have called this narrative the Prometheus variation.[21]

These films concentrate their narratives on the reclusive scientist and his creation, and express themselves with settings that are often artificial. Thus the Prometheus variation comes closer to the structural and thematic pattern of the horror film than to any aspect of the science fiction genre. Accordingly, the many films that constitute the Prometheus variation, notably the myriad Frankenstein films, have been and continue to be misread and misinterpreted as horror films. The truth is that these films remain properly linked with the alien invasion genre. Unlike horror films, which focus on the evil intentions of the scientist and his mad desire for power and control, the Promethean films present a scientist whose intentions are basically good at best and amoral at worst.

The evil, mad scientist of the horror film has a long and distinguished film history, but the Promethean scientist is newer. For the most part, he is a product of the fifties. When Bela Lugosi (Fig. II.15) portrayed the mad Doctor Alex Zorka in Ford Beebe and Saul A. Goodkind's *The Phantom Creeps* (1939), he had a whole array of scientific gadgets, including a belt that made him invisible and a giant robot, and he used these devices to enact a plan of revenge against those he considered responsible for his wife's death. And seventeen years later, when Lugosi played the mad atomic scientist Eric Vornoff in Edward D. Wood, Jr.'s *Bride of the Monster*, also known as *Bride of the Atom* (1956), he was experimenting with isotopes and atom smashers, hoping to create a horde of "atomic zombies" that would conquer the world for him. In both instances, the scientist was motivated not by altruism but by the desire to enslave mankind and rule the world. Both of these films thus resonate with an "evil" presence that puts them into the horror genre. By contrast, Andre Delambre (Al [later David] Hedison) in Kurt Neumann's *The Fly* (1958) works desperately to perfect his teleportation machine; his motive, unlike the motives of Lugosi's characters, is not to rule the world but to improve man's efficiency. Unfortunately, Delambre experiments on himself and inadvertently integrates his own atomic structure with that of an ordinary house fly; the result is a hideous "thing" that, as the advertising copy reads, "was once human— even as you and I." The desire to improve the quality of life—a mark that distinguishes the science fiction genre from the horror genre—also

Fig. II.15. Unlike Boris Karloff, whose characterizations nearly always evoked sympathy from audiences, Bela Lugosi portrayed characters of evil intent and thus became a prominent icon of the horror film and not of the science fiction film.

motivates such experimenters as Professor Walgate in Crabtree's *Fiend without a Face,* Professor Deemer in Arnold's *Tarantula,* and even Dr. Jekyll (Boris Karloff) in Charles Lamont's *Abbott and Costello Meet Dr. Jekyll and Mr. Hyde* (1953).

Another aspect of the Prometheus variation often obscures the distinction between the horror and the science fiction genres: hubris. The scientist experiments for no reason other than the desire to experiment, and often this desire is motivated by the scientist's pride in his own work and knowledge. The question that arises is significant: Is this hubris a symptom of a greater, underlying evil?

To answer this question we need to examine Peter Cushing's portrayal of Baron Victor Frankenstein in the Hammer Films series, beginning in 1957 with Terence Fisher's *The Curse of Frankenstein* (Fig. II.16).[22] Cushing's performance is unlike the portrayals by his predecessors (Colin Clive, Basil Rathbone, Sir Cedric Hardwicke, and others) in that he has replaced the sympathetic scientist with the cold, aloof aristocrat, or what David Pirie describes as a combination of Baudelaire's "dandy" and Oscar Wilde: "an extravagant rebel who alternates between noble defiance and detached cruelty."[23] In these films, Frankenstein is not an altruistic experimenter, but he is not exactly evil, either. We never know his intentions other than his desire to experiment; as Martin Tropp notes, Frankenstein's life is his devotion to science.[24] In Cushing's hands, then, Frankenstein emerges as a haughty, snobbish egoist, devoid of ethics and morality and motivated only by his proud desire to experiment. The issue before us is again a question of intent. We cannot say that the Baron is evil; nor can we say that he is altruistic. What we can say is that he is a vain and selfish man. That is a flaw in the scientist's character, and Jack Matthews describes the result as the "Frankenstein myth, in which a human meddles with the life force, manipulating that which is essentially beyond human understanding, and ultimately being destroyed . . . as a result of his proud

Fig. II.16. Peter Cushing as Baron Frankenstein in Fisher's *The Revenge of Frankenstein* (1958) epitomizes the amoral scientist of the science fiction film who experiments for no other reason than the desire to experiment.

and foolish tinkering, his *hubris*."[25] Hence, Frankenstein and others like him belong to the alien invasion genre and not the horror genre. We must remember that the evil scientist of the horror film is very evil, in characterization and intent, whereas the Promethean scientist either works toward improving the quality of life or experiments for the sake of experimentation.

As noted earlier, the Prometheus variation follows the basic pattern of exposition established by the classical text. In the Prometheus variation, however, the unexplained happenings bring the hero, who is often an authority figure, to society. The hero is usually an outsider, and the mysterious events bring him to the group, be it large city or village. Under the guidance of the hero, society seeks rational explanations for the odd occurrences. The hero usually has a hunch that something beyond human understanding is responsible. Undaunted, and supported by the faith of his girl friend, who is usually a member of the group, the hero soon discovers that a scientist, usually reclusive and aloof, is responsible for the strange events. Before the scientist can corroborate the hero's findings, the invader has marched on society. Here we see, in many instances, the motif in which the scientist and the invader are one and the same. Often this identity is literal, as in the many versions of *Dr. Jekyll and Mr. Hyde* (Fig. II.17), but many films imply only a figurative linkage. Society now turns to the hero for leadership, and by a sudden hunch the hero discovers the method to repel the invader. At this stage, prompted perhaps by the danger involved, the hero and his girl friend are drawn closer together and marriage is imminent. Moreover, society, which once doubted the hero, now eagerly cheers him to victory over the invader. The battle or contest is fought, and society emerges victorious.

Scientific experimentation is at the heart of the Prometheus variation, of course, and thus these films do not, like the classical text films, center their narratives on the invader's impact on society. Rather, they focus on the relationship between the scientist and his creation. While

Fig. II.17. E. A. Dupont, who directed the classic silent film *Variety* (1925), also directed this entry in the Jekyll/Hyde theme of the Prometheus variation.

there usually is no metamorphosis, there is an uncanny bond between the two. This relationship gives much of the meaning and value to the Prometheus variation.

To display the inner workings of the Prometheus variation, I have chosen another Jack Arnold film, which is representative of the type. *Tarantula* (1955), with John Agar, Mara Corday, and Leo G. Carroll, is based on an original television script by Robert M. Fresco, "No Food for Thought," which was an episode of Ziv's *Science Fiction Theatre*. The story tells of "a deadly accident of science," as the advertising copy reads, that unleashes an unusual specimen of tarantula. Having been injected with a special nutrient, it grows into a giant monster that attacks the small town of Desert Rock, Arizona (Fig. II.18).

Professor Gerald Deemer (Carroll) and two associates have secluded themselves in a large house on the outskirts of Desert Rock. Hoping to increase the world's food supply, Deemer experiments with a synthetic nutrient fortified with radioactive isotopes. He tells his new assistant, a young graduate student named Stephanie and called Steve (Corday), that the world will be without sufficient food supplies in a few generations: "I have sought an atomically stable nutritional formula to feed the mass of mankind when it grows too large for the food supply." Unfortunately, the nutrient has dangerous side effects: Injected into animals, it causes giantism.

Adding problems for Deemer are his two associates. Both have injected the nutrient into themselves, attempting to evaluate the nutrients on human tissue. The serum causes an aggravated case of the rare disease acromegaly—progressive enlargement of the face, hands, and feet. Even worse, it slowly deteriorates brain cells, causing insanity. One afternoon, Deemer is attacked by one of his crazed associates; a chair hurled at Deemer misses but shatters the glass on a large terrarium holding a tarantula specimen that is already the size of a large dog. Deemer is knocked unconscious, and the tarantula escapes into the desert. When Deemer awakens he finds his laboratory in shambles, his

Fig. II.18. Monstrous spider in *Tarantula* attacks Desert Rock, Arizona, just before the creature is destroyed by Air Force jets.

associate dead. He has the horrifying realization that he, too, has been injected with the serum.

In this film, experimentation is quite explicit. Indeed, the first half centers on Deemer's efforts to produce the supernutrient, and Deemer is revealed as a good man, a visionary concerned with the future well-being of humanity. Once the spider escapes, this aspect of the narrative overlaps with the second half: the spider's attack on society. There is a sort of merging of the two halves. Arnold crosscuts between Deemer's continued experimentation (despite his acromegaly), and the spider's growing presence in society. Moreover, Deemer's world progressively gets darker, falling away into an abyss of failure and futility. It culminates in the nighttime destruction of Deemer's home by the giant spider and the figurative replacement of Deemer by the spider (Fig. II.19), which kills him. The creation thus becomes an extension of the creator, and certainly the spider symbolizes the dark and uncontrollable side of man. Once the spider demolishes the house and kills Deemer, the narrative then concentrates on the attack of the monster on society and society's efforts to repel it.

Crucial to this narrative is the motif of the flaw. A scientific flaw unleashes the spider; since the nutrient possesses a deadly side effect when used on animal life, the unpredictability of experimentation, the dabbling with forces beyond human understanding and control, is to blame for the death and destruction in society.

The hero of the Prometheus variation—as distinguished from the experimenter like Deemer—is seldom an intellectual. He is an intuitive thinker who exists comfortably in his environment and knows right from wrong. Even in films in which the hero is a scientist (for example, *The Curse of Frankenstein*) he often rejects science for common sense or the morally right hunch that leads to the destruction of the monster. He relies on intuitive thought to meet the challenge of the scientist and his aberrant creation. This pitting of the intuitive hero against the intellectual scientist reflects an attitude of many in the fifties toward the

Fig. II.19. Tarantula manifests Professor Deemer's dark and uncontrollable side, figuratively replacing Deemer by demolishing his house and killing him.

elitism of scientists and intellectuals.[26] Thus the hero of the Prometheus variation often emerges as a figure of the common man, honest, practical, virtuous, moral, and hard-working, the kind of American the audiences of the fifties could identify with and admire.

Matt Hastings (John Agar), the Desert Rock physician, is this kind of hero. He is pragmatic and worldly; he knows his part in the community and is sure of his place in the future. When the giant spider attacks the community, he is the only one who acts—a common characteristic of the hero in these films. As the toll of human life mounts, his actions are motivated by a sense of duty and justice, and he responds to the threat not with scientific inquiry but with practical sense: The creature must be destroyed! Since this reduction of options to just one is so obvious, it can only stand as a flag, a metaphor, for the common sense that permeates these films. Science, it says, with its logic and amorality brings all this death and destruction, while common sense with its morality and justice is the only thing capable of destroying the "thing." Matt Hastings's only recourse, since he cannot handle the situation alone, is to turn to those who can effectively deal with the monster, the U.S. Air Force. In a volley of napalm, the giant spider is burned to a cinder, and society rejoices, knowing that common sense has prevailed. With Deemer and his science out of the way, the people of Desert Rock are once again safe and secure.

If a specific message can be extracted from the Prometheus variation, it lies somewhere in this taboo, this reactionary attitude toward science (Fig. II.20). No matter what the motive or intention of the scientist, these films seem to say, the pursuit of absolute knowledge always brings destruction, not only upon the scientist himself but also upon many innocent persons.

Fig. II.20. Title cards from trailers for a) *Fiend without a Face*, left, and b) *The Unearthly* state succinctly the alien invasion film's attitude toward scientific experimentation.

The alien invasion genre clearly focuses on science, and hence it is "science fiction." But in one aspect it shows us hope and aspiration, in another death and destruction. We can interpret these opposing attitudes toward science not as signs of dissension or confusion but rather in the same way we interpret the classical text and the Prometheus variation, as complementary opposites that make for a sturdy balance. Together they form the alien invasion genre, whose meaning and value ultimately are good and positive—as we shall now see.

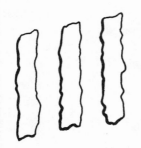

Iconography and Convention

The analysis of the alien invasion film would be incomplete without an examination of the recurrent images that, as Colin McArthur has observed in connection with the gangster film, "set [the film] off visually from other types and are the means whereby primary definitions are made."[1] Such images are referred to as iconography.

An alien invasion film has recurrent images, figures, and objects that unequivocally identify it as belonging to the alien invasion genre; these images also uncontestably distinguish the genre from other genres. I have categorized these recurrent images (and I am using *images* now to include figures and objects) in terms of certain film conventions: the actors, the machinery, the special effects footage, the stock footage, and the landscapes. In addition, I have included as conventions two aspects of the cinema that exist outside the actual film and yet complement the film's existence: the titles and the advertising material, notably the posters.

Iconography as applied to the alien invasion film is social not in the sense that language is social but rather in the sense that an archetype is social. The iconographic images are recognizable, or seem to be recognizable, because of their dynamic relationship to primordial images in the collective (also called transpersonal) unconscious. They are universal symbols ripe with meaning and easily recognized by the human mind. I call the relationship between the film image and the mental image dynamic because it elicits a value response, an intellectual or emotional response, and not merely an acknowledgment of the image. In this sense, as Jung stated, the image speaks to us "chiefly upon the *attitude* of the observing consciousness; for instance, on whether it regards a given fact not merely as such but also as an expression for something unknown."[2]

The Beast, in *The Beast from 20,000 Fathoms,* is a dinosaur, though of a species that is scientifically fictitious.[3] On the one hand, the word *dinosaur* connotes nothing more than a name; nothing in the word itself indicates hostility or viciousness. On the other hand, the Beast-image connotes more than a mere name and certainly more than an animal. The Beast, its snake-like/reptilian quality evoking the archetypal serpent (Fig. III.1), is hostile and vicious, a primordial image that may well be, as Carl Sagan suggests in *The Dragons of Eden,* an unconscious memory of mankind at the mercy of dinosaurs.[4]

Iconography, then, is first of all the "thing" studied, the images that momentarily denote themselves as recognizable because the films repeat them. But iconography is not limited to this denotation, for the images also connote various qualities about themselves and our relationship to them. With this distinction in mind, we can say that the iconographic image is a symbol and not a sign because, as Don Fredericksen points out, "something relatively unknown, neither explained by nor satisfied by concretistic interpretation and its attendant semiotic attitude, generates such imagery."[5]

My approach to iconography stems from two sources. First, it comes from the spectator's recognition of the images as images within the alien invasion film form itself, what McArthur has described as "the continuity over several decades of patterns of visual imagery, of recurrent objects and figures in dynamic relationship."[6] I call these patterns conventions—specifically iconographic conventions to distinguish them from literary or dramatic conventions. A convention is the result of a repetition of screen images that elicits a sort of "we've seen this all before" response. Second, my approach comes from my own conviction that film images are like dream images, and that "images" within the mind correspond to these screen images. Thus, for me, iconography is a dynamic relationship between the images of the screen and the "images" in the unconscious. To study the implications of this claim is to study iconography, and iconography is what I referred to in the previous chapter as "the living myth."

Fig. III.1. Prehistoric monster in Lourié's *The Giant Behemoth* (1959), here capsizing a ferry, resembles the serpent, archetypal symbol of evil and destruction.

The conventions of the alien invasion genre are dominated by iconography. The genre simply did not have enough time to develop conventions through a "continuity over several decades of patterns of visual imagery." The alien invasion film essentially is a product of a single decade, the fifties, though the genre spilled over into the early sixties and a few such films were made in the late seventies and early eighties. Hence, not being able to rely on decades of recurrent images to establish its conventions, the alien invasion film relied on quantity. And, as it happened, the appetite of American cinema audiences was for quantity: Through continued box-office support, they demanded a steady diet of monsters and alien invaders. Conventions were ingrained by sheer mass production. Unlike other genres, with the exception perhaps of the western, the alien invasion genre was established practically immediately. In 1951 and 1952 alone, nine films were "conventionalizing" the genre: *The Thing from Another World, The Man from Planet X, Superman and the Mole Men, The Day the Earth Stood Still, Son of Dr. Jekyll, Abbott and Costello Meet the Invisible Man, The Flying Disc Man from Mars, Radar Men from the Moon,* and *Zombies of the Stratosphere.* And the genre was in full swing in 1953: *It Came from Outer Space, Phantom from Space, Invaders from Mars, The Twonky, War of the Worlds, Abbott and Costello Meet Dr. Jekyll and Mr. Hyde, The Beast from 20,000 Fathoms, Robot Monster, Donovan's Brain, The Neanderthal Man, Invasion USA, The Magnetic Monster,* and *The Lost Planet.*

Thanks to this mass production, the alien invasion genre did not need decades to establish conventions. The conventions were accepted immediately, and iconography is the reason. The interaction between iconography and convention is simply a cause-and-effect relationship. This relationship is best seen in an examination of the actors who dominated the genre and the era.

The Actors

Certainly one of the more intriguing aspects of the alien invasion genre is the near repertory company of male performers who dominated the genre. Like their predecessors in the horror movies of the thirties and forties and their descendants in the late fifties and sixties—Vincent Price, Peter Cushing, and Christopher Lee—these actors became inextricably linked to the genre, not only to the alien invasion film but also to the science fiction film in general and to the science fiction television series of the fifties. In film after film we find the same faces and voices.

Richard Carlson (Fig. III.2), with a strong and convincing pro-

Fig. III.2. Richard Carlson epitomizes the cleancut, intellectual, romantic visionary of the science fiction film.

fessorial presence, played in *It Came from Outer Space, The Magnetic Monster,* and two science fiction adventures, Jack Arnold's *The Creature from the Black Lagoon* (1954) and *Riders to the Stars* (1954), which Carlson himself directed. Carlson's dynamic scientific presence also took him into television, where he shared professorial duties with a real-life University of California professor, Dr. Frank Baxter, in a Bell Telephone science series, *Hemo the Magnificent* (1957), *The Strange Case of the Cosmic Rays* (1957), and *Unchained Goddess* (1958). Although Carlson appeared in only two true alien invasion films, his presence seemed to serve as a model for other actors. It was said that his dynamic portrayal of romantic visionary John Putnam in *It Came from Outer Space* created the quintessential science fiction hero; John Baxter described it as "embodying the cleancut intelligence that audiences demanded in their scientific heroes."[7] The Carlson influence can be sensed in the portrayals of scientists by Arthur Franz in *Invaders from Mars,* Richard Denning in *Creature with the Atom Brain,* and Rex Reason in *This Island Earth* and *The Creature Walks among Us.*

Contrasting with this romantic visionary hero are the genre's other heroes, the practical, "guts 'n glory guys," members of what has been called the Hawksian brotherhood. And it is precisely in a Howard Hawks production that we find the prototype of this action hero. Kenneth Tobey (Fig. III.3) personified the military man of action, Captain Patrick Hendry, in Hawks and Christian Nyby's *The Thing from Another World.*

Tobey repeated this characterization in *The Beast from 20,000 Fathoms,* as Colonel Jack Evans; in *It Came from Beneath the Sea,* as Commander Pete Matthews; and, changing from the military to a tough big-city cop, in Paul Landres' *The Vampire* (1957), as Detective Buck Donnelly. Tobey's hero is a no-nonsense, intuitive, hard-core pro-

Fig. III.3. Kenneth Tobey, in Hawks and Nyby's *The Thing from Another World* (1951), is an intuitive professional who has no time for the romantic visions of scientists when hostile forces threaten the world.

fessional who has no time for romantic visions, particularly when he is faced with a seven-foot-tall, savage monster on the prowl, and little time for the scientific jargon and philosophy that purport to explain the monster and humanity's relationship to it. Baxter describes Tobey's characterization as a tough guy,[8] and this image can be seen repeated in the roles of such military leaders as Tim Holt's naval commander in Arnold Laven's *The Monster That Challenged the World* (1957) and Marshall Thompson's characterizations in *Fiend without a Face, First Man into Space,* and Edward L. Cahn's *It! The Terror from Beyond Space* (1958).

Tobey's influential characterization can be found even outside the lead roles in the alien invasion film. When characterization is centered on the Carlson type, the romantic visionary, then the pragmatic man of action, albeit a bit less forceful, is found in the secondary roles. These secondary roles were usually assigned to Morris Ankrum or Thomas Browne Henry (Fig. III.4), two character actors whose presence in alien invasion films is as predictable as the monsters and invaders them-

Fig. III.4. Two character actors whose presences in alien invasion films are as predictable as the aliens themselves: A) Thomas Browne Henry, left, as General MacIntosh in Nathan Juran's *Twenty Million Miles to Earth* (1957), and b) Morris Ankrum as General Hanley in *Earth vs. the Flying Saucers.*

selves. Indeed, Ankrum appeared in eleven science fiction films, usually playing a military officer: Kurt Neumann's *Rocketship X-M* (1950), *Earth vs. the Flying Saucers*, *The Giant from the Unknown*, *Invaders from Mars*, Bert I. Gordon's *The Beginning of the End* (1957), *The Giant Claw*, Harry Horner's *Red Planet Mars* (1952), Lesley Selander's *Flight to Mars* (1951) as a Martian general, and Kurt Neumann's *Kronos* (1957) as a psychiatrist, for a change. Henry, who slightly resembles Ankrum, appeared as a military officer in *Earth vs. the Flying Saucers* with Ankrum, *Twenty Million Miles to Earth*, *The Beginning of the End* with Ankrum, and Edward Bernd's *Space Master X-7* (1958); in addition, he played secondary roles in Herbert L. Strock's *How to Make a Monster* (1958) and *The Brain from Planet Arous*.

If true "stars" emerged from the alien invasion genre, they are Arthur Franz and John Agar (Fig. III.5), who between them starred in thirteen features. Both actors portrayed characters of the Carlson mold who express a sense of hope for civilization and who connote the reconciliation of science and humanity. On several occasions, however, they eschewed the professorial persona to play tough commanders in the Tobey tradition. This vacillation between the two molds worked well, for both Franz and Agar had physical presences that lent themselves to either characterization with as much credibility as the actors who seemed "typed" to one or the other, and indeed that may be the reason for their repeated popularity.

Despite Arthur Franz's striking performance as Eddie Miller, the psychotic lady-killer, in Edward Dmytryk's *The Sniper* (1952), he will be long associated with science fiction films. Commencing in 1951 as Chief Engineer Jim Barker in Monogram's cinecolor production of *Flight to Mars*,[9] Franz spanned the decade in *Abbott and Costello Meet the Invis-*

Fig. III.5. Stars of science fiction films: A) John Agar, left, as Major Bruce Jay in *Invisible Invaders* and b) Arthur Franz as Professor Stuart Kelston in William Cameron Menzies's *Invaders from Mars* (1953).

ible Man (as the invisible man), *Invaders from Mars*, *The Flame Barrier* (as a tough jungle explorer), *Monster on the Campus*, and *The Atomic Submarine* (as a tough submarine commander). In addition, he co-starred with Marshall Thompson in *The World of Giants*, a syndicated television series of 1959 produced by William Alland.[10]

John Agar, introduced to the screen in 1948 as the rookie cavalry officer O'Rourke in John Ford's *Fort Apache*, found stardom in the alien invasion film in 1955 with Jack Arnold's *Revenge of the Creature*. He went on to more or less dominate the science fiction films of the latter part of the decade: *Tarantula*, Virgil Vogel's *The Mole People* (1956), *The Daughter of Dr. Jekyll*, *Attack of the Puppet People*, *The Brain from Planet Arous*, and *Invisible Invaders*. His science fiction career continued into the sixties as well, establishing Agar as "star" in terms of quantity if not of quality.

Still other faces are seen in numerous alien invasion films (Fig. III.6). Richard Denning first appeared with Richard Carlson in *Creature from the Black Lagoon*, then took solo billing in *Creature with the Atom Brain*, *Target Earth*, *The Day the World Ended*, and *The Black Scorpion*. Jeff Morrow first played in the alien invasion film as the humane Exeter from the planet Metaluna in Joseph Newman's *This Island Earth* (1955). Afterward he offered an interesting performance as the narcissistic Dr. Barton in John Sherwood's *The Creature Walks among Us* (1956), and he ended his fifties career with appearances in *Kronos* and *The Giant Claw*. Still other familiar faces include Peter Graves, Robert Clarke, and several supporting players.[11]

These actors themselves are a convention. In light of McArthur's description of continuity and recurrent objects and figures, we can say that the recognizable screen presences of these actors created a continu-

Fig. III.6. A) Whit Bissell and b) Richard Denning, two of many players who found prominent roles in alien invasion films of the fifties.

ity within the alien invasion genre. Moreover, their screen presences formed an iconography by personifying the mental, symbolic image of the hero, in this case the romantic visionary and the tough guy. McArthur writes: "By the curious alchemy of the cinema, each successive appearance in the genre further solidifies the actor's screen persona until he no longer plays a role but assimilates it to the collective entity made up of his own body and personality and his past screen roles."[12] In this sense, it is practically impossible to separate the actor from the role; he *is* the hero.

The Machinery

The second major convention and the best known iconographic image embedded in the alien invasion film is the machine—the flying saucer in the classical text, the laboratory in the Prometheus variation, and often the military machinery in both types of narrative patterns (although a discussion of military hardware is best saved for an examination of the stock footage convention).

When invaders come from space they invariably arrive in a saucer, a sphere, or a cylindrical flying machine (Fig. III.7). By and large the saucer is the most frequently used vehicle for interstellar travel, having brought aliens to earth in such films as *The Thing from Another World, The Atomic Submarine, The Day the Earth Stood Still, Earth vs. the Flying Saucers, Invaders from Mars, Invasion of the Saucer Men, Invisible Invaders, Plan 9 from Outer Space, This Island Earth, Visit to a Small Planet, The Mysterians,* and *Devil Girl from Mars. The Cosmic Man* and the giant transparent alien in *Attack of the Fifty Foot Woman* came to earth in spheres (actually the same footage in both films), and invaders who came in cylinders include the Martians in *War of the Worlds, The Man from Planet X, Zombies of the Stratosphere,* and *Radar Men from the Moon* (the latter and *The Flying Disc Man from Mars* used the intact sequence of the cylindrical rocket crashing to earth from their 1946 predecessor, *The Purple Monster Strikes*). Saucer, sphere, and cylinder all showed up in the 1956 documentary *Unidentified Flying Objects,* which purported to assemble "actual" footage of flying objects; interestingly, this footage is dominated by the archetypal flying saucer.

As iconography, the saucer/sphere/cylinder flying machines are important because of their relationship to the mandala (Sanskrit for circle), the symbol Jung identified with psychological wholeness and totality. Jung himself saw this relationship in the fifties and wrote about it in *Flying Saucers: A Modern Myth of Things Seen in the Skies.* His thesis is that the vast amount of UFO sightings was due to the anxiety of the

Fig. III.7. Mandala symbol manifested in the flying machines of alien invasion films: A) saucer in *Earth vs. the Flying Saucers,* above left, b) sphere in Nathan Hertz's *Attack of the Fifty Foot Woman* (1958), above right, and c) cylinder, or familiar rocketship, in Fred C. Brannon's *Radar Men from the Moon* (1951).

times. The fifties decade was a time of cold war and international suspicion; disunity, conflict, and confusion; and advanced esoteric technology, exemplified by UniVac (the "thinking machine"), satellites and rockets, the atomic-powered submarine *Nautilus* cruising under the North Pole, and the ultimate weapon, the thermonuclear bomb. The advertising copy for *Rocketship X-M* summed it all up: "The Future is Here!" The future, however, offered a seemingly black and white portrait of the times: humanity on the verge of a second Eden, or humanity on the verge of Armageddon. In such a time of crisis, Jung says, new or old symbols are brought into play. What the mandala symbolized for ancient alchemy, the flying saucer symbolized for modern technology. The flying objects "are to be regarded as *symbols* representing in visual form, some thought that was not thought consciously, but is merely potentially present in the unconscious, in invisible form, and attains visibility only through the process of becoming conscious."[13] Jung sees these flying objects as mandala figures.

The mandala is the archetypal symbol for order. As Jung states, "Experience shows that individual mandalas are symbols of order and that they occur in patients chiefly during times of psychic disorientation or reorientation. As magic circles they bind and subdue the lawless powers belonging to the world of darkness, and depict or create an order that transforms the chaos into a cosmos."[14] Jung explains that mandala symbols occur in the dreams of persons who have never heard of or consciously recognized mandalas, and, significantly, "are widely disseminated in the historical records of many peoples and many epochs. Their significance as symbols of unity and totality is amply confirmed by history."[15]

Indeed, the art of humanity is laden with mandalas. M.-L. von Franz, in her essay "The Process of Individuation," has reported mandala symbols representing wholeness in such diverse cultures as those of the Navajo Indians, who use mandala sand paintings in an attempt to resuscitate their infirm and bring them back into harmony with self, and of various Eastern civilizations, where similar pictures are used for similar purposes. Von Franz writes:

> The contemplation of a mandala is meant to bring an inner peace, a feeling that life has again found its meaning and order. The mandala also conveys this feeling when it appears spontaneously in the dreams of modern men who are not influenced by any religious traditions of this sort and know nothing about it.[16]

The immediate question, in reference to the alien invasion film, is: How can flying saucers bring peace and harmony when their inhabitants, in most cases, are out to conquer our world? This question is answered by examining two valid approaches to the film in general. First, we bring to the film an external approach of simply accepting the drama; our reactions and responses amount to a vicarious experience. In the alien invasion film, specifically, the inhabitants of the saucers arrive and issue a challenge to mankind, and mankind responds by rallying behind its hero and overcoming what appear to be impossible odds. We, the audience—by vicariously experiencing, with the sense of control and catharsis that the cinema offers, the seemingly impossible conditions of the film world—can, however momentarily, confront the real world with a bit more ease. We also bring an interior mode, or psychic approach, to our encounter with the drama. To accept this proposition we must also accept the cinema as art; we must accept Jung's notion that there is an intimate relationship between dream, myth, and art, and that all three serve as media through which the archetypes of the unconscious are brought into harmony with the conscious. Accepting such notions permits one to see a relationship between UFO sightings (or, as Jung calls them, visions) and the cinema that documents, indexes, and presents similar objects to audiences as a collective dream. With these two modes in mind, we can better understand Jung's basic tenet for interpreting the psychic aspects of UFO sightings.

The principle is rather simple. The flying saucer is the iconographic image for the symbol (mandala) of wholeness and totality. Wholeness and totality, furthermore, are representative of individuation. The flying saucer, then, is the vehicle by which the ego assembles the archetypes for full harmony within consciousness. Such actions toward wholeness by the ego (prompted by the archetype of the self) comprise the process of individuation.

To answer our question about how flying saucers can bring harmony when their inhabitants seem malevolent, we need only look at the following scheme: *The flying saucer (mandala) from space (unconscious) brings its inhabitants (archetypes) to earth (conscious mind) where the hero (ego-cum-self) deals with the inhabitants to achieve a proper and harmonious conclusion (individuation).* It is important to recognize that the marauding Martians, attacking invaders, and so on—no matter how malevolent they may seem—are actually positive images. As Jung himself is quick to observe, both good and evil, or at least an awareness of each, are necessary for achieving wholeness. A moral decision, after all, cannot be properly made without a knowledge of both good and evil.

This scheme works not only for the extraterrestrial invasion film but also for the monster-on-the-loose or terrestrial invasion film. But in lieu of a mandala figure these films feature fire, and fire becomes the principal iconographic image of this type of story (Fig. III.8). The mon-

Fig. III.8. Fire symbol of terrestrial invasion story is often seen in an atomic explosion. In this sequence from *The Amazing Colossal Man*, Col. Manning is caught in the middle of an atomic explosion and, as the ads say, he grows and grows "to a giant, to a monster, to a behemoth! When will it stop?"

ster invariably appears by means of fire. Usually it is a man-made atomic blast that either awakens the monster from eons of suspended animation, as in *The Beast from 20,000 Fathoms, The Giant Behemoth,* and *Godzilla, King of the Monsters,* or serves as a cause of giantism or mutation, as in *Them!, Tarantula, The Beginning of the End,* and *The Amazing Colossal Man.* Nature's fire also unleashes the monsters: A volcanic holocaust releases *The Black Scorpion,* and a volcanic eruption at the South Pole is the "action," as the narrator explains, that causes the Arctic earthquake "reaction" that unleashes *The Deadly Mantis* from its icy sepulchre. Like the mandala, fire is a symbol of wholeness and totality. Jung says of the fire symbol:

> The fiery figure is ambiguous and therefore unites the opposites. It is a "uniting symbol," a totality beyond human consciousness, making whole the fragmentariness of merely conscious man. It is a bringer of salvation and disaster at once. What it will be, for good or ill, depends on the understanding and ethical decision of the individual. The picture is a kind of message to modern man, admonishing him to meditate on the signs that appear in the heavens and to interpret them aright.[17]

Hence, *the fiery birth (wholeness) from the unknown (unconscious) brings a monster (archetype, presumably dominated by the evil aspect of the shadow) to earth (conscious mind) where the hero (ego/self) must deal with the monster to achieve a satisfactory conclusion (individuation).*

The Prometheus variation combines both the mandala and fire (Fig. III.9), presenting a double-edged drama of individuation. The mandala is seen in the laboratories: glassy jungles enmeshed in twisting tubes and scattered electronic machinery that literally encircle the scientist. Bernard Robinson's set design for the Hammer Frankenstein series is quintessentially such a place. His intertwined glass tubes, glass bassinets for the assembly of the creature, electric generators pulsating with violent flashes of colored light, traveling arcs, skeletons dangling from open rafters, and diverse specimen jars full of anatomical spare parts all cramped together in a claustrophobic mise-en-scène are indeed a visual delight if in actuality a mixture of biology, physics, chemistry, and magic. Similar laboratories can be seen in *Blood of the Vampire, I Was a Teenage Frankenstein, The Fly, The Gamma People,* and *The Alligator People.* Fire is always present in these laboratories, usually seen, through convention, in the traveling arc (sometimes called Jacob's ladder); this arc of electricity climbing two V-shaped carbon rods dates back to James Whale's *Frankenstein* (1931).

Like its counterpart, the classical text, the Prometheus variation functions according to the individuation scheme: *In the fiery birth in the laboratory (mandala and fire as wholeness) from the unknown (uncon-*

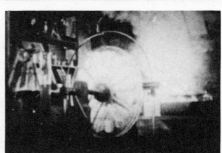

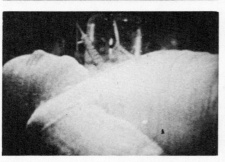

scious) come invaders (archetypes, usually of the evil aspects of the sha-dow) to earth (conscious mind) where the hero (ego/self) must deal with the intruders to achieve a satisfactory conclusion (individuation).

The remaining images carry less significance than the images just discussed, but they are nonetheless very much a part of the visual components of the alien invasion film.

The Special Effects Footage

The creation of the fiery scenes is usually under the skillful guidance of special effects technicians. Special effects are usually divided into two categories, mechanical (often credited as "special") and optical (often credited as "photographic" or "visual"). It is easy to distinguish between the two. Mechanical effects are physical and are nothing more than stage effects—trapdoors, fire troughs, flash powder, and so on—used on a grand, filmic scale. Optical effects are "trick" photography, an illusory practice nearly as old as photography itself but adapted to the moving image. As a movie technique, it dates back to the beginnings of cinema, primarily to the *cinéma merveilleux* of Georges Méliès. Obviously, both categories are concerned with creating illusion.

Alien invasion and other science fiction films hold no monopolies on creating illusion. All movies use some kind of illusory technique, from the obvious spectacle of Atlanta burning in Victor Fleming's *Gone with the Wind* (1939) and Fred Astaire's mind-boggling ceiling/wall dance in Stanley Donen's *Royal Wedding* (1951) to the unobtrusive matte paintings in Orson Welles's *Citizen Kane* (1940) and the subtle process shots in Michael Curtiz's *Casablanca* (1942). What is special about the alien invasion film is that it centers its entire milieu on the special effects illusions. As spectacular as they are, Atlanta's destruction and Astaire's defiance of gravity are not central or crucial to the overall impact and acceptance of the respective films. But for such films as *The Beast from 20,000 Fathoms* and *It Came from Beneath the Sea*, convincing and horrifying special effects cinematography is the very lifeblood.

This kind of image is unique to the movies. The images move only in the sense that they are "recorded movement." The stop-motion creations of Ray Harryhausen, for example, have no movement, no per-

Fig. III.9. Fire is the principal image of the Prometheus variation. In this sequence from Fisher's a) *The Curse of Frankenstein* (1957), lightning b) strikes the roof, (c & d) travels down to the machinery, and e) gives life to the bandaged creature in Frankenstein's laboratory. F) Frankenstein hears the commotion and races in g) to find the creature ambulatory. H) Frankenstein reacts with fear and fascination as (i & j) the creature rips off its facial bandages.

sonality, no life in any reality except that of the film itself. Harryhausen's "kinetic sculptures" are alive only in film.

Likewise, the creations themselves, the monsters and mutations, have no reality except the reality of a dream. The Beast from 20,000 fathoms has no existence except in dream; the flying saucers of a myriad alien invasion films have no accepted reality (only a potential for existence) except the reality of dreams. In this sense, the special effects footage resembles psychic images. The reality of this footage is tied to film only; the reality of the special effects subjects—monsters, mutations, fantastic flying machines—is tied to dream only. It is, then, fitting that most of Harryhausen's alien invasion creations (and, for that matter, most of the creations in the monster-on-the-loose films) are saurians, direct relatives of the serpent, the archetypal symbol of evil. Indeed, even the giant octopus in *It Came from Beneath the Sea* looks more like a snake than an octopus as its seemingly endless tentacle slithers through San Francisco's Fisherman's Wharf.

Alien invasion films, moreover, have the ability to combine reality (live actors) with their unreal special effects footage. Monsters rampage as real people flee the chaos, all in the same frame. By this technique— which only a highly active imagination could evoke—these movies make "real" what we normally perceive as unreal: The images are there on the screen for all to see. In many of these films the reality is revealed through Eisensteinian montage. The special effects images clash against the images of reality, bouncing from illusion to reality and reality to illusion and thereby creating a world that resembles the real world. But *resemble* in this case means something more: The special effects footage, the real footage, and the illusion they create resemble a reality that is composed in part of imaginative, or archetypal, material. Reality itself, of course, contains dreams and symbols, which in some cases seem truer to reality than mere reality does. That is the case also with these films, which seem truer to reality than mere realism. Certainly they seem so to the part of the mind that readily accepts archetypal imagery, though not to the ego that readily rejects this imagery. The point is this: If these films seem crazy and mixed-up, so does reality itself. Such things as dreams, visions, symbols, and even "monsters from the deep" (archetypal imagery from the collective unconscious) do indeed exist.

A movie, particularly the alien invasion film, is a collective dream. The spectators experience flashing archetypal images—serpents and mandalas—that link and connect with identical images in the unconscious. The special effects footage, in most cases, no matter how skillful and convincing or crude and insulting, is the medium through which the iconographic images are linked with the identical images in the

Fig. III.10. Alien in Alex Gordon and Spencer G. Bennet's *The Atomic Submarine* (1959) is one of expert Jack Rabin's special effects for a "restraint budget."

unconscious. The film simply manifests these images. As iconography, special effects visuals record and solidify many of our psychic images. As convention, these visuals are mandatory ingredients in the genre—to appease iconographic hunger, perhaps.

Even when budgets forbade extravagance, the creatures appeared, as evidenced by Roger Corman's inexpensive creatures. In fact, an entire special effects house was set up to aid independent producers driven by the urge to manifest archetypal images but hindered by cost. Studio Film Service, run by Jack Rabin, Irving Block, and Louis De-Witt, dominated the credits of a myriad independent productions through the decade, creating inexpensive yet acceptable special effects for such films as *War of the Satellites, The Giant Behemoth* (portions only; the climactic sequence of the monster marching on London is credited to *King Kong* animator Willis O'Brien and his assistant, Peter Petersen), *The Atomic Submarine* (Fig. III.10), *Invasion USA*, and *Kronos*. The formation of this company to aid independent producers on "restraint budgets," as Jack Rabin describes them,[18] and the acceptance of such "restrained" special effects by the public indicate that special effects were indeed an integral part of the alien invasion film.

The Stock Footage

Stock library footage—strips of film already shot and processed that are available for insertion in current productions—is also a recurring image in alien invasion films. Practically all of them contain some kind of easily recognizable library footage. From the newsreel or docu-

Fig. III.11. Two frequently seen images from stock library footage are the atomic bomb detonation and U.S. government testing of rockets and missiles.

mentary, four dominant images appear in such footage: government rocket, missile, and bomb testing (Fig. III.11); U.S. military maneuvers; the Palomar Observatory; and newsreel coverage of earthquakes, floods, fires, and other natural disasters. Columbia Pictures, through the ingenuity of its producer Sam Katzman, must hold some kind of record among studios for incorporating footage from previous films into its later productions. Ray Harryhausen's footage of the Washington Monument (Fig. III.12) collapsing onto a fleeing crowd, first seen in *Earth vs. the Flying Saucers,* is seen again in *The Giant Claw.* A building collapsing onto a sidewalk full of fleeing citizens, so effective in Warner Brothers's *The Beast from 20,000 Fathoms,* proved no less so in *It Came from Beneath the Sea, Earth vs. the Flying Saucers,* and *The Giant Claw.* Columbia even borrowed the destruction of the Los Angeles city hall from Paramount's *War of the Worlds* for inclusion in *Earth vs. the Flying Saucers.* This studio is not alone in this practice, of course. Republic Pictures released two films in 1958 that are constructed of nothing but library footage. *Satan's Satellites* and *Missile Monsters* are adapted from Republic's 1952 and 1951 serials, *Zombies of the Stratosphere* and *The*

Fig. III.12. Scene of destruction from Sears's *The Giant Claw* (1957) actually is footage borrowed from destruction of Washington Monument in *Earth vs. the Flying Saucers.*

Flying Disc Man from Mars, respectively. Not one foot of film except the titles was new; these films were indeed a film editor's creation.[19]

Newsreel footage helps give the alien invasion film its sense of reality. This footage, coupled with special effects footage, creates a kind of dialectic between reality and illusion. With live performers functioning as drama, special effects footage functioning as illusion, and newsreel footage functioning as an identifiable reality, the films offer not reality itself but its semblance. In *It Came from Beneath the Sea,* Kenneth Tobey as Commander Matthews is drama (and screen reality); Harryhausen's octopus is illusion—the manifestation of an imaginary being; and the newsreel footage of atomic submarines, with its graininess and hand-held jerkiness, is a record of the real world. The newsreel footage, as a document of the spectator's world, serves as the reference point for the real world. The very fact that it is easily recognizable as library footage—its poor quality contrasting sharply with the staged action—and its repetition throughout the film make it a constant reminder that the film is an extrapolation from the known world. This extrapolation usually is evident at the very beginning of the film, as a narrator explicates the state of science and technology while the visuals confirm his words. Such precisely is the opening for *It Came from Beneath the Sea, Twenty Million Miles to Earth,* and *Earth vs. the Flying Saucers,* among many others.

Even when the newsreel footage is not used, extrapolation is still evident, either by narration over special effects footage, as in *Invaders from Mars* (Professor Kelston explains the state of astronomy as we zoom through the universe), or through the use of roll-up titles, a frequent device employed by Allied Artists Pictures. A typical epigraph is seen at the beginning of Spencer G. Bennet's *The Atomic Submarine* (1959):

THE IMPOSSIBLE happens all about us! Jules Verne's super submarine has come true! H. G. Wells' trip to the moon is a certainty!

The atom that couldn't be split has been smashed!

Fantasy explodes in Fact!

OUR STORY deals with ships and atoms, in a war of unbelievable craft, many leagues under an incredible sea . . . in a dream of the future . . . that may be nearer than you think!

A definite sign of America's advancing space technology in the fifties was the Palomar Observatory atop Palomar Mountain in Southern California (Fig. III.13). With its 200-inch Hale telescope, Palomar made headlines as a mighty stride in technology and astronomy. The

Fig. III.13. Palomar Observatory, a mandala image, is used extensively in science fiction films of the fifties, including a representation of the Hall of Science building on the planet Krypton in television's *Adventures of Superman*.

cinema wasted no time exploiting Palomar's potential. The observatory is seen in a number of films, including *Flight to Mars* and *Invaders from Mars*, as a picturesque icon of space technology. Dennis Saleh has observed that "Palomar . . . caused great excitement in the early 50s; it must have been irresistable to include footage of one of Southern California's newest wonders, the enormous telescope rising as the entire dome turns in slow grandeur."[20] With so much attention given to Palomar it is only fitting that it is a sphere.

The most prevalent stock footage is that of military maneuvers and news coverage of real disasters (Fig. III.14). From *War of the Worlds* to *Tarantula* and from *Them!* to *The Mysterians*, footage of military hardware is an easily recognizable and repetitive image. Akin to the machinery discussed earlier, the military tanks, jeeps, cannons, missile launchers, jets, bombers, and so on are listed here because of their relation to the real world. The sight of the massive military hardware marching against the invaders is a rallying point not only for the cinematic characters but also for the spectator; the spectator knew all too well the firepower of America's military might. In small town and big city alike, military exhibitions[21] reminded America that it was strong and ready to meet any intruder. The cinema, too, shows this military strength in action against such incredible odds as the invading monsters and

Fig. III.14. U.S. government footage of military maneuvers is a frequent image in alien invasion films. This scene is from military alert montage in Menzies's *Invaders from Mars*.

aliens. Moreover, the cinema shows the entire population rallying behind the military; it is a modern-day cavalry to the rescue.

Disaster footage is used in a number of films as a link, once again, to reality. The graininess and jerkiness of the footage immediately signal a change from dramatic action. Byron Haskin, in *War of the Worlds*, cuts from illusion (the Martian machines destroying miniatures of recognizable architecture amid staged panic in studio streets) to tinted black and white newsreel footage of refugees fleeing a South American earthquake. This juxtaposition offers the spectator yet another glimpse of the dialectic between reality and illusion.

The Landscapes

An important aspect of the alien invasion genre is, of course, invasion. Creatures and invaders come to earth, and earth is the battlefield for a showdown between alien invaders and humanity. Vivian Sobchack, in her essay "The Alien Landscapes of the Planet Earth: Science Fiction in the Fifties," describes the role the earth plays in the genre:

> We saw the threat as "them" or "it"—the alien as separate from ourselves and the ground beneath our feet. We knew what our world was. Earth and Man were an organic unit, a known quantity, working together to repel the alien "other." Our cities and traffic and technology, our churches and monuments gave an anthropomorphic—and thereby reassuring—face to our planet. These movies suggested that we and the very ground we walked upon were intimately bound together, harmoniously entwined in some metaphysical lovers' embrace.[22]

This "metaphysical lovers' embrace" is best understood in the context of the benevolent side of the earth mother, the archetype that represents the origins of life. It symbolizes the earth itself from which all life is born, and it nourishes and protects its offspring, the "organic unit," humanity and earth. That is the earth mother's benevolent side, which appears in the films of the classical text as humanity is nourished and protected from the extraterrestrial invaders. In Haskin's *War of the Worlds*, although the Martian machines are connected to the earth by invisible power shields, they are in effect airborne, estranged from the earth and in direct contrast to the earthbound army. In another instance, Dr. Marvin's sonic/magnetic ray emanates from the earth, destroying the airborne saucers in the appropriately titled *Earth vs. the Flying Saucers* (Fig. III.15).

The earth mother is not always so benevolent. She can also elicit death and destruction—her dangerous side. In the terrestrial invasion film, she shows both faces: She unleashes the monster upon mankind but then nourishes and protects humanity in its battle with the mon-

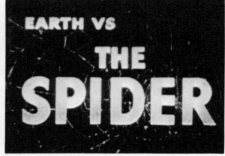

Fig. III.15. Mankind is not alone; as these titles indicate, the entire earth is allied with mankind in the struggle against the invader.

ster. In Nathan Juran's *The Deadly Mantis* (1957), the giant praying mantis is set free from its suspended animation not by an atomic blast but by Mother Nature with an Antarctic volcano that activates earth tremors in the Arctic region. As narrator Marvin Miller explains, "For every action there is an opposite and equal reaction," reminding us that science understands such phenomena. From the vast splitting of ice and the opening of centuries-old ice mountains, a prehistoric insect is born. It unfurls its wings and begins a journey of destruction. Airborne, it is virtually indestructible. It knocks jets from the sky with ease. Nevertheless, somewhat in the manner of the mythical Antaeus, child of the earth, the forces of humanity defeat the invader: Jet planes soar after the creature in scene after scene and seem to get stronger after each contact with the earth. Finally, the aircraft and the earthbound military heroes succeed in driving the mantis into the Holland tunnel, and in a sense we have come full circle: The creature born out of darkness dies in darkness.

This duality of the earth mother is also found in Bert I. Gordon's *The Spider*. A giant tarantula crawls out of a womblike cave and terrorizes a small town. As in *The Deadly Mantis*, atomic technology is not to blame; the spider is a result of "natural mutation." It seems invincible as it marches on the town; but when humanity follows the spider back to the cave, the monster is destroyed: Humanity gives the spider a supercharge of electricity and it impales itself on giant stalagmites. This scenario apparently follows the hermetic doctrine that "to 'return to the mother' was the equivalent of dying."[23]

Titles and Posters

Titles and posters and all advertising material play an important part in recognizing the alien invasion genre. Completely unpretentious, these titles function somewhat like newspaper headlines, encapsulating the entire narrative. The titles also reflect the notion of dehumanization: A "thing" will either destroy you, replace you, or metamorphose you, or an invading army will either enslave you or destroy you; no matter what, as you sensed all along, somehow you are less human.

The titles can be catalogued under two headings: xenophobia (Fig. III.16) and threat (Fig. III.17). They can also be reduced to a single word about the American state of mind in the fifties: paranoia. Andrew Dowdy writes that "Each Saturday night we witnessed the latest hostile surprise created by an environment more capriciously malignant than anything [Joseph] McCarthy promised in his most lunatic moments."[24]

Fig. III.16. Titles tell us that some thing is coming for us.

Fig. III.17. More titles telling us we are threatened.

The paranoia of the era was real, but the exaggerated threats of a communist invasion only "seemed" real. Exploited by McCarthy and his followers and by the newspapers and television (indeed, Richard Carlson himself as real-life FBI undercover agent Herbert A. Philbrick warned us about a communist takeover every week in Ziv's *I Led 3 Lives*), the "red menace" was a daily concern, eliciting fears of the dark and the unknown. But where was it? The answer, of course, was: in the collective conscious of America. Fears of the atomic age, of science itself, fostered a collective neurosis. Much of this fear manifested itself in a collective xenophobia—the fear of anyone (and in this case any-thing) different. To compensate for this imbalance, the movies un-pretentiously and overtly gave the public a manifestation of these fears. But, strangely enough, these fears can be seen as part of the *good* in these films. The fear is clearly linked to the red scare, to everything that is conceived as different; but, as a necessary part of the individuation process, it forms a perfect balance with good to elicit meaning and value, not only in the films but in ourselves as well.

Although the alien invasion film is a product of the fifties, one of its primary iconographic images links it to earlier times. The poster art created for the films owes much to pulp science fiction magazine covers of the thirties and forties (Fig. III.18). Lurid and garish, these posters are artifacts of the halcyon days of American film history. It is no surprise that collectors pay exorbitant sums to own original posters for *The Day the Earth Stood Still* and *Invaders from Mars*. Like the titles, the posters are totally unpretentious. They encapsulate the film through a collage of graphic images and prolix copy. Indeed, movie posters and advertise-ments are a unique art form in combining visual and written expression (Fig. III.19).

Fig. III.18. The best poster art to come out of the alien invasion fifties; bug-eyed monsters and scantily dressed woman owe much to the garish covers of pulp science fiction magazines.

Fig. III.19. Collection of newspaper ads reveals the graphic unpretentiousness of alien invasion films.

One recurring feature of the posters is an emphasis on human subservience. In nearly all the posters in which humans and beasts/invaders are depicted, the human image is small and off in a corner, looking up to the domineering and threatening image of the invader (Figs. III.20, 21, and 22). This image of the diminutive human is repre-

Fig. III.20. Newspaper ad, in addition to its lurid graphics and copy, depicts the humans as diminutive and hence representative of infantile fears manifested by the films themselves.

Fig. III.21. Another example of lurid poster art; presumably, no one ever won the $50,000.

Fig. III.22. Humans are depicted as subservient to the invader. This poster is unusual: It is signed by the artist (upper right corner), Ken Sawyer.

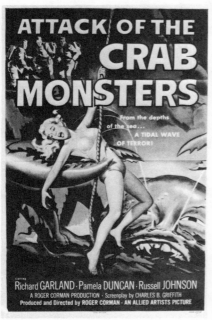

Fig. III.23. Perfect example of the depiction of woman in poster art (and in the films as well): suspended between man and monster and sought after by both as prize.

sentative of yet another motif of the alien invasion film: Infantile fears literally manifested as children. This motif and its child metaphor are discussed in the following chapter.

Another striking and often grotesque poster image is that of the woman (Fig. III.23). She is pictured as helpless, caught in the claws of the monster; but her terrified and screaming countenance is secondary to her state of dress, which is nearly nude. With an emphasis on breast and leg exposure, she is suspended between man and monster, and as such the image is an aberrant yet nonetheless accurate depiction of the woman's role in the alien invasion film: She is object, sought after—as prize—by both man and monster. Given her role as a professional (some are scientists, like Faith Domergue in *It Came from Beneath the Sea* and *This Island Earth*, but most are reporters, physicians, and bureaucrats), the woman emerges at first as an equal. A closer examination reveals that her professional status is merely a ruse to get her near the invader, and once the invader meets her she becomes the archetypal "damsel in distress," and therefore a symbol in the romantic tradition.[25]

The poster art for Edward Ludwig's *The Black Scorpion*, a Warner Brothers release of 1957, pushes the theme to the limit. There are just two images: a close-up of a scorpion's mouth and its lusting eyes, and, standing directly behind the scorpion, bosomy Mara Corday, a one-time *Playboy* playmate, her head turned slightly and a strap from her evening gown falling off her shoulder. So incongruous is this poster that Leslie Halliwell quips: "You couldn't say *The Black Scorpion* was a good film of its kind, but you do have to hand it to the publicity boys."[26]

Meaning and Value

Before we undertake an analysis of the process of individuation, we need to recall the two basic principles underlying Jungian thought: that everything is made up of opposites, and that the psyche is an autonomous, or self-regulating, complex motivated to reconcile opposites. To appreciate these claims, let us suppose, for example, that the conscious contents of the mind become so dominant that the unconscious is repressed totally. The result will be that the unconscious will attempt to return the psyche to a harmonious balance between the conscious and the unconscious. In the patient, this attempt at creating balance is communicated by symbols found in dreams and fantasies. These symbols are manifestations of the overlooked aspects of the psyche, and in our example these neglected aspects originate in the unconscious.

In a similar manner, entire cultures can easily become one-sided. Jung writes that "Every period has its bias; its particular prejudice, and its psychic malaise. An epoch is like an individual; it has its own limitations of conscious outlook and therefore requires a compensatory adjustment."[1] Entire societies can drift into an imbalance in which values of one sort are emphasized at the expense of others. When that occurs, Jung writes, old symbols or entirely new ones arise out of the society, compensating for the maladjusted state. The compensatory symbols for society are traditionally found in the collective dream, or myth. In modern society, myth has been replaced by art and literature. The entire process is precisely the subject of Jung's *Flying Saucers: A Modern Myth of Things Seen in the Skies,* a work that suggests that UFO sightings were the spiritual balance needed to compensate for cold war tensions.

Unlike Freud's rather dismal principles of determinism, Jung's psychology is rooted in the concept that the psyche is intrinsically inclined toward reaching a higher, almost exalted awareness of the nature of all things. A reconciliation of opposites is the goal of the psychic process Jung calls individuation, and the object of this process is to ultimately join the primordial unconscious with consciousness. A major aspect of this process is the emergence and recognition of certain definite archetypal images. Briefly, these images represent: (1) the inferior side of man, which Jung calls the shadow; (2) the opposite sex, which Jung calls the anima in men and the animus in women; (3) the outward, social facade, which Jung calls the persona; and (4) the godlike image that represents individuation, which Jung calls the self. Other archetypal figures may also appear, possessing special meaning for the individual or society—the mandala figures of the fifties, for example. Once these archetypes have been assimilated, uniting the unconscious with the conscious, then the mind has fulfilled its destiny: The ego has been replaced by the individuated Self as the center of the psyche, and perfect balance and harmony are achieved.

I have been necessarily succinct in describing a complex process that has taken volumes to define, but I hope to expand and develop these concepts in examining the archetypal imagery found in films.

With regard to the alien invasion film, it is necessary to distinguish the concept of Self as individuated ego—the result of the individuation process—and the concept of the self as an archetype, or organizing principle of the psyche, whose location is the center of the collective unconscious. The task of individuation is to bring the self archetype out of the depths of the unconscious into consciousness, from darkness to light, where it will replace the ego, transforming the ego into the Self, as the center of a newly formed, unified, whole personality. The Self, the end result of the individuation process, gives meaning and value to the alien invasion film. The films function as symbols of transformation, directing us toward an individuated life. The self archetype is the functioning aspect of the process, and hence it becomes the motivating factor in the films.

In the classical text, the self is a figure, the hero, whose function is to replace the ego as the center of the personality. In the narrative, the hero (self) and the alien invader (shadow) emerge simultaneously, and each struggles for recognition by members of society (ego). Society (now as inflated persona), however, refuses to recognize either, but the heroine (anima) begins mediating between the hero and society. Society continues to reject the hero, however, resulting in repression. The unconscious material grows unstable, finally erupting and causing all kinds of negative, disruptive, and harmful effects. Society (inflated persona) is weakened by the onrush of the monsters and the hero (all the unconscious material), and society seeks the advice of the hero (self, but he may also function at this point as the mana-personality, depending on each film's peculiarities). The hero then deals with the alien invader, and together the heroine and society gather around the hero, who marries the heroine. In other words, both consciousness (society) and the unconscious (heroine-as-anima) gather about the Self, the unifying and harmonizing center of the individuated personality.[2]

In the Prometheus variation, the self archetype is often a presence, an abstract quality that permeates the film. Since the emphasis is on the Promethean scientist, the self archetype is made apparent by factors—including such abstract qualities as ethics and morality—that oppose the scientist's actions. The hero is actually the "self-in-potential"; as such, he remains somewhat in the background, waiting for circumstances—the death of the scientist (death of the ego)—to allow the self to be fully manifested into the hero-as-self figure. Once the hero replaces the scientist as the centerpiece of the narrative (once the self replaces the ego), individuation is complete. The closing image of the hero embracing his girl friend represents this transformation of ego into Self.

The hero myth is significant to analytical psychology because it corresponds to the development of the psyche; "the image of the hero," Joseph Henderson writes, "evolves in a manner that reflects each stage of the evolution of the human personality."[3] Specifically, the hero myth divides into two strands. The first strand is the myth of adaptation. The hero overcomes his (and the world's) situation by adapting to it. The hero is usually revealed as godlike; moreover, he is depicted as the suffering victim, the innocent who dies and is resurrected, leading mankind to a higher degree of understanding and awareness. Such a myth is exemplified for western man by Christ, whose death enables mankind to gain eternal life, "a life not in this world," as Esther Harding writes, "but in a non-material, that is, psychic realm."[4] With respect to the alien invasion genre, this type of hero is usually found in the "martyr" films in which the unfortunate scientist, through no explicit fault of his own, becomes a monster. In Jack Arnold's *Monster on the Campus*, for example, Professor Donald Blake (Arthur Franz) accidentally contaminates his own blood with the blood of a primordial fish; as a result, Blake is transformed into a crazed Neanderthal man. What is important is that Blake realizes that he is the monster society is seeking, and his only option is to destroy himself for the sake of humanity. Similar characters are found in Paul Landres's *The Vampire*, Bert I. Gordon's *War of the Colossal Beast*, and Robert Day's *First Man into*

Space (Fig. IV.1). However, such characterizations are the exception rather than the rule.

The second strand of the hero myth is much more significant to the alien invasion film. It is the myth of the struggle. The hero struggles against agonizing perils, culminating in the fight with the dragon. Once the hero slays the dragon, he discovers the hidden treasure. He discovers his true Self. The psychic development in the myth of the struggle corresponds to adolescence,[5] when a youth must overcome his desire to remain protected, cared for, and cherished by his mother. Members of the alien invasion genre that present the perspective of a young boy—a

Fig. IV.1. In closing scene of *War of the Colossal Beast,* Manning realizes that for the sake of himself and society his only option is to destroy himself. He takes hold of high-voltage lines and in a mystical conclusion slowly passes out of existence.

type we will examine at length later in the chapter—can be viewed in the context of the heroic myth of the struggle. The point of transition, the moment when "boy becomes man," is represented by the fight with the dragon, the alien invader. Harding writes:

> In order to free himself from his bondage to the mother, the youth must conquer his childish dependence and his desire to be loved and cared for without effort on his own part. The myths invariably represent this transition in the form of a battle, a fight against the mother in the guise of a monster, usually a dragon. That is to say, it is not the personal mother, the actual woman, who must be overcome, but the mother archetype. Usually the dragon has imprisoned the beautiful damsel and keeps her shut up in a dungeon, that is, in the unconscious. It is to free this maiden that the hero has to undertake his heroic task. The damsel is, of course, the anima, and the myths show quite clearly what the psychological condition of the youth on the threshold of life is . . . a victory not just over the mother, but far more significantly over his backward longing for his childhood's paradise.[6]

It is important to note that the alien invasion genre is profoundly patriarchal, and its appeal is especially to young boys.

To discover meaning and value in the alien invasion genre, we will examine in detail two films that exemplify the genre: William Cameron Menzies's *Invaders from Mars* and Arthur Crabtree's *Fiend without a Face*. I have chosen these films rather arbitrarily, and I confess they are favorites. But significantly, each film deals with the human mind in a literal sense: the dream of a young boy in one, the horrors of "thought monsters" in the other. This delineation of the "content" of the human mind allows for a secondary interpretation of the films in terms of dream analysis. Young David McLean's dream of marauding Martians can be our dream as well, and as we examine the symbolic references within his dream we simultaneously examine the identical references within our collective dream, the film itself.

This time I will discuss the Prometheus variation before the classical text, since the Promethean film I have chosen for analysis, *Fiend without a Face*, provides an excellent and lucid exhibit of Jung's organized stages of the individuation process.

The American Dream Myth and Science Fiction

The essence of the Prometheus variation is similar to the essence of alchemy. A scientist/philosopher dabbles in the hard and soft sciences in a sometimes vain but often altruistic quest for the answers to the mysteries of life. For the Promethean scientist, his quest leads to an understanding of good and evil, but this knowledge comes at the great expense of innocent lives and is usually marked by the scientist's own death as well.

Alchemy had a strong influence on Jung and his analytical psychology, for Jung developed much of his theory on individuation by intensely studying the ancient alchemical manuscripts. In *Psychology and Alchemy*, he offered comparisons of the myriad symbols associated with alchemical studies and the identical symbols found in dreams, of which the mandala is the prominent transcending symbol. As Antonio Moreno has suggested, Jung discovered that the alchemists were not chemists "but mystics who through the unconscious projection into matter of the contents of the archetypes were expressing in that way the motions of their psyche towards individuation."[7] This process is a quest; Northrop Frye says that it is the very essence of the mythopoeic heroic quest:

> In Jung's book the symbolic structures of alchemy and the heroic quest are united on the Euclidian principle that things equal to the same thing are equal to one another. The "same thing" is Jung's own individuation process, whose general resemblance to the *great work* of alchemy, on its psychological side, is not difficult to demonstrate. But, centuries before Jung was born, the "same thing" to which alchemy and romance were equal was biblical typology. For the Bible was not only the definitive alchemical myth for alchemists, but the definitive grammar of allegory for allegorical poets. Its central structure is that of quest-romance; it tells the story of a progress from creation to recreation through the heroism of Christ in killing the dragon of death and hell and rescuing his bride the Church. Jung would have perhaps have made this point clearer if his own literary experience, being German, had not given so central a place to Goethe.[8]

Frye's biblical allusions are important. The Prometheus variation centers its thematic milieu on a quest for a better and more reliable world. In this way it gets its strength from Jung's alchemical analogies of psychic development and from the myth of the American dream, the possibility of America as the second Eden. Frederic I. Carpenter, in *American Literature and the Dream*, sees the American dream myth as the desire to create a second Eden not in the next world but in the new world of America "where the religious prophecies of Isaiah and the Republican ideals of Plato might be realized."[9]

This version of a "new Eden" was likely given a foundation of truth, as Alvin Toffler has suggested in *The Third Wave*, by the abundance of agriculture in America. However, in yet another quest for "perfection on earth," agriculture soon gave way to the industrialization of America; soon, moreover, industrialization gave way to a newer form of industry, the technological revolution, "the third wave."[10]

The American dream myth as a topic of literary criticism is relatively new, having developed—appropriately enough, considering our concerns—during the 1950s. The fifties decade is seen as a decade of progress; its technological experimentation and innovations, indeed, set Toffler's third wave in motion. Central to this experimentation is the atom. Coming out of the Second World War with its own doomsday machine, the atomic bomb, America, under President Eisenhower, was quick to alter the public's perception of the atom as destructive and negative by implementing the "Atoms for Peace" program, a program that underplayed the total destructive power of atomic fission and promised a better and more reliable world in which to live. The atom was celebrated as crucial not only to the defense of freedom and American ideals but also to a better way of life. The atom signified the end of civilization but also the salvation of civilization.

The love affair with the atom, although dubious in retrospect, opened the way for related experimentation. Computers promised to make man's life more relaxed and leisurely by taking on the burden of menial yet significant labor. Indeed, if the second Eden was not already here, it was just around the corner; however, the corner was to be a far corner. If the American continent itself could no longer reasonably expand into a second Eden, Americans would then take their ideal to yet another, newer world, outer space.

Panicked into action by the Soviet Union's launching into orbit of Sputnik in October 1957, America, the following year, orbited Explorer I, followed by five additional satellites. Space travel was suddenly a reality, and the potential of George Pal's *Destination Moon*, the pseudo-documentary film that introduced the decade, was now within grasp. What it all meant was that the ultimate technological advancement was drawing near; the colonization of space was yet another manifestation of the second Eden.

Inhabiting this second Eden in America was an American Adam, described by R. W. B. Lewis as "an individual standing alone, self-reliant and self-propelling, ready to confront whatever awaited him with the aid of his own unique and inherent resources."[11] Such a character is central to American literary history, originating in Cooper's Natty Bumpo and reaching through the Western tales of Zane Grey, Louis L'Amour, and Clarence E. Mulford. The American Adam, moreover, is the Adam before the Fall. He is morally pure and socially innocent; his drive is for freedom, manifested by his never-ending escape from the confines of civilization and from the corruption that accompanies civilization. His vision is a romantic vision, a quest, it seems, for a perfect world.

Destination Moon and its brethren in exploration, including such noteworthy films as *Rocketship X-M, Forbidden Planet, Conquest of Space*, and *Riders to the Stars*, celebrate the romantic quest of the American Adam (Fig. IV.2). Explorers like Cargraves, Thayer, and Barnes *(Destination Moon)* combine the qualities of Tennyson's Ulysses—the adventurer forever seeking a better world—with the qualities of the new Adam. These explorers will discover a new Eden and then move on to discover even newer ones.

The Prometheus variation offers a different view of the American Adam. Like the one just described, this Adam has a long tradition in American literature. He originates with Hawthorne; indeed, Hawthorne's Dr. Heidegger is a direct ancestor of such filmic scientists as Professor Walgate *(Fiend without a Face)* and Professor Deemer *(Tarantula),* in that each lusts for knowledge; his goal is altruistic, motivated by a desire for absolute knowledge. The Promethean scientist is best described as "Adam falling." He is tempted and seduced by the serpent of curiosity, and he invariably partakes of the forbidden fruit of scientific experimentation ("It Challenged the Supreme Power of the Universe," reads the advertising copy for Kurt Neumann's *The Fly*). Like Eve cursed with a painful childbirth, the Promethean scientist bears a painful delivery of his newly acquired knowledge: He who survives the experiment pays greatly by bearing the guilt of the deaths of innocent lives caused by his experiment. Often, moreover, the scientist's acquisition of knowledge is at the expense of his own life, a reflection of God's curse upon Adam that "in the day thou eatest thereof thou shalt surely die."

The Prometheus variation never shows experimentation in a good light; it leads only to evil. Its milieu is dark, its substance evil. How fitting that this perspective of the American dream should have been observed first by an Englishman, D. H. Lawrence. The latent nightmare within the American dream is described by Lawrence as a "certain tension." He writes that the liberty of Americans "is a thing of sheer

Fig. IV.2. Exploration film celebrates the romantic quest. Cargraves, in *Destination Moon*, tells fellow scientists that his rocketship will make it to the moon and to other worlds as well.

will, sheer tension: a liberty of THOU SHALT NOT. And it has been so
from the first. The land of THOU SHALT NOT."[12] Lawrence sees Americans as escapees from the traditions of evil in Europe, though prisoners
of a greater and more repressive evil in Puritan conscience. Their new
world tradition is, he argues, a tense, if not neurotic, threshold where
the drive for freedom is subjugated by the conscience of Puritan ethics
and morals.[13]

The Prometheus variation is a modern manifestation of "thou shalt
not." Experimentation with modern technology, specifically atomic experimentation, is best left alone (Fig. IV.3). Let us now examine the
Promethean film as it relates to this dream and to Jung's psychology.

Fig. IV.3. Title sequence from coming
attractions trailer of *Cosmic Monsters* reveals the alien invasion genre's attitude
toward the nuclear age.

Fig. IV.4. *Fiend without a Face* poster art deviates from norm by having humans looming over the monster, but the fiend is nonetheless the dominant image.

Fiend without a Face (Fig. IV.4), though produced by an American film company and starring an American actor, Marshall Thompson, was made in England by a British crew under the direction of Arthur Crabtree.[14] Screenwriter Herbert J. Leder based his script on a story called "The Thought Monster" by Amelia Reynolds Long. The film tells of a series of bizarre murders—victims are found with their brains and spinal cords sucked out through two punctures at the base of the neck—near a U.S. Air Force atomic-powered experimental radar station in an isolated Canadian village named Winthrop. The populace blames the Air Force's experimentation with atomic power for the deaths, but the Air Force pleads innocent and launches its own investigation. The Air Force soon discovers that a reclusive scientist "borrows" atomic energy to bolster his experiments in telekinesis; moreover, he has accidentally unleashed "mental vampires" from the repressed unconscious. It seems that these creatures—at first invisible but later becoming visible and materializing into human brains with attached spinal cords—exist in pure energy. They are given animation only by excessive energy emanating from the atomic plant, and they feed by devouring human brains and spinal cords. The chief Air Force investigator, Major Jeff Cummings (Thompson), dynamites the atomic plant, thereby denying the creatures their energy source and leading to their destruction.

Like most films in the Promethean mold, *Fiend without a Face* is structured much like a detective story. Two curious and initially unrelated events near the Air Force base provoke an investigation by Cummings. First, he must find out what causes the mysterious and sudden power drain during their radar experiments. Secondly, Cummings must find the who or what that is responsible for the deaths of three townspeople who lived near the Air Force station. As a science fiction sleuth, Cummings tracks one lead after another to finally stumble across the common denominator, Professor R. E. Walgate (Kynaston Reeves), whose late-night experiments correspond to the hours of the power drain and the time of death for each victim. The steps Cummings takes are intuitive—characteristic of the hero we discussed in a previous chapter. His method of detection is more akin to the "relentless pursuit" style of Sam Spade than to the stringent analytical reasoning of Sherlock Holmes. Early in the film, for instance, Cummings tells his girl friend, Barbara Grisselle (Kim Parker), that Walgate is somehow responsible for the murders; after a chance encounter with Walgate's manuscript, "The Principles of Thought Control," Cummings mutters to her, "It's a hunch, his background and training." The remainder of the film follows Cummings's drive to prove his hunch correct.

Whereas the first part of the film is more or less cerebral, concentrating on discovering the who and the what, the second part is dynamic and emotional, centering on the actual confrontation between the forces of good and evil, the Air Force and the marauding monsters. For this confrontation the film—and many other Promethean films—borrows a popular motif of many Westerns, that of the settlers under siege by Indians or outlaws, as in John Wayne's *The Alamo* (1960) and John Huston's *The Unforgiven* (1960). In *Fiend without a Face* Cummings, Barbara, Walgate, and several others are trapped by the marauding monsters inside Walgate's home (Fig. IV.5). Cummings discovers that the monsters—and there are hundreds of them—are "mortal" and hence can be destroyed by bullets. As Cummings and the others fire at the monsters, holding them off, Walgate offers a plan to destroy the lot. Someone must get through the forest of fiends and shut down the atomic plant. Cummings volunteers; he claims to be the only one who knows the layout of the plant. With great courage, he makes his way through the forest to successfully dynamite the plant. With their power source gone, the monsters dissolve into a putrescent residue.

Fig. IV.5. Monster-brains attack Walgate's home much as marauding Indians or outlaws attack protagonists in westerns.

I want first to examine the film in terms of the American dream myth, a critical theory that is closely related to Jung's notions. *Fiend without a Face*, like all films following the narrative structure of the Prometheus variation, manifests the idea of the fallen Adam by centering its theme and milieu on the inherent dangers of challenging the "thou shalt not" code of the new world. Walgate, exemplary of the Promethean scientist, is seduced by science. He is tempted by experimentation—the desire to reach some perfect order for mankind. As an invalid, suffering from strokes, Walgate searches for the secret of materializing thought to do menial work. He ultimately surmises that if he can stimulate his brain's natural electrical impulses with supplementary power, first by large doses of electricity and then by large doses of atomic radiation, he can "detach thought from . . . [the] unconscious and give it a separate entity." During a violent thunderstorm one evening, he "devised a being into which the thought once released could preserve itself for all humanity . . . something akin to the human brain with life and mobility without the limitations of man's body . . . and like thought itself it was invisible."

Despite this altruistic/Edenic motive—the desire to detach thought so that man can perform untold tasks without ever leaving his chair, to reach that perfect world—Walgate failed to realize that he could not detach and separate his own dark and repressed nature, perhaps his link with the Puritan conscience so crucial to Lawrence's observations. Too late, Walgate admits that he has created a fiend: "There were more than one and each growing more powerful from the atomic radiation . . . a fiend to drain the intellect, to survive and multiply." Walgate, then, exemplifies the fallen Adam, trapped between his desire for freedom and the law of thou shalt not; that "certain tension," as Lawrence calls it, arises and soon snaps, unleashing uncontrollable psychic energy, or, in this instance, unleashing monsters from the repressed unconscious.

The focus is similar to that of another science fiction film of the fifties, Fred McLeod Wilcox's *Forbidden Planet* (1956). Like Morbius, who failed to admit that the monster prowling Altair IV was actually a manifestation of his own id[15] and not a leftover beast from the fallen Krel civilization, Walgate fails to admit that the marauding fiends are manifestations of his own unconscious. Morbius proclaims his innocence, declaring that he is no monster; Commander Adams, however, knows better: "We're all part monsters in our subconscious, so we have laws and religion" (Fig. IV.6). Likewise, Walgate eschews responsibility for his "thought monsters," preferring to think of them as "a new form of [evil] life that nobody understands." Colonel Butler (Stanley Maxted) then tells him differently: "It is my opinion, Professor, that the evil is all in your head." Both Morbius and Walgate are unable to admit their own weaknesses; they are unable to admit that even they are indeed capable of primitive, barbaric thoughts and actions. Their experimentation into the mysteries of life and their quest for absolute knowledge bring to them, as to Adam, death, a reflection of the Promethean myth itself. Morbius collapses from the strain of denying his creation, and Walgate, in a futile attempt to control his creations, enters the forest and is immediately attacked and killed by the pulsating fiends.

If the myth were to end here, its message would be clear: The American dream myth is an illusion, an existential reality of despair and futility; a meaningless death is the reward for any attempt to overcome the rigid conditions of the world. Man, it seems, is at the mercy of a hostile, often violent world with no way out. Certainly, much of American literature is rooted in such a notion; the late writings of Twain are indicative of just such a view.[16] However, the Prometheus variation, like all forms of science fiction, offers more than mere emptiness and futility. Its message is redemption, for, true to its biblical allusions, it delineates not only the Fall but also the redemption of man. It seldom ends its narrative with the destruction of the scientist; rather, it uses the destruction of the scientist as an object lesson, warning us about where the uncontrollable urge to acquire absolute knowledge will lead.[17] Its narrative focuses finally on the uniting image of the hero and

Fig. IV.6. Morbius, left, in *Forbidden Planet* confronts his own dark side as monster from the id begins melting the door to the laboratory.

heroine. This closing image, usually the hero embracing his girl friend, corresponds symbolically to biblical redemption. The Promethean scientist represents "Adam during and after the Fall," and the heroine—a damsel in distress—best represents the Church, or Bride of Christ. Thus the hero represents Christ, and his victory over the monsters represents, as Frye suggested, "recreation through the heroism of Christ in killing the dragon of death and hell and rescuing his bride the Church." Futility and despair are replaced by wonder and awe, salvation and hope.

Alchemy, biblical typology, and the American dream myth as expressed by the Prometheus variation all correspond to the process of individuation. As such, they can be viewed as dramas that play out the psychic struggle for the realization and fulfillment of a unique existence. *Fiend without a Face*, then, is a drama of individuation, and the characters of the film have archetypal analogues. Major Cummings as hero functions as the self archetype and Barbara Grisselle, with respect to her role as Cummings's girl friend and Walgate's secretary, functions as the soul-image, the anima. Professor Walgate is best understood in terms of the ego, especially since he is the centerpiece of the narrative. We can also view the stages of the individuation process as revealed by the Prometheus narrative. Not only do the characters function as archetypal images, but also their functions within the film—the action itself—correspond to Jung's organized stages of the individuation process; to watch *Fiend without a Face* is to watch the process in action.

Jung has stated that the individuation process is divided into two parts, which correspond to the first and second halves of life. As Jolande Jacobi summarized it:

> The task of the first half is "initiation into outward reality." Through consolidation of the ego, differentiation of the main function and of the dominant attitude type, and the development of an appropriate persona, it aims at the adaptation of the individual to demands of his environment. The task of the second half is a so-called "initiation into inner reality," a deeper self-knowledge of humanity, a "turning back" *(reflectio)* to the traits of one's nature that have hitherto remained unconscious or become so. By raising these traits to consciousness the individual achieves an inward and outward bond with the world and the cosmic order. . . . When he [Jung] speaks of the "individuation process," it is this latter part that he has primarily in mind.[18]

Like the individuation process, *Fiend without a Face* can be divided into two parts. The first part, relatively short and only incidental to the narrative, introduces the world of "outward reality." In a pre-credits sequence (Fig. IV.7), Crabtree uses technology—various static shots of aircraft, radar scanners, and other military hardware at the Air Force base—as a sign of man's outward, conscious adaptation to his environ-

Fig. IV.7. Pre-credits sequence in *Fiend without a Face* presents duality of outside (conscious) reality and inner (unconscious) reality. A) MGM trademark first reminds us that it is only a film, b) then a long shot establishes the air base; (c & d) aircraft represent man's conquest of his outer world. E) Guard reacts to Mach-1 flights overhead, f) and trails in sky offer further evidence of man's conquest of his environment. G) This calm setting is interrupted by strange sounds heard by guard; (h & i) radar scanners and the atomic plant provide signs of the persona. J) Guard then starts for the forest to investigate the strange sounds; k) dark forest represents the unconscious. L) Jacques Grisselle, in the forest, watches aircraft overhead and also hears the strange sounds. M) Guard hears a scream, and the strange sounds fade away; n) the archetypes have erupted from the unconscious.

ment. Moreover, throughout the film Crabtree uses the base and the village of Winthrop as symbolic of "consciousness," nearly always showing them in daylight. The second part, the "initiation into the inner reality," is the narrative itself. It, too, originates in the pre-credits sequence. As Crabtree shows us the domineering, impressive images of the military hardware, we become aware of strange sounds.[19] Crabtree then cuts away from the Air Force base to the forest nearby. There, the eerie sounds increase in volume and a man is suddenly struck down. Crabtree thus contrasts the forest, the haven for the fiends, with the Air Force base. The forest, always dark, represents the unconscious, the very place where the individuation process begins. Jung writes that "the forest, dark and impenetrable to the eye, like deep water and the sea, is the container of the unknown and the mysterious. It is an appropriate synonym for the unconscious. Trees, like fishes in water, represent the living contents of the unconscious."[20]

The first stage of the individuation process leads, as Jacobi writes, to the experience of the shadow, "symbolizing our 'other side,' our 'dark brother,' who is an invisible but inseparable part of our psychic reality."[21] The shadow is literally invisible; the fiends are, as the title indicates, faceless, and they are heard but not seen until the film's climax. Moreover, as shadow figures, the fiends take on a dual function. First, in the context of the film we are watching, as a detached symbolic representation of psychic energy, the fiends are archetypal symbols of evil. They are representations of all the inferior, animalistic passions associated with the darker side of the human psyche. Second, in the context of Walgate's own personal dilemma, the fiends represent the psychic entity called the personal shadow, the repressed material of his personal unconscious. Thus, the notion of evil itself can be differentiated from the psychic notion of "inferiority," or the inferior dimension of the personality. That is not to say, however, that such a differentiation is mutually exclusive; for each is a reflection of the other. To deal effectively with the collective evil, Jung says, one must first assimilate his own personal shadow; he must recognize his own inferior side, and by so doing acknowledge his own imperfection. Antonio Moreno writes:

> Recognition of the shadow leads to the modesty we need in order to acknowledge imperfection. A modest man knows that whatever is wrong in the world is in himself, and if he only learns to deal with his own shadow he has done something for the world. Failure to recognize the archetype, Jung says, has brought white-man and the whole world to the brink of destruction. . . . The first condition for moral health is therefore humility; recognition of the shadow is a reason for it, for genuine fear of the abysmal depths of man. This recognition is important because our dark side is not harmless; it brings the archaic psyche, the whole world of archetypes, into direct

contact with the conscious world and mind. The shadow lurks behind every neurotic dissociation, and can only be annexed to consciousness if the corresponding unconscious contents are made conscious. Consequently, it is imperative to discover our shadow, because insofar as it is conscious there is always a possibility of correction; if repressed there is no possibility at all, and, on the contrary, it is liable to burst forth suddenly in a moment of awareness, upsetting the ego and breeding neurosis.[22]

The assimilation of the shadow is the message of Crabtree's film, for despite Cummings's dominance in the film, Walgate is the central figure. When he is not on camera, he is discussed. The fiends themselves are but an extension of Walgate; created "from" him, not "by" him, they are born out of his own mind. And before the fiends can be properly disposed of, Walgate himself must assimilate them. As he denies the fiends, they grow stronger and more deadly, but when he finally admits that it is he who unleashed them, they are suddenly manageable. At this point Crabtree allows the fiends to become not only visible but vulnerable as well. Once Walgate humbles himself, Crabtree is saying (true to Moreno's description), Walgate is able to discover truth. He discovers what is wrong with the outside world (the village). The "secret learned"—that is, what Walgate's problem actually is—is not important. Rather, the act of discovery itself gives to the observer the meaning and value inherent in the film, for in a real sense we are dealing more with "the way," the process, than with the result, although the result is individuation.

As noted, the fiends are animated human brains with attached spinal cords that propel them along (Fig. IV.8). The fiends without faces are as repulsive as any monster that ever graced the screen. With their whiplike spinal cords, their affinity with the snake is visually intact, and their appearance is in keeping with Jung's own words:

> The lower vertebrates have from earliest times been favourite symbols of the collective psychic substratum, which is localized anatomically in the subcortical centres, *the cerebellum and the spinal cord. These organs constitute the snake* [my italics].[23]

Although the fiends spring from Walgate's mind and momentarily inhabit his home, they actually come from the forest. The first killing, for instance, takes place in the forest near the Air Force base. The killing of a farmer and his wife takes place inside their barn, the fiends attacking from the wooded area nearby. The fourth killing, that of the Mayor, takes place inside his home after the fiends break in, coming once again from the nearby woods. Crabtree uses the forest as representative of the unconsicous; it is always dark and forbidding, even during daylight hours. It is fitting that the fiends come from the forest, from trees, since

Fig. IV.8. With their whiplike spinal cords, the fiends are linked to the archetypal serpent.

the very image of the tree traditionally suggests a duality: the tree of the knowledge of good and evil, and the tree of life. This dual nature suggests the parallel worlds of knowledge (the tree of the knowledge of good and evil) and living, or the conquest of death (the tree of life).[24] In the context of the film, these parallel worlds are represented by Walgate and Cummings.

The symbolic relationship between Walgate and the tree of the knowledge of good and evil has already been suggested, particularly in discussing Walgate in terms of Adam. Specifically, Walgate's fiends leave his laboratory and discover their true haven in the forest (Fig. IV.9). Visually, in the film's climax, the fiends slink up and down the trees, coiling and writhing in arrogance like the serpent of Eden itself. Moreover, the fiends in appearance are nearly indistinguishable from the barren and twisted branches and roots of the trees. Most important, however, is Walgate's death in the forest, for it comes at the moment he leaves the house and enters the forest. The fiends leaping from the trees, attack him, knocking him to the ground, where they kill him. Walgate's death, the film is saying, comes with the gaining of the knowledge the serpent of the tree offered to man.

Fig. IV.9. A) Fiends, the archetypal material of the unconscious, erupt from the forest into consciousness by breaking through boarded-up windows of Walgate's home.

Cummings, too, is associated with the forest. He is seen on several occasions surrounded by trees. And during the siege of the Walgate house, he is the only one who knows the way back through the forest to the atomic plant (Fig. IV.10). Cummings, however, is associated not with the tree of the knowledge of good and evil but with the tree of life, itself a symbol of Christ, just as the hero of romance is symbolically linked with Christ. Such an association suggests redemption, and redemption is Cummings's function in the film. J. E. Cirlot deals with this aspect:

> Why does God not mention the Tree of Life to Adam? Is it because it was a second tree of knowledge or is it because it was hidden from the sight of Adam until he came to recognize it with his new-found knowledge of good and evil—of wisdom? We prefer the latter hypothesis. The Tree of Life, once discovered, can confer immortality; but to discover it is not easy. It is "hidden," like the herb of immortality which Gilgamesh seeks at the bottom of the sea, or is guarded by monsters, like the golden apples of the Hesperides.[25]

What the tree of the knowledge of good and evil brought to man (death) will be overcome by what the tree of life brings, life itself. Cummings, as Christ-figure, enters the forest, slays the monster guarding the tree of life, and returns to the Walgate house with the promise of life. The return trip through the forest back to the house reveals the forest as no longer a dark and forbidding presence but a pleasant and idyllic landscape; light rays shine through the branches. In the mythic sense, having conquered death, Cummings/Christ returns to claim his bride, Barbara/Church.

The forest/tree image is also significant to the individuation process. With so much energy exerted in the forest milieu, it is fitting that in addition to representing the unconscious, where individuation begins, the forest also represents libido, the psychic energy that provides much of the force for the process of individuation.[26]

We need now to turn our attention back toward consciousness. Any discussion of consciousness necessitates a discussion of ego as well. In

Fig. IV.10. Cummings, making his way toward the atomic plant, fights off fiends near the air base at the forest's edge.

Fig. IV.11. A) Air base and b) village of Winthrop are associated with light (conscious) and the forest with darkness (unconscious) until the final moments of the film, when all are seen in the new light of individuation.

the film, Walgate appears as the ego figure, and consciousness is best represented, as noted earlier, by the Air Force base and the village of Winthrop, since both are nearly always associated with light (Fig. IV.11).

If we agree that ego rules the conscious world, then we can see how Professor Walgate represents ego. We know that, though a recluse, he is accepted by members of the community. He is a dominant figure (perhaps it is Crabtree's staging or actor Reeves's frame, but at any rate he is quite prominent) at the funeral of Jacques Grisselle, Barbara's brother and the fiends' first victim. And during the town meeting organized to discuss the killings, Barbara, as Walgate's representative, is able to suppress the hostility between the angry villagers and the confused Air Force by suggesting that Walgate will mediate between them. However, he never actually does so. This lack of drive and purpose, coupled with his seclusion and his sickly appearance, suggests that he is a very weak and frightened man—a weak ego. Walgate is unable to deal adequately with unconscious material. He then falls outward, as it were, and compensates for his weakness by inflating his persona, thereby repressing totally the unconscious material. He reaches a point where he is unable to differentiate between his persona, the outward perception of himself (the "brilliant scientist" incapable of evil thoughts and deeds), and his own true being.[27] As he grows weaker and his persona solidifies at the center of consciousness (propelled there by the villagers' refusal to accept him as the one responsible for the killings), the unconscious material grows all the more powerful and dangerous, culminating in an overpowering shadow that literally runs amok. True to Jung's theories, however, the overdeveloped persona is compensated by the anima. As Moreno describes it:

The persona, the ideal picture of a man, is inwardly compensated by the feminine weakness; as the individual outwardly plays the strong man, he becomes inwardly a woman, the anima. Hence, it is the anima that reacts and compensates the persona by playing a decisive role in stripping off the mask of the mere social; the gradual strengthening of the anima simultaneously parallels the gradual weakening of the persona.[28]

The recognition and experience of the anima is the second stage of the individuation process. In the film, the second stage is marked by a shift of attention from Walgate to Barbara (Fig. IV.12). As Walgate grows weaker and secludes himself from the village and the Air Force, Barbara grows stronger and her presence in the film becomes quite dominant. As anima figure, she mediates between Walgate (ego) and Cummings (representing here the unconscious material, specifically the self). Indeed, her role is that of both Walgate's personal secretary and confidant and Cummings's girl friend. She introduces Cummings to Walgate and later allows Cummings access to Walgate's papers and notebooks. She also brings to Walgate-as-ego much of the unconscious material; besides introducing Cummings to Walgate, she supports Cummings's later accusations against him. She, too, comes to believe that somehow the professor is responsible for the strange deaths and that he must come to grips with his own imperfection. At this stage, she (anima) becomes assertive yet compassionate, demanding that the imperfections be made conscious and hence realized. As mediator, Barbara also deals with Cummings, rejecting him on two separate occasions: Following his altercation with the town constable, she orders Cummings out of her home, and after Cummings upsets the professor with barbed questions about his work, she again orders him out. She is rejecting what can be best described as an overzealous self pushing its way to consciousness without regard for the reconciliation of unconscious material, especially the reconciliation of the shadow, since at this stage in the film the shadow is still dark and unrecognized.

In the third stage of the individuation process, Professor Walgate

Fig. IV.12. As Walgate grows weaker and secludes himself, Barbara grows stronger and becomes the mediator between Walgate (ego consciousness) and Cummings (unconscious material).

again comes to the fore. About two-thirds of the way into the film, just prior to the climax, Walgate literally takes on the guise of the wise old man, the archetype of the father, the spiritual factor of the unconscious. Moreno writes:

> The archetype of the spirit appears in situations in which insight, understanding, good advice, determination and planning are needed, but cannot be mastered on one's own resources. The archetype compensates this state of spiritual deficiency by contents designed to fill the gap. The wise old man means reflection, knowledge, insight, wisdom, and cleverness. He also represents moral qualities which manifest the spiritual character of this archetype, such as good will and the readiness to help. On the other hand, he also manifests the ambivalent character of his nature and is capable of working for either good or evil, which decision depends upon man's own free will.[29]

Professor Walgate, then, emerges in the final moments of the film as not only ego but also wise old man (Fig. IV.13). The Promethean scientist is usually portrayed by an elderly actor whose presence is scholarly; British stage actor Kynaston Reeves embodies just such a presence. Walgate's function at this stage resonates with the wise old man archetype: Walgate attracts to his side Cummings, Barbara, Colonel Butler, Captain Chester (Terence Kilburn), and several others who seek his advice in dealing with the marauding monsters. In a voice-over flashback (reflection, as Moreno says), Walgate recounts the origin and development of the fiends and offers insight into the method by which they can be destroyed: "Shut down your atomic plant," he insists, and the others readily agree. Furthermore, by recounting the creation of the fiends, Walgate-as-ego confesses and acknowledges his own imperfection: "I had created a fiend," he laments, finally admitting his true nature. The film then offers a gathering of archetypal material: Cummings-as-self and Barbara-as-anima are now accepted and brought into Walgate's confidence (into ego-consciousness); the shadow becomes visible and, most importantly, manageable (Fig. IV.14).

Fig. IV.13. Walgate, in voice-over flashback, becomes the image of the archetypal wise old man.

Fig. IV.14. As soon as Walgate admits that he created the fiends, they become a) visible and, most importantly, b) manageable: they are mortal.

Following his confession, the fiends launch their attack on the house, and Walgate runs into the forest in a futile attempt to control them. This moment of confrontation brings out two significant aspects of analytical psychology: the mana-personality and what Esther Harding calls the death of the ego.

The death of the Promethean scientist is the pivotal point of the film, since it not only looks back to the issue of the fallen Adam, the Promethean myth itself, but also looks forward to the final stage of the individuation process. Death comes to the Promethean scientist because of his acquisition of knowledge that can be best described as absolute or omniscient. All along the scientist has searched for the answer to the riddles of the universe, and once he locates the answers, these films are saying, death takes him for looking upon the face of God, as it were. Much of this drive for the acquisition of knowledge springs from the wise old man archetype, for it is this archetype that raises the mana-personality—"extraordinary power"—into consciousness. According to Jacobi, "To possess mana means to have power over others, but it also involves the danger of becoming arrogant and vainglorious."[30] And the Promethean scientist is often depicted as just such an arrogant and vainglorious figure; Peter Cushing's portrayal of Baron Frankenstein is exemplary of this characterization. In *Fiend without a Face*, the scientist has already been seduced by the potent energy of the wise old man archetype to such a degree that he is unable to distinguish himself from this powerful, unconscious force. He sees himself as a superman, a magician, or even a friend of God. The film comes very close to being what Sobchack refers to as the horror/science fiction hybrid, since the distinction between the evil intent of the horror film scientist—his desire to rule the world and enslave mankind—and the altruistic intent of the science fiction scientist is obscured by nuances of characterization.

At the proper time, usually just after what I call the exposition scene and just prior to the scientist's death, the mana-personality erupts and possesses the scientist. He has the sudden realization that he created the monsters in the first place and believes as well that he can control them (Fig. IV.15). As Walgate tells Barbara, "They're my creations, perhaps I can control them." He then confronts the fiends and is killed. Colonel Butler remarks, "That was a brave man," suggesting that Walgate exhibited courage in what actually was a rather stupid attempt to overpower the fiends. If individuation is to take place, the mana-personality must be distinguished from ego; as Jacobi writes, "the forces that have been activated in the individual by these insights become really available to him only when he has learned in all humility to distinguish himself from them."[31] The scientist's death, then, symbolically reveals the problem of an undifferentiated personality, namely one-sidedness, or an unbalanced psyche.

On a more positive note, the confrontation between the monsters and the scientist reveals what Harding calls the death of the ego:

> It is the case of "the king is dead, long live the king!" If the attitude is right, and the ego is willing to be sacrificed and to submit to a higher authority, then the symbols of healing begin to appear in the dreams, but if the attitude is wrong, then disastrous symbols take over the stage.

The attitude here is right;[32] for, as Harding continues, "the symbols arising from the unconscious must be realized as truly belonging to his own condition and must be explored and handled from that point of view."[33] In this sense, Walgate's death takes on yet another meaning; symbolically, Walgate dies in order to live. He accepts the fiends as his own, and his attempt to control them is a conscious gesture reflecting the realization that the fiends (symbols) in the forest (unconscious) truly belong to his own condition. In this sense, Colonel Butler's remark can

Fig. IV.15. Walgate attempts to control the fiends, a) leaving his house to b) confront them in the forest.

Fig. IV.16. Walgate is killed by the fiends, but since psychic energy cannot be destroyed, it is now directed toward Cummings; the ego (Walgate) is replaced by the Self (Cummings).

be taken literally. Walgate was indeed a brave man, one who did overcome the persona and face the heretofore threatening symbols of the unconscious.

Walgate-as-figure dies (Fig. IV.16), but psychic energy cannot be destroyed; it is merely redirected to another form. The narrative now concentrates solely on Cummings; the ego is replaced by the Self. Thus the final moments of the film correspond to the final stage of the individuation process, the realization of the Self, or the individuated ego: "Only when this midpoint is found and integrated," Jacobi writes, "can one speak of a well-rounded man. For only then has he solved the problem of his relation to the two realms which make up every man's life."[34] The two realms are the unconscious and the conscious, and the Self stands at the center of these realms, harmonizing and balancing the contents of each, creating a total and whole personality. Cummings and Barbara embrace as the other survivors gather around them. Doctor Bradley (Peter Madden), the village physician, tells Cummings that the whole town will now cooperate, suggesting that conscious and unconscious material has been reconciled. With the fiends destroyed and the hero at the center of the narrative, individuation is complete (Fig. IV.17).

The alien invasion film functions more like a dream than do many films in other genres. We have already seen the part iconographic images play here. In addition, the alien invasion film owes much of its dreamlike quality to what are best described as lapses in narrative logic. Like the rather unstructured events of dreams, and certainly like the rapid jump cuts of experimental film, many scenes and sequences in alien invasion films are seemingly devoid of rational development and sensible continuity. *Fiend without a Face* is certainly exemplary of this condition; the odd juxtaposition of scenes, for example, in which Crabtree dissolves in the middle of a conversation between Walgate and Cummings to the hunters in the forest, denies logic. Moreover, there are

Fig. IV.17. As in all alien invasion films, the hero and the heroine are united at the end; once the conscious and unconscious have come together and are balanced and the Self stands at the center governing the two realms, the personality is complete and whole.

two obvious gaps in the narrative that can bewilder the viewer. The first comes in the cemetery scene (Fig. IV.18). Cummings, without any explanation whatsoever, descends into the Mayor's crypt only to find himself trapped there by a frightened Professor Walgate. Later, Walgate confesses that he entered the crypt to examine the Mayor's body in order to confirm his own suspicions that the fiends were responsible for the deaths; Cummings, however, never once mentions any reason for his visit to the crypt. The second gap comes when Barbara suddenly and without any apparent reason changes her attitude toward Cummings; it appears that between reels, as it were, Barbara's hostility has changed to amity, even love. One might attribute such seeming nonsense to poor scripting or poor editing, but I connect it with the notion of the dream. The alien invasion film can be best understood and appreciated in the context of what Jung calls the visionary mode, or an artist's raw material "that derives its existence from the hinterland of man's mind, as if it had emerged from the abyss of prehuman ages, or from a superhuman world of contrasting light and darkness."[35]

To fully understand and appreciate the value of the visionary mode, we need to distinguish it from the psychological mode, or what Jung describes as material from man's conscious life:

> All this is assimilated by the psyche of the poet, raised from the commonplace to the level of poetic experience, and expressed with the power of conviction that gives us a greater depth of human insight by making us vividly aware of those everyday happenings which we tend to evade or to overlook because we perceive them only dully or with a feeling of discomfort. The raw material of this kind of creation is derived from the contents of man's consciousness, from his eternally repeated joys and sorrow, but clarified and transfigured by the poet.[36]

The psychological mode refers to the type of story in which the writer raises his material into a psychological context. Much of contemporary American cinema is both presented and viewed in terms of the psychological mode. Often, popular critics praise films for their "realism," a

Fig. IV.18. Anomalous cemetery scene, which nonetheless functions symbolically as a descent into the unconscious.

term used to describe a kind of naturalism in the sense that the films eschew artifice for a documentary quality that purports to reveal "truths about the real world." Here, films, to be considered good, must adhere to strict critical principles, nebulous and capricious though they may be. Films, for example, must be made on location in color in natural lighting, or at least have that look about them; studio sets and back-lot facades are no longer acceptable in terms of aesthetic value. Characterization, moreover, must avoid "types" and present "real" characters who are neither good nor bad but just are; characters as one-dimensional symbols or metaphors are considered absurd. This is the psychological mode taken to the extreme, but it is important because this extreme attitude by popular critics has led to ridicule of the alien invasion films of the fifties. Filmmakers reflect this critical attitude by either remaking the films (for example, John Carpenter's *The Thing* and Tobe Hooper's *Invaders from Mars*) to fit these critical principles and thereby repudiate the meaning and value inherent in the films, or reworking the original films into self-mocking burlesques. Andrew Solt and Malcolm Leo's *It Came from Hollywood*, for example, is a compilation of scenes from past science fiction and horror films, but any reverence due the films is nullified by the added sarcastic mocking of the various comics narrating the film, most of whom came from the sardonic television program *Saturday Night Live*.[37]

On the other hand, there are writers who do not show their characters in a psychological light; they present us with what we have already described as polarized characters. This presentation, Jung notes, allows room for analysis and interpretation, especially with regard to the psychic background. Such a story is "constructed against a background of unspoken psychological assumptions, and the more unconscious the author is of them, the more this background reveals itself in unalloyed purity to the discerning eye." The visionary mode refers to those works in which we are astonished, confused, bewildered, put on our guard or even repelled; we demand commentaries and explanations. We are reminded of nothing in everyday life, but rather of dreams, nighttime fears, and the dark, uncanny recesses of the human mind. The public for the most part repudiates this kind of literature, unless it is crudely sensational, and even the literary critics find it embarrassing.[38]

The visionary mode does not apply uniquely, as Jung's description may suggest, to experimental or avant-garde works; Jung himself cites detective fiction and English fiction in the tradition of H. Rider Haggard as good examples of narratives devoid of psychological intentions. Moreover, he writes that "literary works of highly dubious merit are often of the greatest interest to the psychologist."[39] What Jung is claiming is that the visionary mode begs for the systematic analysis of its psychic meaning, its psychic background. As such, the alien invasion film should not be dismissed merely on the feeble grounds that the films are "unreal," outdated, or "camp." Rather, they should be examined and appreciated for their archetypal/visionary expression.

The gaps in the narrative of *Fiend without a Face* take on meaning when examined in the context of the visionary mode. The cemetery scene is rich with symbols of transformation. Cummings makes his way through the conventional images of fear and death: the gravestones, the coffins, the crypt itself (Fig. IV.19). He descends into the crypt, where he finds Walgate's discarded pipe on the lid of the Mayor's coffin. Cummings returns to the surface with the evidence to finally confront Walgate. Irrespective of Cummings's motivations or lack of motivations, in archetypal terms we can claim—just as we claim with the images of dreams—that Cummings's descent into the crypt is a *nekyia,* a term Edward F. Edinger borrowed from Homer's *Odyssey* to describe "an encounter with the collective unconscious."[40] Cummings then returns a more knowledgeable man to the realm of the conscious. In this instance, relative to our scheme of individuation, Cummings-as-self is ready to fight the ego for psychic dominance.

Barbara's change of attitude toward Cummings, too, reflects psychic meaning. The behavior change occurs at the crucial town meeting, and with respect to our scheme of individuation, we can claim that when the anima realizes that the ego is rejecting the unconscious material (Walgate's boycott of the meeting), she begins to assist the self archetype (Cummings) in reconciling the conscious (the villagers) with the unconscious (Cummings-as-self and the fiends).

An anonymous critic said of *Fiend without a Face* at the time it was released: "Easily one of the goriest horror pictures [sic] in the current cycle, it oozes and gurgles with Grand Guignol blood and crunching

Fig. IV.19. Despite Cummings's lack of motivation for visiting the Mayor's crypt, in a symbolic sense he has an encounter with the collective unconscious and emerges from the crypt a more knowledgeable man.

Fig. IV.20. Highly stylized gore of decomposing fiends.

bones . . . the macabre effects will satisfy even the most jaded of the bloodthirsty."[41] Such a description is indeed fitting; *Fiend without a Face*, unlike most films of the alien invasion genre, is explicit in its handling of gore. Anyone who has seen the film can attest to its blatant bloodletting; blood is wildly pumped out of the wounded fiends, and the scenes of decomposition are indeed repulsive (Fig. IV.20). However, these scenes are so stylized and withdrawn from the cinema norm of violence (even by today's standards) that they take on yet another dimension of the dream: an improbability seen with a reference to reality. The blood from the fiends is, after all, our own blood.

The Child Archetype and Science Fiction

William Cameron Menzies's *Invaders from Mars* is a direct descendant of Wells's prototypical story idea: The invaders from Mars come to earth bent on enslaving humanity. There is nothing benevolent or innocent about these aliens; their very appearance—green, bulbous-eyed giants controlled by a disembodied "supreme intelligence"—evokes fear and revulsion. All this is certainly the stuff of which comic books and pulp magazines are made, but underlying the "cheap thrills" exterior is a serious, poignant, and beautifully designed and photo-graphed symbolic expression of individuation: It falls nicely into Harding's myth of the struggle as it pertains to adolescence. In an archetypal sense, *Invaders from Mars* is a narrative dream that takes its "sleeping" audience on a journey through the netherworld, where unconscious and conscious meet; with the self archetype as guide, we are treated to a gathering of archetypal material, a rush of entropy, and a transformation that not only transforms the ego into an individuated Self but also shapes and coalesces our own consciousness into a new awareness.

At the core of this process of individuation is a twelve-year-old boy, David McLean (Jimmy Hunt), and the visions of children (Fig. IV.21). Sightings of UFOs, monsters, and alien beings by a small child are a frequent and important motif of the alien invasion genre. Thomas Disch, the American "New Wave" science fiction writer, once observed that science fiction is nothing more than a segment of children's literature. He based his observation solely on empirical evidence: The golden age, he said, is between ten and fourteen, when "we" first begin to read science fiction. He added that most of the "classics" of the literature are about children.[42] The merits of this argument have been challenged, but his assessment, when applied to the alien invasion film of the fifties, is uncontestable. This genre is indeed a segment of children's drama—more precisely, of young boys' drama, since they dominate the genre. A child, usually a boy between nine and thirteen, has been essential to the narratives of no fewer than fourteen films: *The Black Scorpion*, *The Colossus of New York*, *The Day the Earth Stood Still*, *Dinosaurus*, *Gorgo*, *The Invisible Boy*, *The Monolith Monsters*, *The Rocket Man*, *The Space Children*, *Tobor the Great*, *Twenty Million Miles to Earth*, *The Vampire*, *Village of the Damned*, and *Invaders from Mars*. In roughly fifteen additional films[43] children appeared in prominent scenes, from Sandy De-scher's unforgetable little girl lost in *Them!* to Patty Duke's walk-on in *The 4-D Man*. Dennis Saleh writes:

Fig. IV.21. Jimmy Hunt as David McLean in *Invaders from Mars* epito-mizes child archetype figure.

The child is a potent figure of identification, always a version of ourselves. In the perspective of science fiction, the magic, invention, and excitement of a child's world is like the promise of unpredictable tomorrows. The
child can believe anything, and tomorrow is where anything can happen.
Tomorrow makes children of us all. . . . The child's fragile place in the world
is like humanity's fragile place in time and in the universe.[44]

Saleh is correct, particularly about identification. The child in the alien
invasion film, and certainly most potently in *Invaders from Mars*, is a
figure of audience participation in two ways. First, the films are presented from a child's perspective, as we have noted. Second, and certainly more important, the child represents the self archetype, and its
function in the alien invasion film is to overpower the persona, recognize the shadow, and replace the ego as the center of consciousness; in
other words, the child archetype sets in motion the process of individuation. In this context, the child's function is of supreme importance, for,
as Jung remarks, he

represents not only something that existed in the distant past but also
something that exists *now;* that is to say, it is not just a vestige but a system
functioning in the present whose purpose is to compensate or correct, in a
meaningful manner, the inevitable one-sidedness and extravagances of the
conscious mind . . . our differential consciousness is in continual danger of
being uprooted; hence, it needs compensation through the still existing
state of childhood.[45]

This compensation, or correction, is precisely the functioning role
of David McLean. David, as we shall see, potently assimilates and
reconciles psychic material, personified by the invaders and by other
characters in the film. David's role takes on yet another dimension, the
childhood motif. His actions are definitely heroic, and as such he becomes a formidable opponent of the marauding Martians. Such a description is viewed by Jung as the motif of "smaller than small yet
bigger than big." He writes that such a motif "complements the importance of the child by means of its equally miraculous deeds." Jung
continues:

The motifs of "insignificance," exposure, abandonment, danger, etc. try to
show how precarious is the psychic possibility of wholeness, that is, the
enormous difficulties to be met with in attaining this "highest good." They
also signify the powerlessness and helplessness of the life-urge which subjects every growing thing to the law of maximum self-fulfillment, while at
the same time the environmental influences place all sorts of insuperable
obstacles in the way of individuation.[46]

There is yet another significant correlation between this presentational quality, the child archetype, and the proper understanding

of the alien invasion genre: the emphasis on narrative action. As discussed earlier, the alien invasion genre eschews characterization for an
emphasis on plot. What mainstream critics describe as "characters in
conflict with characters," or the development of characterization, is not
crucial to the aesthetic meaning and value of the alien invasion film;
"conflict," the tension between absolute opposites, is the essential element. Likewise, the child at play is not concerned with development, or
growth, of character; rather, the child is concerned with wondrous
adventures, or narrative action, for his "character" to experience, and
this "play-action," like the action in the alien invasion film, is reduced
to opposing absolutes of good and evil, evil in the psychological sense
and not in the theological sense. Hence, the alien invasion film is a sort
of sophisticated child's play, a symbolic expression deriving its form
and meaning from the collective unconscious. The genre is not childish
but childlike, and accordingly its meaning is sophisticated and complex
behind a surface of rather simplistic design.

The child represents the self archetype overpowering the persona
for conscious recognition by the ego. We identify with the child, as
Saleh writes, because the child represents the unconscious seeking
proper and needed recognition. The ego, however, inflated by its
identification with the persona, forbids any such recognition because,
as Jacobi writes, the psyche of modern man, particularly western man,
has overemphasized the conscious side. Western man, for one reason or
another, has repressed the unconscious to such a degree that the persona, the "public character" or facade, has become a dictatorial agent
for the ego. This is obviously one-sided and therefore a threat to true
well-being. The answer lies in rediscovering what Jacobi calls "the land
of childhood":

> We must . . . realize that despite its undeniable successes the rational
> attitude of present-day consciousness is, in many human respects, childish-
> ly unadapted and hostile to life. Life has grown desiccated and cramped,
> crying out for the rediscovery of the fountainhead. But the fountainhead
> can only be rediscovered if the conscious mind will suffer itself to be led
> back to the "land of childhood," there to receive guidance from the uncon-
> scious as before. To remain a child too long is infantile, but it is just as
> childish to move away and then assume that childhood is no longer visible
> because we do not see it.[47]

If man does indeed rediscover his "land of childhood," then he can also
discover the secret of an individuated life, and that is why the child is
such a potent symbol for the process of individuation. Jesus told his
disciples that the kingdom of God is for those who come to God as
children; he told Nicodemus that to gain entry into the kingdom of God

a man must be "born again." Jung interprets these admonitions as descriptions of individuation; indeed, Jung derives his meaning of "whole" and "wholeness" from the German *heilen* and *heilig*, "to make holy," "to heal." The presumption is that understanding the meaning of existence, understanding our true "selves," is to become a child again—"born again"—and to discover reality in terms of a child's inward manifestations of life's complexities, or finding our truest "self" by raising the infantile contents to consciousness, thereby integrating them. This circular motion is geometrically similar to the mandala, the symbol of wholeness and totality.

Invaders from Mars (Fig. IV.22) may be divided into three parts that roughly correspond to points in the process of individuation. First, the arrival of Martians is analogous to the point at which unconscious material begins to make its presence known. Second, David's attempt to convince the citizens that the Martians have landed is analogous to the eruption of the self archetype into consciousness, which is compensated for by the eruption of the shadow. Third, the resolution or reconciliation is analogous to the point at which the self archetype finally overpowers the ego and reconciles the unconscious with the conscious.

As I pointed out earlier, I have discussed the Promethean variation example first because *Fiend without a Face* is much more lucid and yet more complex in its relationship to the process of individuation than is the classical text example, *Invaders from Mars*. The reason for this will become clear as I unravel the inner workings of the film. It is well to remember that character analogues are often charged with multiple meanings and hence may become confusing. The task is to follow the characters in the narrative and delineate their functioning quality—what they do, where they are, who is with them—with respect to their places in the film. In this sense, we are examining the archetypal image as made manifest not only by the character but also by the environment and the situation.

In general, we can ascribe archetypal analogues to the principal characters in the film. As I have suggested, David McLean is the self archetype, and the film is a working out of the individuation process, since the narrative follows David's efforts to convince the citizens of his community that Martians have landed and are taking over people. The ego, for the most part, is manifested by Professor Stuart Kelston (Arthur Franz); he is the object of David's search. The anima figure is best represented by Dr. Patricia Blake (Helena Carter), who is the first to assist David in his efforts to reach Kelston. The wise old man is Colonel Fielding (Morris Ankrum), the image of wisdom and insight. That leaves the shadow figure, and herein lies the strength of the classical text. Its

Fig. IV.22. Advertising art for *Invaders from Mars*, like that for *Invasion of the Saucer Men*, owes much to pulp magazine covers.

narrative is centered on a "good guy versus bad guy" confrontation, but this confrontation is not apocalyptic, as in the horror film; it is the depiction of a combat for the ego by two volatile archetypes: the shadow and the self (Fig. IV.23). This combat is not necessarily one with a victor in the sense that one is vanquished; rather, the struggle is to assimilate the shadow, to recognize and integrate it. When that occurs, the battle is won and individuation is complete.

The first part of the classical text narrative reveals the struggle by the unconscious material to be made known, and it is often played out by elucidating the tensions between the unconscious and consciousness. Menzies opens his film with a recurring alien invasion motif, the epigraph (Fig. IV.24). As the camera travels through space, the narrator (Franz) questions humanity's presumption upon its role in the cosmos:

> The heavens, once an object of superstition, awe, and fear, [are] now a vast region for growing knowledge. The distance of Venus, the atmosphere of Mars, the size of Jupiter, and the speed of Mercury, all this and more we know. But their greatest mystery the heavens have kept secret: What sort of life if any inhabits these planets? Human life like ours or life extremely lower on the scale or dangerously higher?
>
> Seeking the answer to this timeless question, forever seeking, is the constant preoccupation of scientists everywhere; scientists at great universities and modest homes; scientists of all ages.

This scene is the starting point for the individuation process. Menzies immediately sets up opposites, the most notable of which is sky (heaven) and earth, unconscious and conscious. Menzies sets up yet another pair of opposites by showing us the sleeping David while the narration speaks of "scientists at great universities and modest homes; scientists of all ages." What can be learned from this juxtaposition of image and sound is that the answer to the nature of things is not necessarily found in ego-consciousness, and particularly not in the persona. The great scientist can be interpreted as the persona, since the term evokes images of outward appearance or label.

Also in this opening sequence, Menzies foreshadows the confrontation that will bring the self out of the unconscious and into consciousness. Menzies establishes the warmth, security, and compassion that permeate the McLean family. An alarm clock awakens David, and it also awakens his father. George McLean (Leif Erickson) enters his son's bedroom and finds David gazing through a telescope. George orders his son to bed. "But Dad," David pleads, "Orion is in its zenith and it won't happen again for six years." The smile of a proud father appears, and George joins his son at the telescope (Fig. IV.25). Finally, Mary McLean (Hillary Brooke) enters and orders them both to bed. By avoiding open

Fig. IV.23. Meeting of self and shadow archetype: David confronts disembodied Martian intelligence.

Fig. IV.24. Titles, with emphasis on depth, indicate the film may have been shot in a 3-Dimension process, although no one seems to know for certain.

spaces and allusions to vastness (and preferring tight shots), Menzies visualizes the closeness of the family. This is David's world, a view of wholeness free from harm and discomfort. It is an important image relative to the process of individuation. To fully grasp its meaning, we must step back and look on it in a literal as well as a figurative sense. David not only represents the self archetype but adolescence as well, and both manifestations tell us much. As an archetypal figure David is shown safe and secure in what is best described as the unconscious (his home), an image that will be made clear in a moment. Menzies is foreshadowing a most important element of the individuation process: the differentiation of self and ego, or unconscious and conscious. For the personality to become whole, the self must free itself from the security of its own home, the unconscious. Such a task involves much suffering and pain for the patient, and Jung is quick to point out that individuation is a dangerous and often tragic task.[48] The self must be made conscious; it must differentiate itself from the ego and then replace the ego as the center of the personality. As a boy about to enter manhood, David must also break the bonds and free himself from the warmth and security that is home. Menzies thus prepares us for the opposing factors that come next in the film.

David falls asleep but is awakened by a violent thunderstorm; when he gets out of bed to close the window he sees a flying saucer landing in the sand pit behind his home (Fig. IV.26). Menzies has now broken the secure mood by the lightning that illuminates David's bedroom; the wailing wind also fills the room, flapping the curtains about, until David manages to reach the window. The warmth and security has been invaded by the shadow.

Fig. IV.25. Warmth and security of a happy home is played out by a) David and his father, George McLean, sharing a telescope, and b) David's mother, Mary, ordering her astronomers to bed.

Earlier I stated that the force that gives the film its meaning and value in the classical text is found in the confrontation between the self and the shadow. To fully appreciate this notion, we must distinguish the shadow from other archetypal material. We can say with certainty two things about the shadow: First, the process of individuation begins when the patient becomes aware of his shadow. Second, everyone possesses a shadow, since no one is perfect and all good; hence, the shadow is the sum total of our negative, unpleasant, inferior qualities. The shadow, however, is not necessarily evil; it is the unadapted, inferior aspect of the personality, and, as Jung points out, it is the hidden center of the personality filled with the entire historical aspects of the unconscious, including the animal passions of our primordial heritage.[49]

The shadow must be understood in the context of the personal shadow and the shadow archetype. This distinction is important. Jung makes a rigid distinction between the two on the basis of their origins: "Whereas the contents of the personal unconscious are acquired during an individual's lifetime, the contents of the collective unconscious are invariably archetypes that were present from the beginning."[50] Jacobi points out that the personal shadow stems from the "personal darkness, personifying the contents (sometimes positive) of our psyche that have been rejected and repressed or less lived in the course of our conscious existence."[51] The personal shadow needs to be integrated with the entire psyche, to become part of the psyche and not rejected by the psyche; only then will the individual be complete. There is also the shadow archetype. It is the deadly and dangerous aspect of mankind, since its origin is in the dark, primeval aspects of the human condition. When the shadow archetype appears, Jung says, even the most "hard-

Fig. IV.26. A) David awakens a second time to see b) a flying saucer descending into the sand pit behind his home.

boiled rationalist is not immune from the shattering nightmares and
haunting fears" that make up the substance of the shadow archetype.
Sometimes, Jung states, the contents of the collective unconscious in
their shadow form assume "grotesque and horrible forms in dreams and
fantasies."[52]

The shadow in *Invaders from Mars* is seen in both aspects. The
personal shadow is manifested in George McLean; the dangerous shadow archetype is represented by the Martians (Fig. IV.27). A third factor
here is the *nekyia*, the encounter with the collective unconscious.

After David sees the saucer landing, he runs into his parents' bedroom and reports the sighting. George suggests that David was just
dreaming. David returns to bed, but George, a rocket research scientist
at Coral Bluffs Proving Grounds, tells Mary that he had better investigate. "There have been rumors," he says, acknowledging a common
suspicion of the people of the fifties that flying saucers were buzzing
top-secret government installations. George leaves the house and makes
his way to the sand pit. As he approaches the knoll, an eerie sound is
heard and Menzies cuts to a close shot of the sand falling into itself,
forming a hole. George then disappears behind a tree.

This scene introduces the major image in the film, the sand pit and
its eerie musical sound effect (Fig. IV.28).[53] The image serves much like
the Gothic cemeteries of horror films. Constructed inside a studio, with
forced perspective in a fashion similar to the bizarre expressionism of
Robert Wiene's *The Cabinet of Dr. Caligari*, it is a desolate and dreary
place. The scene not only looks like a Gothic cemetery; it also functions
like one: Vile monsters are lingering below. This is the place of the
Martians, an underground fortress. It functions as the unconscious,
particularly the collective unconscious, for below the sand can be found
the shadow archetype, the Martian invaders. They are vile and corrupt,

Fig. IV.27. Manifestations of the shadow: a) George McLean as the personal shadow and b) the Martians as the dangerous shadow archetype.

dangerous and terrifying. The "Martian intelligence," what Sergeant Rinaldi describes as "mankind developed to its ultimate intelligence," with its tentacled arms resembling a serpent, takes on the connotation of the absolute ruler of darkness, the devil. The whole scene expresses a pathological one-sidedness that needs no integration but rather rejection or conquest. Only then can the psyche assimilate the personal shadow.

George McLean now emerges (literally from the sand pit) as the personal shadow (Fig. IV.29). He appears as a consequence of what happens when the personal shadow is not recognized or assimilated but is allowed to fall back into the collective unconscious. There, the shadow archetype gathers all sorts of unconscious material and subsequently bursts into consciousness, where it can do much harm. The secret of coming to grips with it is to merely recognize or acknowledge it but not integrate it. The formidable task is to reject the shadow archetype and thereby facilitate the integration of the personal shadow. This task involves much suffering and pain in a spiritual sense; it is difficult for one to admit that one has an inferior side.

George emerges from the sand pit a changed man, and the warmth and security with which Menzies opened the film is in shambles. The self (David) is now forced out of the unconscious (the secure home) to fulfill its destiny, that is, to initiate individuation. David's task is to force the citizens (the ego, including Kelston and everyone else in the film) to reject the Martians (shadow run amok). Once that is done, George-as-personal-shadow can be assimilated.

One description of the ego is "doorkeeper to the psyche." The ego stands at the center of the psyche looking both forward and backward,

Fig. IV.28. Major image of Menzies's film: the sand pit, an expressionistic membrane between conscious and unconscious realms.

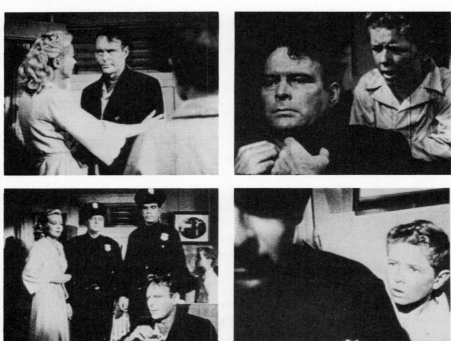

Fig. IV.29. The warmth and security of the McLean home is shattered by intrusion of the invaders. A) Following a long absence, George returns home from the pit a changed man; b) he is cold and hostile to Mary and David, and David observes a peculiar X scar on his neck. C) Police officers, also returning from the pit, act in similar fashion, telling Mary coldly that they found nothing at the pit. D) David notices the same scar on the officers that he saw on his father.

to consciousness and the unconscious. In this sense, we can ascribe the ego figure to Professor Kelston. Kelston-as-ego is alluded to early in the film; he is discussed frequently during David's plight; and he is the object of David's pursuit. But the ego fails to respond to the self's call, and accordingly the persona is inflated to such a point that the ego is swallowed by it. To see how this works, let us first examine the persona and then the ego with respect to the anima.

The persona takes on various guises in *Invaders from Mars*. Initially, the persona is manifested by David's father; he squelches David's story of the saucer sighting by dismissing it as merely a dream or illusion. Like the persona ordering the ego to repress "threatening impulses," George orders David to dismiss the sighting. Later, George becomes the manifestation of the personal shadow, and therefore the psychic energy is transformed into another entity, the "adult world." David is quite literally at the mercy of doubting, conscious-oriented, rational adults who dismiss his sighting as sheer fancy, fostered by "trashy" science fiction magazines. To emphasize this point, Menzies gives us stark, rapid images (Fig. IV.30): First, Mrs. Wilson scolds David for "telling stories"; next, Jim, the gas station attendant, placates David before

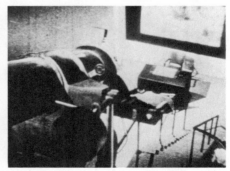

Fig. IV.30. Frightened, David searches for his friend Professor Kelston, and Menzies accelerates the action. A) Mrs. Wilson scolds David for lying about her daughter, Kathy, who has returned from the pit, also changed and with the tell-tale cold expression. B) Jim, the gas station attendant, tries to calm David while Jim calls David's father. C) David tries to call Kelston at the observatory, but d) the observatory is empty.

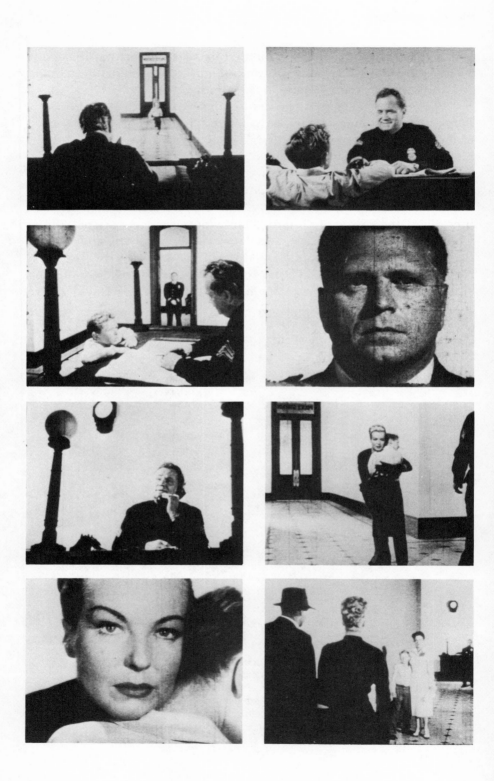

calling his father; and then the police literally hold David prisoner for being a child "out of control." It is not until the anima, the soul-image (Blake), enters the scenario that David finds comfort.

The inflated persona is almost vicious in its efforts to reject the self; moreover, the ego, if not rejecting, is at least refusing to acknowledge the self. Kelston is not available, and excuses for his absence are meaningless, since what matters is the fact that he is nowhere to be found. It is not until the anima enters the drama that we finally see Kelston.

At this point we need to consider the scene in the police station (Fig. IV.31), a pivotal point in the narrative. The scene is often lauded by critics; Vivian Sobchack describes it as "a setting as visually jolting and alien as any other-worldly planet."[54] It is certainly a masterwork of deep-focus, mise-en-scène style, and its image is so striking and memorable that it attests to Menzies's skill not only as designer but director as well. Confused and frustrated, frightened and helpless, David runs to every child's friend, the cop. From a high angle, shooting over the shoulder of the desk sergeant, Menzies introduces his police station: In forced perspective, it is a Caligariesque chamber, with empty, washed-out walls and a long, tunnel-like corridor stretching from the door to the desk. The sergeant's desk is a monolithic structure, with two light globes on standards at either side of the sergeant. The desk and the sergeant are overpowering, even to adults; seen against David's diminutive figure they become objects of terror. The station contrasts sharply with the warmth of David's home. Now, for the first time, David's helplessness is dramatized rather than suggested by mise-en-scène. Menzies, foreshadowing the climax inside the Martian cave, shows David lost and helpless in the police station, running up to the desk in desperation just as he will run up to the Martian intelligence in desperation in the final reel.

The police station becomes yet another milieu for Menzies's continual emphasis on duality. If the police station is the home of every child's friend, he seems to say, then every child's enemy is not far away. The

Fig. IV.31. Highly praised police station sequence. A) After learning that Kelston is not available, David runs to the police station for help and b) explains his dilemma to the desk sergeant. C) Suddenly, in a beautifully symmetical deep-focus mise-en-scène, the chief appears, and d) David (and we) discover that the cold expression worn by David's father, the police officers, and Kathy is on the chief's face as well. E) After David notices the X scar on the chief's neck and is sent to a cell to calm down, the sergeant calls Dr. Blake. F) David's mother arrives, g) wearing the same cold expression, h) but Dr. Blake takes custody of David, fearing for his emotional state.

threatening atmosphere of the station has a threatening occupant, the chief. David demands to see the chief, and after a brief verbal bout with the desk sergeant, the chief appears. David runs to him and together they enter the chief's office. David tells him the story of the landing and his father's strange behavior. "Are you George McLean's boy?" the chief asks. David answers and then sees the curious X scar on the nape of the chief's neck—the same mark he saw earlier on his father's neck. David panics, but is subdued by the sergeant. The chief orders David to a jail cell pending the arrival of his parents. However, even though the threatening station holds this threatening figure, the chief, it also holds the child's "friend"; the sergeant, somewhat puzzled by the chief's cold behavior and genuinely concerned about David's well-being, calls Dr. Blake.

This rather lengthy exposition of the police station scene is necessary to fathom the film. Several things happen here. First, as I mentioned, it is the pivotal point in the narrative, the point at which the adults become aware of the Martian threat. Second, it introduces Dr. Blake, a pivotal character with respect to the narrative and the scheme of individuation as well. Third, David finally—with the aid of Blake—finds Kelston, and we, too, are introduced to him (Fig. IV.32). Fourth, Menzies slows the pace for some exposition and insight.

Of importance at this point is the function of Dr. Blake. It is she who finally overpowers the doubting society. In addition, she literally refuses to let David return to his parents, preferring that he go directly to Kelston and explain what has happened. What can be seen in this sequence is an analytic correlation: Blake as anima has come under the influence of the self. Even more important is her overpowering of the persona, something that is not literally shown but nonetheless happens, much in the same way that Barbara Grisselle in *Fiend without a Face* suddenly changes her behavior. We seem to "know it" and thus experience it a priori. Blake as anima is the opposite pole of the persona. Jung writes that "if the persona is intellectual, the anima will quite certainly

Fig. IV.32. The object of David's search: Professor Kelston (ego).

be sentimental."[55] Blake is sentimental and views the outside world through the lenses of the irrational functions, whereas the persona has grounded itself in the rational functions, repudiating such things as flying saucers. Blake's role with respect to the anima is also explained by her mediation between Kelston and David. Jacobi writes that "the persona is the mediating function between the ego and the outside world and the soul-image [anima/animus] the corresponding mediating function between the ego and the inner world."[56] Again, it is appropriate that she brings David to Kelston (Fig. IV.33).

We need to recall the special attributes of the self archetype. First, it is the archetype of order and unification. It draws to itself all the other archetypes and binds them into a harmonious whole. Second, it is often at odds with the persona, the public mask. Third, the self is often referred to as the "god-archetype," since its true nature is nearly divine. Fourth, it is often depicted in myth and art in the figure of the child. David is the unifying, orderly factor in the film, and inside the observatory (a mandala figure), David brings Colonel Fielding, the army commander, the wise old man, to Kelston (Fig. IV.34).

In the classical text, the wise old man figure often appears as a military commander, usually played by Morris Ankrum. Unlike the wise old man in the Prometheus variation, who soon becomes the mana-personality, this figure in the classical text is always good and

Fig. IV.33. The three significant character analogues: David as self, Kelston as ego, and Pat as anima.

Fig. IV.34. Archetype of the wise old man, manifested by Col. Fielding.

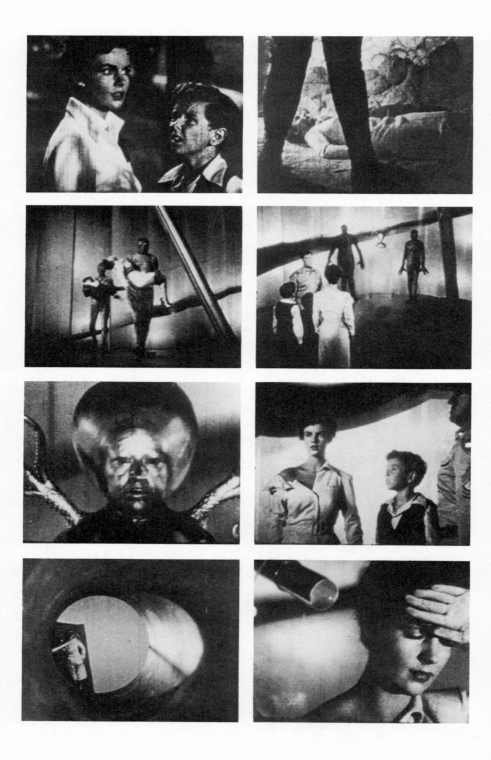

remains a positive influence. He brings with him all the knowledge and wisdom, insight and cleverness needed to aid the hero in defeating the invader. Thus Colonel Fielding arrives at the sand pit bearing all the knowledge needed to defeat the Martians. Interestingly, when David is taken captive by the Martians, he cries for help by calling to Colonel Fielding and not to Kelston. His cry of "Colonel Fielding, Colonel Fielding," heard over and over again during the siege of the Martian stronghold, suggests that the wise old man in its positive sense represents the moral and spiritual qualities needed to boost the self into consciousness.

With this psychological dramatis personae in order, we can turn our attention to the action of the film. As discussed in a previous chapter, the alien invasion film is structured much like a detective thriller; a good three-quarters of the narrative delineates the chase, or quest, for the alien invaders as well as the means by which to repel them. The final quarter is taken up by the climax and resolution, which, according to the scheme of individuation, is the point at which individuation takes place.

The climax of *Invaders from Mars* is a dynamic interpolation of fast-paced images (Fig. IV.35). With the abduction of David and Blake, Menzies returns to furious action. The central images are the parallel action between Blake's near "rape" by the mind-controlling machine and the penetration of the subterranean Martian lair by the U.S. Army. Blake is ultimately rescued by Kelston, and Colonel Fielding activates a time bomb inside the Martian craft. Fielding and David and a company of soldiers are trapped inside the tunnel. In a scene resembling a ritual of manhood, David frees the group by operating a stolen Martian ray gun, opening an escape tunnel.[57]

What we have psychologically in the climactic tunnel sequence is the self (David) pulling the archetypes together and allowing the ego (Kelston) to pass them into consciousness (Fig. IV.36). Kelston has escaped the tunnel and stands at the hole, literally pulling out first Blake (and thereby receiving the onrush of unconscious material into consciousness) and then the fleeing soldiers (more material). The persona is no longer inflated; the adult world is actively involved in the

Fig. IV.35. As film reaches its climax, Menzies offers more stark, rapid images in tunnel sequence. A & B) Pat and David are taken captive by Martians, c) and the mutants carry them to d) the chamber of e) the Martian intelligence. F) Sergeant Rinaldi, captured earlier, explains that the Martians are bent on taking over the earth. G & H) Pat is prepared for takeover by the machine that leaves the X scar on the neck.

Fig. IV.36. Kelston and Pat pull David out of the Martian lair; in psychic terms, the ego and anima pull the Self into its proper place at the center of the psyche.

"land of childhood," assimilating the archetypes; the Martian threat is not just the fantasy of a boy inspired by "trashy" science fiction magazines, but quite real.

Of particular importance to the classical text is the assimilation of the shadow. The Martians are destroyed, and we can interpret that as rejecting the shadow archetype—rejecting it, not repressing or ignoring it. We have acknowledged its existence. Once the Martians are destroyed, George McLean returns to his normal state. The personal shadow has been saved from the shadow archetype of the collective unconscious; moreover, since George survives and is assimilated with the remaining figures, the personal shadow has been integrated. The final image at this stage in the film is Kelston and Blake together in the daylight with David conspicuously missing. The self has been integrated into an individuated Self. With respect to Harding's ideas about masculine psychology, David has won his battle with the "dragon," and his transition into manhood is complete. David is replaced by Kelston.

The final scene has been an issue of controversy, not only in an aesthetic sense but also because the "definitive version" of *Invaders from Mars* seems to be nonexistent.[58] The print I viewed ends in the following manner: David awakens from this nightmare and is again sent to bed. He lies there for several moments, then jumps out of bed and sees the saucer landing once more. However, the soundtrack plays not the music of the Martian's craft but the clear and distinct roar of turboprop airplane engines. Jean-Luc Godard once remarked that when visuals conflict with the film's soundtrack, trust what you see. Nowhere is this admonition more appropriate than in Menzies's film. Total individuation has indeed been reached as we see the mandala descending; we are, as it were, born again. We are born again into the metaphor of the child. We hear the persona telling us that it is just an airplane, but we see the self telling us that it is more than an airplane: It is a wondrous mandala coming from the unconscious with archetypes for individuation.[59]

Conclusion

Can films with such titles as *The Crawling Eye, Attack of the Fifty Foot Woman, Gog,* and *The Blob* transcend their exploitative absurdity to genuinely express true meaning and value to their audiences? This question is now answered. Meaning and value in the alien invasion film are assessed by articulating its parts in terms of the individuation process. These films, like dreams, are rich in symbolic images and events that are best interpreted by applying analytical psychology and myth criticism.

As I have stated, it does us no good to ignore a very real aspect of alien invasion films: their ridiculousness. These films have many components; their "cheap thrills" titles and lurid advertisements are only a small portion of their exploitative world. But this very ridiculousness gives strength to the films; their characters and events—heretofore considered absurd—often help to elicit the meaning and value of the films. We can censure the films for their simple-minded reduction of events and characters to hackneyed and torpid formulas—and thereby miss much of the worth in the films. Or we can discover meaning in these films by raising their "absurdity" to a manageable and meaningful level, by seeing in these films—through their simple plot outlines and polarized, stereotyped characters—the meaning and value that arises from their simplicity. The films are visionary in the Jungian sense, and therefore they beg for systematic analysis of their meaning and value in the context of the individuation process. The films offer us meaning and value through the symbolic power of their images and events. The alien invasion film, then, is a massive symbol of life's own destiny.

Notes

I. Science Fiction and Horror

1. Paul Michael, ed., *The American Movies Reference Book: The Sound Era*, p. 29.

2. Alan Frank, "Screen Trips," in *The Encyclopedia of Science Fiction*, p. 75.

3. Most science fiction historians and critics recognize Georges Méliès as the originator of cinematic fantasy, horror, and science fiction. For an appreciation of Méliès's contributions to fantasy film, see Paul Hammond, *Marvellous Méliès*.

4. Vivian Carol Sobchack, *The Limits of Infinity: The American Science Fiction Film*, pp. 53 and 54.

5. William Johnson, "Journey into Science Fiction," in *Focus on the Science Fiction Film*, p. 1.

6. Philip Strick, *Science Fiction Movies*, p. 4.

7. Jeff Rovin, *A Pictorial History of Science Fiction Films*, p. 9.

8. Sobchack, pp. 26 and 27.

9. Carlos Clarens, *An Illustrated History of the Horror Film*, pp. 119 and 120.

10. Among the myriad Freudian critics are D. L. White, "The Poetics of Horror: More Than Meets the Eye"; Robin Wood, "The Return of the Repressed"; and Harvey R. Greenberg, *The Movies on Your Mind*. Freudian analyses of science fiction films are found in Margaret Tarratt, "Monsters from the Id," and Frank D. McConnell, "Song of Innocence: *The Creature from the Black Lagoon*."

11. Stanley Solomon, *Beyond Formula: American Film Genres*, p. 112.

12. Stuart M. Kaminsky, *American Film Genres: Approaches to a Critical Theory of Popular Film*, p. 131.

13. Greenberg, pp. 197–199.

14. Solomon, p. 115.

15. Kaminsky, p. 144.

16. Tarratt, p. 38.

17. Susan Sontag, "The Imagination of Disaster," in *Hal in the Classroom: Science Fiction Films*, pp. 25 and 26.

18. Johnson, p. 1.

19. Solomon, p. 115.

20. By the term *horror film* I mean *Gothic film*. This term distinguishes those films that have historically been molded out of supernatural stories, e.g., films about werewolves, vampires, ghosts, demons, etc., from films dealing with slaughter and gore, the so-called "mad-slasher" films. To my thinking such films as Hitchcock's *Psycho* and John Carpenter's *Halloween* are "thrillers" and not horror movies in the traditional sense. Denis Gifford writes that "an element of fantasy is essential to the true horror film: the impossible rather than the improbable" (*A Pictorial History of the Horror Movies*, p. 13).

21. Elizabeth MacAndrew, *The Gothic Tradition in Fiction*, pp. 47 and 48; 109.

22. MacAndrew, p. 49.

23. Often these extremes of characterization are located within one individual. Universal's *Wolf Man* series, for instance, maintained an inner conflict in Lawrence Talbot (Lon Chaney). Talbot was consistently in physical and psychological turmoil because of his werewolf curse, and accordingly many of the films delineated Talbot's quest for help from a Dr. Frankenstein surrogate who would eventually (in Erle C. Kenton's *House of Dracula* [1945]) free Talbot's soul from the hideous curse.

24. David Pirie, *A Heritage of Horror: The English Gothic Cinema 1946– 1972*, p. 51.

25. MacAndrew, p. 25.

26. Alain Silver and James Ursini, *The Vampire Film*, p. 124.

27. Maurice Beebe, "The Universe of Roderick Usher," in *Poe: A Collection of Critical Essays*, p. 123.

28. Sobchack, *The Limits of Infinity*, p. 59.

29. It is interesting to note the difference between Sherman's *The Lady and the Monster* and Felix Feist's *Donovan's Brain* (1953), both based on Curt Siodmak's novel, *Donovan's Brain*. The horror version (Sherman) presents Erich von Stroheim, dressed up considerably like Dr. Praetorius in *The Bride of Frankenstein*, as a sinister doctor experimenting with keeping a "dead" businessman's brain alive. The film includes an old castle in the best tradition of horror films, and Richard Arlen's "zombie" characterization of a servant owes much to the zombies of Victor Halperin's *White Zombie* (1932). Feist's version eschews the expressionism, the Gothic castle, and the "zombie" for a straightforward narrative about Dr. Patrick Corey's efforts to keep the brain alive for the benefit of medical science and humanity. When Corey discovers that no good can come from such an experiment, he destroys the brain and vows to keep his discovery a secret.

30. E. M. Forster, *Aspects of the Novel*, pp. 69–79.

31. John Baxter, *Science Fiction in the Cinema*, pp. 7 and 8.

32. Kingsley Amis, *New Maps of Hell*, p. 44.

33. Running parallel to the science fiction film of the fifties was a peculiar breed of film that I call the technological drama. These films concentrate on mechanical hardware the same way science fiction often does, but here the technological marvels, mostly aircraft, are used as milieu for a personal story about a test pilot or scientist. Some of the best of this type are Anthony Mann's *Strategic Air Command* (1955), Mervyn LeRoy's *Toward the Unknown* (1956), and Robert D. Webb's *On the Threshold of Space* (1955). The aerial sequences in these films use VistaVision and CinemaScope to great advantage and are visually impressive. Other films worth considering are Gordon Douglas's *The McConnell Story* (1955), Richard Donner's *The X-15* (1959), and Francis Lyon's *Bailout at 43,000* (1957), which screenwriter Paul Monash adapted from his original television play presented on CBS's *Climax* in 1956. The original of this type of film is most likely Stuart Heisler's *Chain Lightning* (1949) with Humphrey Bogart. The technological drama, in addition to Monash's drama, was also seen on television in Ivan Tors's *The Man and the Challenge* (1959–60), a half-hour series dramatizing experiments in human and machine endurance by research scientist Glenn Barton (George Nader).

34. See Rollo May, *Man's Search for Himself*.

35. Don Fredericksen, "Jung/Sign/Symbol/Film, Part One," p. 63.

36. Sobchack, *The Limits of Infinity*, p. 63.

II. Myths and Motifs of the Monster Movie

1. See Carl G. Jung and C. Kerenyi, *Essays on a Science of Mythology*, for a discussion of mythologem.

2. Mircea Eliade, *Myth and Reality*, p. 2.

3. Antonio Moreno, *Jung, Gods, and Modern Man*, p. 15.

4. C. G. Jung, *Psychological Types*, p. 436.

5. Jolande Jacobi, *The Psychology of C. G. Jung*, p. 12.

6. For an analysis of psychological types and film, see Don Fredericksen, "Two Aspects of a Jungian Perspective Upon Film: Jung and Freud; The Psychology of Types."

7. Jacobi, p. 12.

8. I am indebted to my friend Gary W. Coville for allowing me access to his unpublished essay, "Notes Toward a Theory of Detective Fiction."

9. I am indebted to Will Wright's *Sixguns and Society: A Structural Study of the Western* for its systematic analysis of a similar narrative pattern.

10. See Robert Scholes and Eric S. Rabkin, *Science Fiction: History-Science-Vision*, pp. 17–25.

11. Dennis Saleh, *Science Fiction Gold: Film Classics of the Fifties*, p. 69.

12. See John Baxter, *Science Fiction in the Cinema*, pp. 114–128, for an appreciation of the works of Jack Arnold.

13. *Time* (July 6, 1953), p. 86.

14. Although the film's story is credited to Ray Bradbury's "The Foghorn," the relationship between the film and the story is slight. There is a scene in which the Beast rises up out of the ocean and topples a lighthouse, the milieu of the story, but the subtlety and gentle romance of the story are not in the film.

15. The dominant motif of the alien invasion genre is the contest, and since it is widely accepted that fiction, whether prose, theatre, or film, is constituted of conflict, a distinction between conflict and contest is necessary. Granted, conflict forms narrative; the movement of any story is accelerated by the force of conflict, and conflict is often considered synonymous with story. However, as Jack Matthews suggests (*Archetypal Themes in the Modern Story*, pp. 5 and 6), the contest is a mode of conflict in which "it constitutes a primordial situation, a truly archetypal theme." Moreover, he writes:

> While a single character may experience "inner conflict," it would be strange indeed to speak of his "inner contest." In the Contest, there are two characters of comparable power who more or less knowingly enter some sort of arena in a struggle with each other. Often this struggle is highly symbolic, insofar as characters themselves seem vested with larger meaning. (p. 5)

With such an operating definition of contest, then, it is clear that the contest motif is the principal underlying motif of the alien invasion genre. There is a contest between society and the invader. "Society," here, often takes the form of a small circle of humanity, as in Hawks and Nyby's *The Thing from Another World* and Edward L. Cahn's *It! The Terror from Beyond Space*, but for the most part it takes the form of an entire population, as in Lourié's *The Beast from 20,000 Fathoms* (the population of New York), Robert Gordon's *It Came from Beneath the Sea* (the population of San Francisco), and Byron Haskin's *War of the Worlds* (the population of the world). The invader (opponent in this contest) takes the form of either an extraterrestrial individual (Klaatu in Wise's *The Day the Earth Stood Still*), group ("invaders"), or thing (*The Blob*), or a terrestrial invader such as the resurrected dinosaur (*The Beast from 20,000 Fathoms*) or mutated insect (*Them!*). The arena is mostly the American city; however, a number of films have taken place in small towns (Arnold's *It Came from Outer Space* and *Tarantula* and Nathan Hertz's *The Brain from Planet Arous*, for example).

16. Brian Murphy, "Monster Movies: They Came from Beneath the Fifties," p. 42.

17. See Stuart Samuels, "The Age of Conspiracy and Conformity: *Invasion of the Body Snatchers*," in *American History/American Film: Interpreting the Hollywood Image,* pp. 203–217.

18. See, for example, Andrew Dowdy, *The Films of the Fifties: The American State of Mind.*

19. For an excellent discussion of amplification and film, see Don Fredericksen, "Jung/Sign/Symbol/Film: Part Two." His subject is Basil Wright's *Song of Ceylon.*

20. *Superman and the Mole Men* is an elusive film; prints are seemingly nonexistent. The film, however, has been edited into a two-part episode of *The Adventures of Superman* TV series. For an interesting discussion of the TV series see Gary Grossman, *Superman: From Serial to Cereal.*

21. The Prometheus myth in the context of the alien invasion film is outlined by Radu Florescu, *In Search of Frankenstein,* pp. 220 and 223.

22. Hammer Films produced six Frankenstein films between 1957 and 1972, all featuring Peter Cushing as the Baron and all but one (*The Evil of Frankenstein* [1964], Freddie Francis) directed by Terence Fisher. What is interesting about this series is that it is not the monster that continues to roam from film to film, as in the Universal series, but the Baron himself, creating a new creature in each film.

23. David Pirie, *A Heritage of Horror: The English Gothic Cinema 1946– 1972,* p. 70.

24. Martin Tropp, *Mary Shelley's Monster: The Story of Frankenstein,* p. 126.

25. Matthews, p. 308.

26. See Richard Hofstadter, *Anti-Intellectualism in American Life* and *The Paranoid Style in American Politics.*

III. Iconography and Convention

1. Colin McArthur, *Underworld USA,* p. 24.

2. C. G. Jung, *Psychological Types,* pp. 473–476.

3. For one reason or another, the Beast is called a rhedosaur, a dinosaur that never existed; however, the most important thing about the Beast is that it resembles a mythological dragon more than a dinosaur.

4. Carl Sagan, *The Dragons of Eden: Speculations on the Evolution of Human Intelligence,* pp. 138–141.

5. Don Fredericksen, "Jung/Sign/Symbol/Film, Part One," p. 169.

6. McArthur, p. 23.

7. John Baxter, *Science Fiction in the Cinema,* p. 116.

8. Baxter, p. 105.

9. *Flight to Mars* is not exactly an alien invasion film; rather, it is a film of space exploration. I mention it here because the basis of its narrative is a plan by Martians to invade the earth, a sort of "planning an invasion" film.

10. William Alland was a staff producer at Universal-International specializing in genre films. The science fiction films he made with director Jack Arnold are visually impressive and atmospheric. Before becoming a producer at Universal he was a member of Orson Welles's Mercury Theatre; he is best remembered, perhaps, for his role of Thompson, the reporter, in Welles's *Citizen Kane* (1940). It should also be noted that Marshall Thompson's film roles are surpassed by his television roles. In addition to *World of Giants,* Thompson starred in no fewer than seven episodes of Ziv's *Science Fiction Theatre* and was a regular, playing Major Devery, in *Men into Space,* a space exploration series of 1959–60 starring William Lundigan as Colonel Ed McCauley, a role similar to

his role in Richard Carlson's *Riders to the Stars* (1954). *World of Giants* co-star Arthur Franz also has an impressive list of television credits, having appeared in five episodes of *Science Fiction Theatre* as well as playing roles in *Men into Space*.

11. The list of iconographic performers does not stop here. Robert Cornthwaite's striking performance as the amoral Professor Carrington in *The Thing from Another World* was only a prelude to Peter Cushing's narcissistic Frankenstein; Cornthwaite, however, was not to repeat such a characterization in his next two films, Howard Hawks's pseudo science fiction comedy, *Monkey Business* (as Dr. Zoldeck), and *War of the Worlds* (as Pacific-Tech scientist Dr. Pryor), but was cast as scientists nonetheless. John Zaremba portrayed scientists in *The Magnetic Monster*, *Earth vs. the Flying Saucers*, *Twenty Million Miles to Earth*, and *Frankenstein's Daughter*. Finally, Peter Brocco appeared in *Radar Men from the Moon*, *Francis Goes to the Races* (as Dr. Mayberry), *The Atomic Kid*, *Invaders from Mars*, *Tobor the Great*, and many additional films in the sixties, including *Our Man Flint* as Dr. Qu, almost always as a scientist. I mention these four performers here because they have uncanny resemblances to each other: tall, thin, and gaunt, with high foreheads of caricatured scientists. In terms of their physical presences, we can say that one figure, this "scientist," has appeared in a substantial number of alien invasion films. Still another performer who can be identified with the alien invasion film is Whit Bissell, first seen in 1947 in Jules Dassin's *Brute Force* as Tom Lister, the taciturn prisoner who commits suicide. Bissell is often seen as a mild-mannered, introverted scientist (Dr. Thompson in *Creature from the Black Lagoon*, Dr. Briggs in Sam Newfield's *Lost Continent* [1951], and Dr. Pangborn in *The Atomic Kid*), but he is also capable of using this reticence as a force of dominance and cruelty as evidenced by his portrayals of Professor Frankenstein and Dr. Brandon in *I Was a Teenage Frankenstein* and *I Was a Teenage Werewolf*, respectively. Like his counterparts above, he also has an impressive list of television credits, including appearances in *Science Fiction Theatre*, *Man and the Challenge*, and *Men into Space*.

The horror movie stars of the thirties and forties seem not to have fared well with the alien invasion genre. Only John Carradine seemed to find a niche, as it were, in the genre, and he was relegated to mostly supporting roles. Carradine did star as the scientist in *The Unearthly*, and he appeared as the title character in *The Cosmic Man*; however, his roles were purely secondary in *The Black Sleep* and *Invisible Invaders*. Lon Chaney, Jr., portrayed the Frankenstein monster in an episode of the 1952 television anthology series, *Tales of Tomorrow*, and he played the title role in *The Indestructible Man*, a role very similar to the one he played in George Waggner's *Man-Made Monster* (1941), which was reissued in 1952 under the title *Atomic Monster*. Chaney's roles in *The Black Sleep*, *The Cyclops*, and *The Alligator People* were purely secondary. Vincent Price, after portraying the mad sculptor Jarrod in Andre de Toth's *House of Wax* (1953), was just beginning his association with horror movies by appearing in three alien invasion films, *The Fly*, *The Return of the Fly*, and *The Tingler*. The two undisputed stars of the horror movies, Boris Karloff and Bela Lugosi, were conspicuous because of their near absence. Karloff played Dr. Jekyll in a spoof, *Abbott and Costello Meet Dr. Jekyll and Mr. Hyde*, in 1953 but was not seen again until he played Dr. Frankenstein in the updated *Frankenstein 1970* (1958). Lugosi, whose absence was due in part to illness, played a butler in *The Black Sleep*; a vampire who controls a robot in the British film *Old Mother Riley Meets the Vampire* (also known as *Vampires over London*), produced in 1952 but not released in the United States until the mid-sixties under the title *My Son the Vampire*; and a mad scientist in *The Bride of the Monster*. His final appearance (actually no more than a walk-on) was in *Plan 9 from Outer Space*. He died in 1956.

12. McArthur, p. 24. Nowhere is this assimilation of actor and character more obvious than in the spate of B westerns produced in the thirties and forties. Heroes Gene Autry and Roy Rogers merely played themselves. Two films of the Rogers series, *Bells of Rosarita* (1945) and *Trail of Robin Hood* (1950), actually had Rogers calling his studio, Republic, and securing the aid of Republic western stars (Alan "Rocky" Lane, "Wild Bill" Elliott, et al.) in bringing the villains to justice.

13. C. G. Jung, "Flying Saucers: A Modern Myth of Things Seen in the Skies," *Civilization in Transition*, p. 325.

14. C. G. Jung, *Aion: Researches into the Phenomenology of Self*, p. 32.

15. Jung, *Aion*, p. 31.

16. M.-L. von Franz, "The Process of Individuation," in *Man and His Symbols*, p. 213.

17. Jung, "Flying Saucers," p. 389.

18. For a brief discussion of Studio Film Service, see Paul Mandell, "Of Beasts and Behemoths: The Fantastic Films of Eugene Lourié, Part 2: *The Giant Behemoth*," p. 55.

19. The use of stock footage is nearly as old as the cinema itself, and the alien invasion genre holds no market on the practice. I would venture, however, that the most frequently used stock footage of any genre is the footage of lizards-as-dinosaurs from Hal Roach's 1940 film, *One Million B.C.*, of which portions are said to have been directed by D. W. Griffith. The fighting lizards and volcanic upheaval have been seen in such diverse works as Jungle Jim movies, Superman television episodes, Tarzan movies, and even an *Encyclopaedia Britannica* television commercial, but nearly the entire film can be seen in Edward Bernds's *Valley of the Dragons* (1961), a free adaptation of Jules Verne's *Off on a Comet*.

20. Dennis Saleh, *Science Fiction Gold: Film Classics of the Fifties*, p. 81.

21. Television was also telling us daily that America was strong and ready for any invader. Such programs as *Air Power, Flight, Navy Log, The Silent Service*, and *The Big Picture* depicted America's invulnerability.

22. Vivian Sobchack, "The Alien Landscapes of the Planet Earth: Science Fiction in the Fifties," in *Science Fiction Films*, p. 51.

23. J. E. Cirlot, *A Dictionary of Symbols*, p. 207.

24. Andrew Dowdy, *The Films of the Fifties: The American State of Mind*, p. 160.

25. For a discussion of the symbolic functions of the "damsel in distress" in romantic literature, see Northrop Frye, *The Secular Scripture: A Study of the Structure of Romance*, pp. 65–93.

26. Leslie Halliwell, *The Filmgoer's Companion*, 4th ed., p. 533. He reproduces the ad.

IV. Meaning and Value

1. C. G. Jung, "Psychology and Literature," *The Spirit in Man, Art, and Literature*, p. 98.

2. This outline of the individuation process corresponds roughly to my schema offered in chapter II.

3. Joseph L. Henderson, "Ancient Myths and Modern Man," in *Man and His Symbols*, p. 112.

4. M. Esther Harding, *The I and the Not I: A Study in the Development of Consciousness*, p. 214. See also pp. 177–215 for the "death of ego" in the context of metaphysical reality.

5. For discussions of Jung's ideas about adolescent masculine psychology, see M. Esther Harding, "The Inner Conflict: The Dragon and the Hero," *Psychic*

Energy: Its Source and Its Transformation, pp. 241–302; Erich Neumann, *The Origins and History of Consciousness;* and Robert A. Johnson, *He: Understanding Masculine Psychology.*

6. Harding, *The I and the Not I*, pp. 156 and 158. As I have stated, science fiction's appeal has been primarily to young boys, and perhaps because of the abolition of the production code of self-regulation, the modern science fiction film has followed the path of its mainstream counterparts by damning any and all restrictions. Unfortunately, by adhering to this form of expression, the film rigidly locks itself into an adolescent attitude. By emphasizing such adolescent traits as gratuitous profanity and voyeurism, the film evades the transcending symbolic function—"slaying the dragon"—of the early science fiction films for a stagnant litany affirming the blessings of adolescence. As such, the more recent films do little to break the bond with the childhood paradise; rather, they are saying that adolescence is a paradise combining the best of both worlds, i.e., the best of the adult world with the unaccountability of childhood. Such a view is reinforced by the many publications oriented to the science fiction film now available (see n. 37). Not only do these magazines endorse the content of the contemporary science fiction film as "real" and therefore "good," but the writers also reflect the very form of the films themselves by shunning standard English for street-wise colloquialism. For example, in a review of Ridley Scott's *Alien*, Jeffrey Frentzen, *Cinefantastique* (8:4 [1979], p. 24), describes Scott's skill at creating and maintaining suspense by saying that "he [Scott] has you by the balls at frame one, and won't let go." Even the popular writer Stephen King, in *Danse Macabre*, is caught up in this locker-room style. Modern science fiction, unfortunately, has apparently become the literature of adolescent delinquency.

7. Antonio Moreno, *Jung, Gods, and Modern Man*, p. 82.

8. Northrop Frye, "Forming Fours," in *Northrop Frye on Culture and Literature: A Collection of Review Essays*, p. 128.

9. Frederic I. Carpenter, *American Literature and the Dream*, p. 128.

10. See Alvin Toffler, *The Third Wave*, and James Oliver Robertson, *American Myth, American Reality*, for assessments of American myth and culture.

11. R. W. B. Lewis, *The American Adam*, p. 5.

12. D. H. Lawrence, *Studies in Classic American Literature*, p. 5.

13. In a much darker and more sombre dress, this Adam appears in the characters of such diverse writers as Poe, Dreiser, Melville, Twain, Crane, and Hemingway. He is not an adventurer seeking a newer and better world, but rather the Adam after the Fall, a caricatured manifestation of the darker side of paradise whose knowledge of good and evil brings with it the reality of despair and futility. This Adam is a character like Huck Finn who finds solace on the river but who also realizes that he cannot sail the river forever; he must always return to shore.

14. *Fiend without a Face* has an interesting international background. The film was co-produced by Amalgamated Productions Inc. and Producers Associates. Amalgamated was an American company formed by film executive Richard Gordon in the 1950s for the purpose of co-producing a series of films in England with established British production companies. It made seven films, all of them with one or more American stars whom Amalgamated brought to London. Gordon, himself British and the brother of Alex Gordon, who was one of the founders of American International Pictures, then formed Producers Associates as a British company for the purpose of producing his own films. One of the five films made by Producers Associates was *Fiend without a Face*.

Specifically, *Fiend without a Face* was produced as a British film by Producers Associates in partnership with Amalgamated Productions. Amalgamated was used as the conduit to supply the services of American actor Marshall Thompson and the rights to the original story and screenplay, all U.S. dollar expenditures. The entire film was shot in England, even though the film's setting is Canada. The magnificent special effects were created in Munich, Germany, by two stop-motion experts with whom Gordon was acquainted.

In addition to *Fiend without a Face,* Amalgamated and Producers Associates produced a second alien invasion film, *First Man into Space,* directed by Robert Day and again starring Marshall Thompson. Of the remaining three films produced by Producers Associates, two were horror films, *The Haunted Strangler* (released on a double bill with *Fiend without a Face*) and *Corridors of Blood* (produced in 1959 but not released in the United States until 1962), both starring Boris Karloff and directed by Robert Day, and the third film was a spy thriller, *The Secret Man,* starring Thompson, John Loder, and Anne Aubrey and directed by Ronald Kinnoch, who would later produce an alien invasion film, *Village of the Damned.* All these films were financed by Gordon's companies, but after he sold the distribution rights of *Fiend without a Face* to Metro-Goldwyn-Mayer, MGM fully financed *First Man into Space.*

The original story for *Fiend without a Face* was written in the 1930s by Amelia Reynolds Long. Called "The Thought Monster," it was published in the pulp magazine *Weird Tales.* Gordon purchased the rights from Long's agent, Forrest J. Ackerman, the world's leading exponent of fantasy film fandom and curator of the "Ackerman Archives," a massive collection of horror, science fiction, and fantasy memorabilia.

Gordon relates a wonderful anecdote about his experience in dealing with MGM, a big studio accustomed to big budgets. He told me that when he made the deal with MGM to release *Fiend without a Face,* MGM's legal department examined all the underlying documents and discovered that Gordon bought the story from Long for $500. MGM, not used to such "paltry sums," refused to release the film until Gordon got written confirmation from Long that she did in fact relinquish all rights to Gordon for a total amount of $500.

15. The use of the Freudian term *id* is taken directly from the film. Doctor Ostrow, after experimenting with the Krel mind amplification machine, warns Commander Adams to beware of the monsters from the id.

16. Twain's "The Mysterious Stranger" is indicative of this dark, existential strain of American literature. At the close of the story, the stranger tells the narrator that

> there is no God, no universe, no human race, no earthly life, no heaven, no hell. It is all a dream—a grotesque and foolish dream. Nothing exists but you. And you are but a *thought*—a vagrant thought, a useless thought, a homeless thought, wandering forlorn among the empty eternities.

The narrator then affirms the stranger's assessment of the world: "He vanished and left me appalled; for I knew, and realized that all he had said was true." Compare that with Scott Carey's closing sentiments in Jack Arnold's *The Incredible Shrinking Man:*

> I looked up, as if somehow I would grasp the heavens. The universe, worlds without number, God's silver tapestry spread across the night. And in that moment I knew the answer to the riddle of the infinite: I had thought in terms of Man's own limited dimension. I had presumed upon nature; that existence begins and ends is Man's conception, not nature's. And I felt my body dwindling, melting, becoming nothing. My fears melted away and in their place came acceptance. All this vast majesty of creation, it had to mean something. And then I meant something, too. To God there is no zero. I still exist.

The true nature of science fiction is, indeed, the sense of wonder and hope.

17. An idea first suggested by M. A. Goldberg, "Moral and Myth in Mrs. Shelley's *Frankenstein.*"

18. Jolande Jacobi, *The Psychology of C. G. Jung*, pp. 108 and 109.

19. The fiends are stop-motion models of human brains with attached spinal cords that propel them along. The fiends, moreover, emit a unique sound effect: a combination of heartbeat, slurping, sucking, and pounding. Actually, it is indescribable and must be heard to appreciate its uniqueness.

20. C. G. Jung, *Alchemical Studies*, p. 194.

21. Jacobi, p. 109.

22. Moreno, p. 43.

23. C. G. Jung, *The Archetypes and the Collective Unconscious*, p. 166.

24. J. E. Cirlot, *A Dictionary of Symbols*, p. 330.

25. Cirlot, p. 330.

26. For a valuable assessment of archetypal landscape, see Alex Aronson, *Psyche and Symbol in Shakespeare*, pp. 212–228.

27. Jacobi, p. 30.

28. Moreno, p. 53.

29. Moreno, p. 58.

30. Jacobi, p. 126.

31. Jacobi, p. 126.

32. The attitude was wrong for Constable Gibbons. He was too one-sided, too determined to prove that Cummings and the Air Force were responsible for the killings. As such, Gibbons was overwhelmed in this instance by the shadow archetype, breaking out of the collective unconscious (the forest) with a vengeance.

33. Harding, p. 214.

34. Jacobi, p. 127.

35. Jung, *The Spirit in Man, Art, and Literature*, p. 90. For a discussion of amplification and visionary film, see Don Fredericksen, "Jung/Sign/Symbol/Film, Part One" and "Jung/Sign/Symbol/Film, Part Two."

36. Jung, *The Spirit in Man, Art, and Literature*, p. 89.

37. In the wake of the *Star Wars* success, magazines oriented to science fiction films have flooded newsstands, and books dealing exclusively with science fiction films are sharing library space with books dealing with horror films. Unfortunately, most of these periodicals and books merely list films, either by chronology or by arbitrary labels ("space flight," "future," "monsters," etc.), and reveal more about the authors' capricious likes and dislikes than about the films themselves. Of the many books available, two deal specifically with science fiction of the fifties: Dennis Saleh's *Science Fiction Gold: Film Classics of the Fifties* and Bill Warren's *Keep Watching the Skies: American Science Fiction Movies of the Fifties*. Saleh limits himself to fourteen films he considers important contributions to the genre; his descriptions and commentaries shed some insight into the films and their times. Warren's book is an expensive two-volume exercise in completeness; it has a wealth of factual production histories and illustrations and little else. As for periodicals, most of them, including Frederick S. Clarke's slick and expensive *Cinefantastique* and Kerry O'Quinn's *Starlog* and *Fangoria* (the latter being an exploitative, atrocious magazine full of color scenes of gore from the "splatter" movies) are merely auxiliary pressbooks for film producers.

38. Jung, *The Spirit in Man, Art, and Literature*, pp. 88 and 91.

39. Jung, *The Spirit in Man, Art, and Literature*, pp. 87 and 88.

40. Edward F. Edinger, *Melville's Moby Dick: A Jungian Commentary*, p. 149.

41. Quoted in Forrest J. Ackerman's review of the film in *Famous Monsters of Filmland*, No. 37 (February 1966), p. 32.

42. Quoted in Joseph D. Olander and Martin Harry Greenberg, Introduction, *Ray Bradbury*, p. 9.

43. Children appear in key scenes in *Attack of the Puppet People, The Blob, The Crawling Eye, The Spider, The Fly, The 4-D Man, It Came from Outer Space, The Monster That Challenged the World, The Return of the Fly, Robot Monster, Them!, The Thirty Foot Bride of Candy Rock, The Twonky*, and *X–The Unknown*.

44. Dennis Saleh, *Science Fiction Gold: Film Classics of the Fifties*, p. 77.

45. Jung, *The Archetypes and the Collective Unconscious*, p. 162.

46. Jung, *The Archetypes and the Collective Unconscious*, p. 166.

47. Jacobi, p. 80.

48. Jung, *The Archetypes and the Collective Unconscious*, p. 32.

49. C. G. Jung, *Aion: Researches into the Phenomenology of the Self*, p. 266.

50. Jung, *Aion*, p. 8.

51. Jacobi, p. 112.

52. C. G. Jung, *Psychology and Alchemy*, p. 32.

53. Adding substance to the chill of the sand pit is the accompanying sound, "an acapella chant of a dissonant, eerie four-note melody by a choir of sixteen voices" (Saleh, p. 79).

54. Vivian Carol Sobchack, *The Limits of Infinity: The American Science Fiction Film*, p. 87.

55. C. G. Jung, *Psychological Types*, p. 468.

56. Jacobi, p. 119.

57. The chase inside the Martian tunnel is very similar to Menzies's design and direction of the cave sequence in David O. Selznick's 1939 production of *The Adventures of Tom Sawyer*. With Tom and Becky trapped inside the cave and at the mercy of the murderous Injun Joe, Tom—like David—is forced into manhood by saving himself and Becky from the evil killer. Tom emerges from the cave a changed person. Also, the design of the fence and pit area is similar to Menzies's design for the opening sequence of Sam Wood's *Our Town* (1940).

58. Saleh writes in *Science Fiction Gold:*

> Here begins two different versions of the film's conclusion. In the original film David thrashes in bed as the explosion occurs, ending the montage of scenes. It was all a dream and he goes back to sleep, until he wakes to see the saucer again, and the film ends. Six months after its U. S. release, the ending was changed and more footage shot for European distribution. The saucer explodes taking off and Kelston and Pat put David to bed, sans dream. The reasoning was a dream ending would not play well with European audiences. For even more realism, several additional minutes of talk at the observatory were shot, expanding the scientific discussion about Mars and including a display of kinds of flying saucers. The definitive version of the film, edited in 1976 by a film distributor making new prints, combines the additional observatory footage with the restored dream ending. (p. 85)

The nontheatrical print I used for my analysis differs from the television print. The television version contains footage of the escape montage that is missing from the nontheatrical print; moreover, neither the print I used nor the television print I viewed fits the description Saleh attributed to the "definitive version." Finally, it would be interesting, indeed, to speculate on the meaning of the scene in which Kelston and Pat and not the parents put David to bed, as the European version is said to have, but film prints being as they are, often spliced and edited for the most inane reasons, film scholars are left with whatever print they can obtain and a lot of wondering.

59. By *individuation*, I mean the conscious realization and fulfillment of one's own unique being. Edinger, in *Melville's Moby Dick*, explains that the process is "associated with typical archetypal imagery and leads to the experiencing of the Self as the center of personality transcending the ego . . . producing the awareness that the ego is subordinate to a more comprehensive psychic entity" (p. 148). As suggested, individuation is a complex and difficult task; indeed, Jung said that only Jesus and Buddha ever achieved an individuated personality. The concept is not to be discussed lightly, for it is most profound and perhaps the greatest thing that can ever happen to an individual. Hence, I want to state that I am not using this process in a carefree or frivolous manner when applying it to the alien invasion film; what we discover in the films is inherently there.

Bibliography

Amis, Kingsley. *New Maps of Hell*. New York: Ballantine Books, 1960.

Aronson, Alex. *Psyche and Symbol in Shakespeare*. Bloomington: Indiana University Press, 1972.

Baxter, John. *Science Fiction in the Cinema*. New York: The Paperback Library, 1970.

Beebe, Maurice. "The Universe of Roderick Usher." In *Poe: A Collection of Critical Essays*. Ed. Robert Reagan. Englewood Cliffs: Prentice-Hall, Inc., 1967.

Carpenter, Frederic I. *American Literature and the Dream*. New York: Philosophical Library, 1955.

Cirlot, J. E. *A Dictionary of Symbols*. Trans. Jack Sage. New York: Philosophical Library, 1962.

Clarens, Carlos. *An Illustrated History of the Horror Film*. New York: G. P. Putnam's Sons, 1967.

Coville, Gary W. "Notes Toward a Theory of Detective Fiction." Unpublished essay.

Dowdy, Andrew. *The Films of the Fifties: The American State of Mind*. New York: William Morrow and Company, Inc., 1975.

Edinger, Edward F. *Melville's Moby Dick: A Jungian Commentary*. New York: New Directions, 1978.

Eliade, Mircea. *Myth and Reality*. Trans. Willard R. Trask. New York: Harper and Row Publishers, 1963.

Everson, William K. *Classics of the Horror Film*. Secaucus: The Citadel Press, 1974.

Florescu, Radu. *In Search of Frankenstein*. Boston: New York Graphic Society, 1975.

Forster, E. M. *Aspects of the Novel*. London: Edward Arnold Ltd., 1958.

Frank, Alan. *Horror Movies*. London: Octopus Books Ltd., 1974.

————. *Horror Films*. London: Octopus Books Ltd., 1977.

————. "Screen Trips." In *The Encyclopedia of Science Fiction*. Ed. Robert Holstock. London: Octopus Books Ltd., 1978.

Franz, M.-L. von. "The Process of Individuation." In *Man and His Symbols*. Ed. C. G. Jung. New York: Doubleday and Company, Inc., 1964.

Fredericksen, Don. "Jung/Sign/Symbol/Film, Part One." *Quarterly Review of Film Studies* 4, No. 2 (Spring 1979), pp. 167–192.

————. "Jung/Sign/Symbol/Film, Part Two." *Quarterly Review of Film Studies* 5, No. 4 (Fall 1980), pp. 459–479.

————. "Two Aspects of a Jungian Perspective Upon Film: Jung and Freud; The Psychology of Types." *Journal of the University Film Association* XXXII, Nos. 1 and 2 (1980), pp. 49–57.

Frye, Northrop. *The Secular Scripture: A Study of the Structure of Romance*. Cambridge: Harvard University Press, 1976.

————. "Forming Fours." In *Northrop Frye on Culture and Literature: A Collection of Review Essays*. Ed. Robert D. Denham. Chicago: University of Chicago Press, 1978.

Gifford, Denis. *A Pictorial History of the Horror Movies*. London: The Hamlyn Publishing Group Ltd., 1973.

Goldberg, M. A. "Moral and Myth in Mrs. Shelley's *Frankenstein*." *Keats-Shelley Journal* 8 (1959), pp. 27–38.

Greenberg, Harvey R. *The Movies on Your Mind*. New York: E. P. Dutton and Company, Inc., 1975.

Grossman, Gary. *Superman: Serial to Cereal*. New York: Popular Library, 1976.

Halliwell, Leslie. *The Filmgoer's Companion*. 4th ed. New York: Avon Books, 1974.

Hammond, Paul. *Marvellous Méliès*. London: The Gordon Fraser Gallery Ltd., 1974.

Harding, M. Esther. *The I and the Not I: A Study in the Development of Consciousness*. Princeton: Princeton University Press, 1965.

———. *Psychic Energy: Its Source and Its Transformation*. Princeton: Princeton University Press, 1973.

Henderson, Joseph L. "Ancient Myths and Modern Man." In *Man and His Symbols*. Ed. C. G. Jung. New York: Doubleday and Company, Inc., 1964.

Hofstadter, Richard. *Anti-Intellectualism in American Life*. New York: Alfred A. Knopf, 1963.

———. *The Paranoid Style of American Politics and Other Essays*. New York: Alfred A. Knopf, 1965.

Jacobi, Jolande. *The Psychology of C. G. Jung*. New Haven: Yale University Press, 1979.

Johnson, Robert A. *He: Understanding Masculine Psychology*. New York: Harper and Row Publishers, 1977.

Johnson, William. "Journey into Science Fiction." In *Focus on the Science Fiction Film*. Ed. William Johnson. Englewood Cliffs: Prentice-Hall, Inc., 1972.

Jung, C. G. *Aion: Researches into the Phenomenology of the Self*. Trans. R. F. C. Hull. 2d ed. Collected Works 9ii. Princeton: Princeton University Press, 1968.

———. *Alchemical Studies*. Trans. R. F. C. Hull. Collected Works 13. Princeton: Princeton University Press, 1967.

———. *The Archetypes and the Collective Unconscious*. Trans. R. F. C. Hull. 2d ed. Collected Works 9i. Princeton: Princeton University Press, 1969.

———. *Civilization in Transition*. Trans. R. F. C. Hull. 2d ed. Collected Works 10. Princeton: Princeton University Press, 1970.

———. *Psychological Types*. Trans. R. F. C. Hull. Collected Works 6. Princeton: Princeton University Press, 1971.

———. *Psychology and Alchemy*. Trans. R. F. C. Hull. 2d ed. Collected Works 12. Princeton: Princeton University Press, 1968.

———. *The Spirit in Man, Art, and Literature*. Trans. R. F. C. Hull. Collected Works 15. Princeton: Princeton University Press, 1971.

———, and C. Kerenyi. *Essays on a Science of Mythology*. Trans. R. F. C. Hull. Princeton: Princeton University Press, 1949.

Kaminsky, Stuart M. *American Film Genres: Approaches to a Critical Theory of Popular Film*. New York: Dell Publishing Company, Inc., 1974.

Lawrence, D. H. *Studies in Classic American Literature*. New York: The Viking Press, 1973.

Lewis, R. W. B. *The American Adam*. Chicago: University of Chicago Press, 1955.

MacAndrew, Elizabeth. *The Gothic Tradition in Fiction*. New York: Columbia University Press, 1979.

McArthur, Colin. *Underworld USA*. New York: The Viking Press, 1972.

McConnell, Frank D. "Song of Innocence: *The Creature from the Black Lagoon*." *Journal of Popular Film* 2 (1973), pp. 15–28.

Manchel, Frank. *Terrors of the Screen.* Englewood Cliffs: Prentice-Hall, Inc., 1970.

Mandell, Paul. "Of Beasts and Behemoths: The Fantastic Films of Eugene Lourié, Part 2: *The Giant Behemoth.*" *Fantastic Films* (March 1980), pp. 34–38, 55, 57, 60.

Matthews, Jack, ed. *Archetypal Themes in the Modern Story.* New York: St. Martin's Press, 1973.

May, Rollo. *Man's Search for Himself.* New York: W. W. Norton and Company, Inc., 1953.

Michael, Paul, ed. *The American Movies Reference Book: The Sound Era.* Englewood Cliffs: Prentice-Hall, Inc., 1969.

Moreno, Antonio. *Jung, Gods, and Modern Man.* Notre Dame: University of Notre Dame Press, 1970.

Murphy, Brian. "Monster Movies: They Came from Beneath The Fifties." *The Journal of Popular Film* 1 (Winter 1972), pp. 31–44.

Neumann, Erich. *The Origins and History of Consciousness.* Trans. R. F. C. Hull. Princeton: Princeton University Press, 1973.

Olander, Joseph D., and Martin Harry Greenberg. Introduction. *Ray Bradbury.* Ed. Olander and Greenberg. New York: Taplinger Publishing Company, 1980.

Pirie, David. *A Heritage of Horror: The English Gothic Cinema 1946–1972.* New York: Avon Books, 1974.

Prawer, S. S. *Caligari's Children: The Film as Tale of Terror.* New York: Oxford University Press, 1980.

Robertson, James Oliver. *American Myth, American Reality.* New York: Hill and Wang, 1980.

Rovin, Jeff. *A Pictorial History of Science Fiction Films.* Secaucus: The Citadel Press, 1975.

Sagan, Carl. *The Dragons of Eden: Speculations on the Evolution of Human Intelligence.* New York: Random House, 1977.

Saleh, Dennis. *Science Fiction Gold: Film Classics of the Fifties.* New York: Comma Books, 1979.

Samuels, Stuart. "The Age of Conspiracy and Conformity: *Invasion of the Body Snatchers.*" In *American History/American Film: Interpreting the Hollywood Image.* Ed. John E. O'Connor and Martin A. Jackson. Frederick Ungar Publishing Company, 1979.

Scholes, Robert, and Eric S. Rabkin. *Science Fiction: History-Science-Vision.* New York: Oxford University Press, 1977.

Silver, Alain, and James Ursini. *The Vampire Film.* New York: A. S. Barnes and Company, Inc., 1975.

Sobchack, Vivian Carol. "The Alien Landscapes of the Planet Earth: Science Fiction in the Fifties." In *Science Fiction Films.* Ed. Thomas R. Atkins. New York: Monarch Press, 1976, pp. 49–61.

———. *The Limits of Infinity: The American Science Fiction Film.* New York: A. S. Barnes and Company, 1980.

Solomon, Stanley. *Beyond Formula: American Film Genres.* New York: Harcourt Brace and Jovanovich, Inc., 1976.

Sontag, Susan. "The Imagination of Disaster." In *Hal in the Classroom: Science Fiction Films.* Ed. Ralph J. Amelio. Dayton: Pflaum Publishing, 1974, pp. 22–38.

Strick, Philip. *Science Fiction Movies.* London: Octopus Books Ltd., 1976.

Tarratt, Margaret. "Monsters from the Id." *Films and Filming* 17, No. 3 (December 1970), pp. 34–42, and 17, No. 4 (January 1971), pp. 40–42.

Time. Review of *It Came from Outer Space.* July 16, 1953, p. 86.

Toffler, Alvin. *The Third Wave.* New York: William Morrow and Company, Inc., 1980.

Tropp, Martin. *Mary Shelley's Monster: The Story of Frankenstein.* Boston: Houghton Mifflin Company, 1971.

Warren, Bill. *Keep Watching the Skies: American Science Fiction Movies of the Fifties.* Vol. I. Jefferson, N.C.: McFarland and Company, Inc., 1982.

White, D. L. "The Poetics of Horror: More Than Meets the Eye." *Cinema Journal* 10, No. 2 (1971), pp. 1–18.

Wood, Robin. "The Return of the Repressed." *Film Comment* (July-August 1978), pp. 25–32.

Wright, Will. *Sixguns and Society: A Structural Study of the Western.* Berkeley: University of California Press, 1975.

Filmography

Several works on the history of the science fiction film found in the bibliography include filmographies that list many of the films I have listed here. I have used this published data as the basis for this filmography of the alien invasion film; however, I have attempted to correct and add to much of the data as well as offer annotations when appropriate in an effort to be as complete in the space allotted and as accurate as possible. This subsequent information has been compiled from various sources, including the opening credits of each film, pressbooks, newspaper and magazine advertisements and reviews, and production and release data found in various trade publications.

Because of space limitations, this filmography lists only the principal production credits and leading players for films released in the United States between roughly 1949 and 1961.

One final comment. Several features and shorts have been included here even though I was unable to view them. They are clearly marked as such; I have included them because catalog descriptions and trade announcements indicate an alien invasion theme.

Abbott and Costello Meet Dr. Jekyll and Mr. Hyde

Production Universal, *Director* Charles Lamont, *Producer* Howard Christie, *Screenplay* Lee Loeb and John Grant, *Story* Sidney Fields and Grant Garrett, *Photography* George Robinson, *Special Photography* David S. Horsley, *Music Supervision* Joseph Gershenson, *Art Direction* Bernard Herzbrun and Eric Orbom, *Editor* Russell Schoengarth, *Distribution* Universal-International.

Cast: Bud Abbott (Slim), Lou Costello (Tubby), Boris Karloff (Dr. Henry Jekyll), Craig Stevens (Bruce Adams), Helen Westcott (Vicky Edwards), Reginald Denny (The Inspector), John Dierkes (Batley), Eddie Parker (Mr. Hyde).

Black and White; 76 minutes; released August 1953.

Abbott and Costello Meet the Invisible Man

Production Universal, *Director* Charles Lamont, *Producer* Howard Christie, *Screenplay* Robert Lees, Frederic I. Rinaldo, and John Grant, *Story* Hugh Wedlock, Jr., and Howard Snyder, *Photography* George Robinson, *Special Photography* David S. Horsley, *Music Supervision* Joseph Gershenson, *Art Direction* Bernard Herzbrun and Richard H. Riedel, *Editor* Virgil Vogel, *Distribution* Universal-International.

CAST: Bud Abbott (Bud Alexander), Lou Costello (Lou Francis), Arthur Franz (Tommy Nelson [The Invisible Man]), Sheldon Leonard (Morgan), Nancy Guild (Helen Gray), William Frawley (Detective Roberts), Adele Jergens (Boots Malone), Gavin Muir (Dr. Philip Gray), George J. Lewis (Torpedo), Sid Saylor (Waiter), Bobby Barber (Sneaky), Sam Balter (Radio Announcer).

Black and White; 82 minutes; released March 1951.

The Alligator People

Production Associated Producers, *Director* Roy Del Ruth, *Producer* Jack Leewood, *Screenplay* Orville H. Hampton, *Story* Orville H. Hampton and Charles O'Neal, *Photography* Karl Struss, *Music* Irving Gertz, *Art Direction* Lyle R. Wheeler and John Mansbridge, *Editor* Harry Gerstad, *Distribution* Twentieth Century-Fox.

CAST: Bruce Bennett (Dr. Eric Lorimer), Beverly Garland (Joyce Webster), George Macready (Dr. Mark Sinclair), Lon Chaney (Mannon), Richard Crane (Paul Webster), Frieda Inescort (Mrs. Hawthorne), Douglas Kennedy (Dr. Wayne McGregor).

Black and White in CinemaScope; 74 minutes; released August 1959 on double bill with *The Return of the Fly*.

Associated Producers was one of the many corporate names for the production/distribution wing of theatre chain magnate Robert L. Lippert. He began his production and distribution activity in the mid-forties, calling his company first Action Pictures and later Screen Guild Productions. In 1949 he formed Lippert Pictures and was involved in many coproductions with England's Hammer Films. In the mid-fifties he formed Regal Films, which shot its features in Regalscope, another name for 20th-Fox's CinemaScope, and supplied Fox with second features and exploitation double bills, like *Kronos* and *She Devil*. Associated Producers eventually gave way in the sixties to Lippert Films Ltd., again coproducing with a British firm headed by Jack Parsons. Traditionally, Lippert's output has been genre pieces, mainly horror/science fiction and melodrama.

The Amazing Colossal Man

Production Malibu Productions, *Producer-Director* Bert I. Gordon, *Screenplay* Mark Hanna and Bert I. Gordon, *Story* Bert I. Gordon, *Photography* Joseph Biroc, *Special Photography* Bert I. Gordon and Flora M. Gordon, *Music* Albert Glasser, *Art Direction* No credits other than Set Decorations by Glen Daniels, *Editor* Ronald Sinclair, *Distribution* James H. Nicholson and Samuel Z. Arkoff through American International Pictures.

CAST: Glenn Langan (Lt. Col. Glenn Manning), Cathy Downs (Carol Forrest), William [later John] Hudson (Dr. Paul Lindstrom), James Seay (Col. Hallock), Larry Thor (Dr. Eric Coulter), Russ Bender (Richard Kingman), Lynn Osborne (Sgt. Taylor), Hank Patterson (Henry), Edmund Cobb (Dr. McDermott), Frank Jenks (Delivery Man).

Black and White; 81 minutes; released September 1957 on double bill with *The Cat Girl*.

Bert I. Gordon, or "BIG," made several "giant monster" films in the late fifties for American International Pictures. *The Amazing Colossal Man* is his best; Gordon actually elicits pathos out of the character played by Langan, a task all the more impressive since most alien invasion films shun characterization for action. As evidenced by the credits, Gordon not only produces and directs his own stories, but creates the special effects as well. Many fan magazines, caught up in the "best of the worst movies" fad, berate Gordon's films, especially his "shoddy" special effects. Gordon's films at best are interesting, and his special effects are passable; he hardly deserves the scorn leveled by many of the fan publications.

The Amazing Transparent Man
Production Miller Consolidated Pictures (MCP), *Director* Edgar G. Ulmer, *Producer* Lester D. Guthrie, *Story and Screenplay* Jack Lewis, *Photography* Meredith M. Nicholson, *Special Photography* Roger Lewis, *Music* Darrell Calker, *Art Direction* Ernst Fegté, *Editor* Jack Ruggiero, *Distribution* American International Pictures.
CAST: Douglas Kennedy*(Joey Faust), Marguerite Chapman (Laura), James Griffith (Krenner), Ivan Triesault (Dr. Ulof), Red Morgan (Julian), Carmen Daniel (Maria), Edward Erwin (Drake), Jonathan Ledford (Smith), Norman Smith (First Security Guard), Patrick Crenshaw (Second Security Guard).
Black and White; 56 minutes; released July 1960 on double bill with *Beyond the Time Barrier*.
    Reportedly, Ulmer directed this film and *Beyond the Time Barrier* at the same time at the Texas state fairgrounds. *Beyond the Time Barrier* was shot during the morning and *The Amazing Transparent Man* in the afternoon.

The Astounding She Monster
Production Hollywood International Pictures, *Producer-Director* Ronnie Ashcroft, *Story and Screenplay* Frank Hall, *Photography* William C. Thompson, *Music* Gunther Kauer, *Distribution* American International Pictures. No other credits available.
CAST: Robert Clarke (Dick Cutler), Kenne Duncan (Nat Burdell), Marilyn Harvey (Margaret Chaffee), Jeanne Tatum (Esther Malone), Ewing Brown (Brad Conley), Shirley Kilpatrick (The She Monster).
Black and White; 60 minutes; released February 1958 on double bill with *Viking Women and the Sea Serpent*.

The Atomic Kid
Production Mickey Rooney, *Director* Leslie H. Martinson, *Producer* Mickey Rooney, *Screenplay* Benedict Freedman and John Fenton Murray, *Story* Blake Edwards, *Photography* John L. Russell, *Music* Van Alexander, *Art Direction* Frank Hotaling, *Editor* Fred Allen, *Distribution* Republic Pictures.
CAST: Mickey Rooney (Blix Waterbury), Robert Strauss (Stan Cooper), Elaine Davis [credit title includes "Mrs. Mickey Rooney"] (Audrey Nelson), Bill Goodwin (Dr. Rodell), Whit Bissell (Dr. Edgar Pangborn), Hal March (FBI Agent "Ray"), Peter Leeds (FBI Agent "Bill"), Peter Brocco (Mr. Mosley).
Black and White; 86 minutes; released December 1954.

The Atomic Man (British: *Timeslip*)
Production Todon Productions/Merton Park Studios, *Director* Ken Hughes, *Producer* Alec C. Snowden, *Story and Screenplay* Charles Eric Maine [from his novel, *The Isotope Man*], *Photography* A. T. Dinsdale, *Musical Director* Richard Taylor, *Art Direction* George Haslam, *Editor* Geoffrey Muller, *Distribution* Allied Artists Pictures Corporation.
CAST: Gene Nelson (Mike Delaney), Faith Domergue (Jill Friday), Joseph Tomelty (Inspector Cleary), Peter Arne (Stephen Rayner), Vic Perry (Vasquo), Donald Gray (Maitland), Charles Hawtry (Scruffy), Lance Maraschal (Editor).
Black and White; 77 minutes (British version: 93 minutes); released in USA March 1956 on double bill with *Invasion of the Body Snatchers*.

The Atomic Monster (Reissue title of *Man-Made Monster* [1941])
Production Universal, *Director* George Waggner, *Producer* Jack Bernard, *Screenplay* Joseph West, *Story* ["The Electric Man"] H. J. Essex, Sid Schwartz, and Len Golos, *Photography* Elwood Bredell, *Special Photography* John P. Fulton, *Musical Director* Charles Previn, *Art Direction* Jack Otterson, *Editor* Arthur Hilton, *Distribution* Realart Pictures.

Cast: Lionel Atwill (Dr. Regas), Lon Chaney (Dan McCormick), Anne Nagel
(June Lawrence), Frank Albertson (Mark Adams), Samuel S. Hinds (Dr.
Lawrence).

Black and White; 60 minutes; re-released 1953.

The Atomic Monster, or *Man-Made Monster*, is just one of the many
Universal features reissued in the late forties and early fifties by Realart
Pictures. Of particular note here is the title change from the original *Man-
Made Monster* to *Atomic Monster* to capitalize on the atomic era. James H.
Nicholson, Realart's sales manager, later with Samuel Z. Arkoff founded
American International Pictures.

The Atomic Submarine

Production Gorham Productions, *Director* Spencer G. Bennet, *Producer* Alex
Gordon, *Screenplay* Orville H. Hampton, *Story* Jack Rabin and Irving Block,
Photography Gilbert Warrenton, *Special Photography* Jack Rabin, Irving
Block, and Louis DeWitt, *Music* Alexander Laszlo, *Art Direction* Daniel Haller
and Don Ament, *Editor* William Austin, *Distribution* Allied Artists Pictures
Corporation.

Cast: Arthur Franz ("Reef" Halloway), Dick Foran (Captain Dan Wendover),
Brett Halsey (Carl Nelson), Tom Conway (Sir Ian Hunt), Paul Dubov (Lt.
David Milton), Bob Steele (Griff), Victor Varconi (Dr. Clifford Kent), Selmer
Jackson (Admiral Terhune), Sid Melton (Chester), Joi Lansing (Julie).

Black and White; 72 minutes; released December 1959.

One of several science fiction films produced in association with special
effects experts Jack Rabin, Irving Block, and Louis DeWitt. Rabin headed
Studio Film Service, a small company that created special effects for independent producers on "restraint budgets." In this instance, it is reported by
many sources that the one-eyed alien monster is actually Irving Block's fist
and arm decorated as a monstrous cyclops. Other Rabin-Block-DeWitt coproductions include *Kronos* and *War of the Satellites*. Alex Gordon was associated
with Nicholson and Arkoff during the infant stages of American International
Pictures. Gordon's Golden State Productions was responsible for several
financial hits for AIP: *The Day the World Ended, Apache Woman, The She
Creature, Voodoo Woman,* and *Runaway Daughters*. Gordon's brother,
Richard, headed Producers Associates, the organization responsible for *Fiend
without a Face*.

Attack of the Crab Monsters

Production Los Altos Productions, *Producer-Director* Roger Corman, *Story and
Screenplay* Charles B. Griffith, *Photography* Floyd Crosby, *Music* Ronald Stein,
Art Direction No credits, *Editor* Charles Gross, Jr., *Distribution* Allied Artists
Pictures Corporation.

Cast: Richard Garland (Dale Brewer), Pamela Duncan (Martha Hunter),
Richard Johnson (Hank Chapman), Leslie Bradley (Dr. Karl Weingard), Mel
Welles (Jules Devereaux), Richard Cutting (Dr. James Carson), Beach Dick-
erson (Ron Fellows), Ed Nelson (Ensign Quinlan).

Black and White; 62 minutes; released March 1957 on double bill with *Not of
This Earth*.

Attack of the Fifty Foot Woman

Production Woolner Brothers, *Director* Nathan Hertz, *Producer* Bernard Wool-
ner, *Story and Screenplay* Mark Hanna, *Photography* Jacques Marquette, *Music*
Ronald Stein, *Art Direction* No credits, *Editor* Edward Mann, *Distribution*
Allied Artists Pictures Corporation.

Cast: Allison Hayes (Nancy Archer), William [later John] Hudson (Harry
Archer), Roy Gordon (Dr. Cushing), Yvette Vickers (Honey Parker), Ken
Terrell (Jessup Stout), George Douglas (Sheriff Dubbitt), Otto Waldis (Dr.

von Loeb), Frank Chase (Charlie), Eileen Stevens (Nurse), Dale Tate (Commentator), Tom Jackson (Prospector), Mike Ross (Tony).
Black and White; 66 minutes; released May 1958 on double bill with *War of the Satellites*.

Attack of the Giant Leeches
Production Balboa Productions, *Director* Bernard Kowalski, *Producer* Gene Corman, *Story and Screenplay* Leo Gordon, *Photography* John M. Nicholas, Jr., *Special Photography* No credits, *Music* Alexander Laszlo, *Distribution* American International Pictures.
CAST: Ken Clark (Steve Benton), Yvette Vickers (Liz Walker), Jan Shepard (Nan Greyson), Michael Emmet (Cal Moulton), Tyler McVey (Doc Greyson), Bruno VeSoto (Dave Walker), Gene Roth (Sheriff Kovis), Dan White (Slim Reed), George Cisar (Lem Sawyer).
Black and White; 62 minutes; released October 1959 on double bill with *A Bucket of Blood*; the film is advertised as *The Giant Leeches*.

Gene Corman is Roger's brother, and screenwriter Gordon is also an actor, usually in "meaner than the devil" villainous roles in westerns and crime films.

Attack of the Puppet People
Production Alta Vista Productions, *Producer-Director* Bert I. Gordon, *Screenplay* George Worthing Yates, *Story* Bert I. Gordon, *Photography* Ernest Laszlo, *Special Photography* Bert I. Gordon and Flora M. Gordon, *Music* Albert Glasser, *Art Direction* No credits, *Editor* Ronald Sinclair, *Distribution* James H. Nicholson and Samuel Z. Arkoff through American International Pictures.
CAST: John Agar (Bob Westley), John Hoyt (Mr. Franz), June Kenney (Sally Reynolds), Michael Mark (Emil), Jack Kosslyn (Sgt. Patterson), Marlene Willis (Laurie), Ken Miller (Stan), Laurie Mitchell (Georgia), Scott Peters (Mac), Susan Gordon (Agnes), June Jocelyn (Brownie Leader), Jean Moorehead (Janet), Hank Patterson (Doorman), Hal Bogart (Mailman), Troy Patterson (Elevator Operator), Bill Giorgia (Janitor), George Diestal (Switchboard Operator), Jamie Foster (Ernie), Mark Lowell (Salesman).
Black and White; 78 minutes; released August 1958 on double bill with *War of the Colossal Beast*.

The title is curious, since the puppet people are victims of scientific experimentation and not a threat. Many sources say the original title was *The Fantastic Puppet People*.

Screenwriter George Worthing Yates single-handedly, as it were, created the myth of the alien invasion film. A one-time newspaper reporter, Yates came to Hollywood in 1939, writing for various studios. In 1954, he found his niche writing the story for *Them!* From that point on, he was responsible for no fewer than nine science fiction films: *It Came from Beneath the Sea, Conquest of Space, Earth vs. the Flying Saucers, Frankenstein 1970, War of the Colossal Beast, The Spider, Attack of the Puppet People, The Flame Barrier*, and *Space Master X-7*. His name is frequently misspelled as George *Worthington* Yates.

Battle in Outer Space (Japanese: *Uchi dai Senso*)
Production Toho Company Ltd., *Director* Inoshira Honda, *Producer* Tomoyuki Tanaka, *Screenplay* Shinichi Sekizawa, *Story* Jotaro Okami, *Photography* Hajime Koizumi, *Special Photography* Eiji Tsuburaya, *Music* Akira Ifukube, *Art Direction* No credits, *Editor* No credits, *Distribution* Columbia Pictures.
CAST: Ryo Ikebe (Dr. Katsumiya), Kyoka Anzai (Etsuko), Koreya Senda (Professor Adachi), Yoshito Tsuchiya (Koichi Adachi), Hisaya Ito (Kogure), Kozo Nomura (Rocket Commander), Harold Conway (Dr. Immerman).

Filmed in Eastman Color and Tohoscope; 90 minutes; (Japanese version: 93 minutes); released June 1960.

Some sources claim this film is a sequel to *The Mysterians* (1959). It is one of many Japanese science fiction films that received popular acclaim in the late fifties and sixties. Prior to *Godzilla* (q.v.), the Japanese cinema was seen in America only in fashionable art houses and was represented principally by the works of Mizoguchi and Ozu. Following the enormous success of *Godzilla*, western audiences also discovered the popular culture side of the Japanese cinema.

Beast from Haunted Cave
Production Filmgroup, *Director* Monte Hellman, *Producer* Gene Corman, *Story and Screenplay* Charles B. Griffith, *Photography* Andy Costikyan, *Music* Alexander Lazslo, *Art Direction* No credits, *Editor* Anthony Carras, *Distribution* Filmgroup.
CAST: Michael Forest (Bill), Sheila Carol (Gypsy), Frank Wolff (Alex), Richard Sinatra (Marty), Wally Campo (Byron), Chris Robinson (The Beast).
Black and White; 65 minutes; released October 1959 on double bill with *The Wasp Woman*.

One of several extremely low-budget films produced by Roger and Gene Corman's Filmgroup organization. Three films in the series, this one, *Creature from the Haunted Sea*, and *The Last Woman on Earth* are interesting if only for their unique story motif: All involve small groups of eccentrics involved with an "eccentric" event, such as beasts and creatures suddenly running amok and the end of civilization.

The Beast from 20,000 Fathoms
Production Mutual Pictures of California, *Director* Eugene Lourié, *Producers* Jack Dietz and Hal E. Chester, *Screenplay* Lou Morheim and Fred Freiberger, *Story* Ray Bradbury, *Photography* Jack Russell, *Special Photography* Ray Harryhausen, *Music* David Buttolph, *Art Direction* Eugene Lourié, *Editor* Bernard W. Burton, *Distribution* Warner Brothers.
CAST: Paul Christian [later Paul Hubschmid] (Prof. Tom Nesbitt), Paula Raymond (Lee Hunter), Cecil Kellaway (Dr. Thurgood Elson), Kenneth Tobey (Col. Jack Evans), Donald Woods (Capt. Phil Jackson), Jack Pennick (Jacob Bowman), Ross Elliott (George Ritchie), King Donovan (Dr. Ingersoll), Frank Ferguson (Dr. Morton), Lee Van Cleef (Cpl. Stone), Steve Brodie (Loomis).
Black and White (sources say early released prints were tinted sepia); 80 minutes; released June 1953.

One of the first motion picture efforts to extensively use television as an advertising medium.

The Beast of Hollow Mountain (Mexican: *El Monstruo de la Montana Hueca*)
Production Nassour Brothers (USA)/Peliculas Rodriguez (Mexico), *Directors* Edward Nassour and Ismael Rodriguez, *Producers* Edward and William Nassour, *Screenplay* Robert Hill, Ismael Rodriguez, and Carlos Orellane, *Story* Willis H. O'Brien, *Photography* Jorge Stahl, Jr., *Special Photography* Henry Sharp, Jack Rabin and Louis DeWitt, *Music* Raul Lavista, *Art Direction* Jack DeWitt, *Editors* Holbrook Todd, Maury Wright, and Fernando Martinez, *Distribution* United Artists.
CAST: Guy Madison (Jimmy Ryan), Patricia Medina (Sarita), Carlos Rivas (Felipe Sanchez), Eduardo Noriega (Enrique Rios), Mario Navarro (Panchito), Pascual Garcia Pena (Pancho), Julio Villareal (Don Pedro), Lupe Carriles (Margarita).

Filmed in DeLuxe Color and CinemaScope; 81 minutes; released August 1956.

The Beast with a Million Eyes

Production San Mateo Productions, *Director* David Kramarsky, *Producer* Roger Corman, *Story and .Screenplay* Tom Filer, *Photography* Everett Baker, *Special Photography* Paul Blaisdell, *Music* John Bickford, *Art Direction* Albert Ruddy, *Editor* Jack Killifer, *Distribution* Palo Alto Productions through American Releasing Corporation.

CAST: Paul Birch (Alan Kelly), Lorna Thayer (Carol Kelly), Dona Cole (Sandy Kelly), Dick Sargent (Larry), Chester Conklin (Ben Webber), Leonard Tarver (Mute).

Black and White; 78 minutes; released January 1956 (some sources say October 1955, and still other sources say it was released on double bill with *Day the World Ended*).

American Releasing Corporation was the initial corporate title for American International Pictures.

The Beginning of the End

Production AB-PT Pictures, *Producer-Director* Bert I. Gordon, *Story and Screenplay* Fred Freiberger and Lester Gorn, *Photography* Jack Marta, *Special Photography* Bert I. Gordon and Flora M. Gordon, *Music* Albert Glasser, *Art Direction* Walter Keller, *Editor* Aaron Stell, *Distribution* Republic Pictures.

CAST: Peter Graves (Ed Wainwright), Peggy Castle (Audrey Ames), Morris Ankrum (Gen. Arthur Hanson), Thomas Browne Henry (Col. Pete Sturgeon), James Seay (Capt. Barton), Richard Benedict (Cpl. Jim Mathias), Than Wyenn (Frank Johnson), John Close (Maj. Everett), Pierre Watkin (Taggart), Frank Wilcox (Gen. Matthew Short).

Black and White (posters claim "HorrorScope"); 74 minutes; released June 1957 on double bill with *The Unearthly*.

AB-PT Pictures was the production wing of the American Broadcasting-Paramount Theatres chain. As far as can be discerned, *The Beginning of the End* and *The Unearthly* are the only two films produced by this short-lived organization. They were two of the last films to be released by Republic Pictures.

The Black Scorpion

Production Amex Productions, *Director* Edward Ludwig, *Producers* Jack Dietz and Frank Melford, *Screenplay* David Duncan and Robert Blees, *Story* Paul Yawitz, *Photography* Lionel Lindon, *Special Photography* Willis H. O'Brien and Pete Petersen, *Music* Paul Sawtell, *Art Direction* Edward Fitzgerald, *Editor* Richard Van Enger, *Distribution* Warner Brothers.

CAST: Richard Denning (Henry Scott), Mara Corday (Teresa), Carlos Rivas (Arturo Ramos), Mario Navarro (Juanito), Carlos Muzquiz (Dr. Velasco), Pascual Pena (Jose de la Cruz), Fanny Schiller (Florentina), Pedro Galvan (Father Delgado), Arturo Martinez (Major Cosio).

Black and White; 88 minutes; released October 1957.

The Black Sleep

Production Bel-Air, *Director* Reginald LeBorg, *Producer* Howard W. Koch, *Screenplay* John C. Higgins, *Story* Gerald Drayson Adams, *Photography* Gordon Avil, *Special Photography* Jack Rabin and Louis DeWitt, *Music* Les Baxter, *Art Direction* Bob Kinoshita, *Editor* John F. Schreyer, *Distribution* United Artists.

CAST: Basil Rathbone (Sir Joel Cadman), Akim Tamiroff (Odo), John Carradine (Borg/Dr. Behemond), Bela Lugosi (Casimir), Lon Chaney (Mungo/Dr. Munro), Herbert Rudley (Dr. Gordon Ramsey), Patricia Blake (Laurie), Sally Yarnell (Nancy), Tor Johnson (Curry), George Sawaya (K-6), Claire Carleton (Miss Daly).

Black and White; 81 minutes; released June 1956 on double bill with *The Creeping Unknown;* reissued in 1963 as *Dr. Cadman's Secret.*

The Blob
Production Tonylyn Productions, *Director* Irvin S. Yeaworth, Jr., *Producer* Jack H. Harris, *Screenplay* Theodore Simonson and Kate Phillips, *Story* Irvine H. Millgate, *Photography* Thomas Spalding, *Special Photography* Barton Sloane, *Music* Ralph Carmichael, *Art Direction* William Jersey and Karl Karlson, *Editor* Alfred Hillman, *Distribution* Paramount Pictures.

CAST: Steven [later Steve] McQueen (Steve Andrews), Aneta Corsaut (Judy Martin), Earl Rowe (Dave), Olin Howlin (Old Man), Steven Chase (Dr. Hallen), John Benson (Burt), Vince Barbi (George), Audrey Metcalf (Mrs. Martin), Keith Almoney (Danny Martin).

Color by DeLuxe; 85 minutes; released October 1958 on double bill with *I Married a Monster from Outer Space;* reissued in mid-sixties by Jack H. Harris.

Blood of the Vampire (British)
Production Tempean Films, *Director* Henry Cass, *Producers* Robert S. Baker and Monty Berman, *Story and Screenplay* Jimmy Sangster, *Photography* Monty Berman, *Music* Stanley Black, *Art Direction* John Elphick, *Editor* Douglas Myers, *Distribution* Universal-International.

CAST: Donald Wolfit (Dr. Callistratus), Barbara Shelley (Madeleine), Vincent Ball (Dr. John Pierre), Victor Maddern (Carl), William Devlin (Kurt Urich), Andrew Foulds (Wetzler).

Filmed in Eastman Color; 85 minutes; released in USA November 1958 on double bill with *Monster on the Campus.*

This strange little film seems to work both sides of the fence. The introductory scenes are pure horror film showing the staking of a vampire and the subsequent removal of the stake by a demented slave, bringing the vampire back to life. The remainder of the film is pure science fiction, following Dr. Callistratus ("the vampire") as he experiments on prison inmates in an attempt to find a cure for his undisclosed malady.

The Bowery Boys Meet the Monsters
Production Allied Artists, *Director* Edward Bernds, *Producer* Ben Schwalb, *Story and Screenplay* Elwood Ullman and Edward Bernds, *Photography* Harry Neumann, *Special Photography* Augie Lohman, *Music Director* Marlin Skiles, *Art Direction* David Milton, *Editors* Lester A. Sansom and William Austin, *Distribution* Allied Artists Pictures Corporation.

CAST: Leo Gorcey (Slip Mahoney), Huntz Hall (Sach), Lloyd Corrigan (Anton Gravesend), Ellen Corby (Amelia Gravesend), John Dehner (Derek Gravesend), Laura Mason (Francine Gravesend), Bernard Gorcey (Louis Dumbrowsky), Paul Wexler (Grissom), David Condon (Chuck), Bennie Bartlett (Butch).

Black and White; 66 minutes; released June 1954.

I have not seen this film, and it may be more of a horror film than an alien invasion film. I have included it here because of ambiguous plot descriptions found in various books on science fiction film.

The Brain Eaters
Production Corinthian Films, *Director* Bruno VeSota, *Producer* Edwin Nelson, *Story and Screenplay* Gordon Urquhart, *Photography* Larry Raimond, *Special Photography* No credits, *Music* Tom Johnson, *Art Direction* Burt Shonberg, *Editor* Carlo Lodato, *Distribution* American International Pictures.

CAST: Edwin Nelson (Dr. Kettering), Alan Frost (Glenn), Jack Hill (Senator Powers), Joanna Lee (Alice), Jody Fair (Elaine), David Hughes (Dr. Wyler), Robert Ball (Dan Walker), Greight Phillips (Sheriff), Orville Sherman

(Cameron), Leonard Nemoy [sic] (Protector), Doug Banks (Doctor), Henry Randolph (Telegrapher).
Black and White; 60 minutes; released October 1958 on double bill with *The Spider*.

The Brain from Planet Arous
Production Marquette Productions, *Director* Nathan Hertz, *Producer* Jacques Marquette, *Story and Screenplay* Ray Buffum, *Photography* Jacques Marquette, *Special Photography* No credits, *Music* Walter Greene, *Art Direction* No credits, *Editor* Irving Schoenberg, *Distribution* Howco-International Pictures.
Cast: John Agar (Steve), Joyce Meadows (Sally Fallon), Thomas B. Henry
  (John Fallon), Henry Travis (Col. Frogley), Kenneth Terrell (Colonel in
  conference room), Tim Graham (Sheriff Paine), E. Leslie Thomas (Gen.
  Brown), Bill Giorgio (Russian).
Black and White; 71 minutes; released December 1958 on double bill with *Teenage Monster*.
  "Nathan Hertz" is reportedly a pseudonym for Nathan Juran, an art director turned director for such features as *Twenty Million Miles to Earth*, *The Deadly Mantis*, and the delightful fantasy, *The Seventh Voyage of Sinbad*. Presumably, the name "Hertz" is applied to films of dubious merit.

Caltiki, the Immortal Monster (Italian: *Caltiki, Il Mostro Immortale*)
Production Galatea (Italy)/Climax Pictures (USA), *Director* Robert Hampton, *Producer* Bruno Vailati, *Story and Screenplay* [Credits say "Based on an ancient Mexican Legend"] Philip Just, *Photography* John Foam, *Special Photography* Mario Bava, *Music* Roman Vlad, *Art Direction* No credits, *Editor* Salvatore Billitteri, *English Version* Lee Kresel, *Distribution* Samuel Schneider through Allied Artists Pictures Corporation.
Cast: John Merivale (Prof. John Fielding), Didi Sullivan (Ellen), Daniela
  Rocca (Linda), Gerard Herter (Max), Daniel Pitani (Bob), Gay Pearl
  (Dancer).
Black and White; 76 minutes; released September 1960.
  The film was shot in Italy and some of the names have been anglicized, e.g., Robert Hampton is Riccardo Freda.

The Cape Canaveral Monsters
Production CCM, *Writer-Director* Phil Tucker, *Producer* Richard Greer, *Photography* Merle Connell, *Special Photography* Modern Film Effects, *Music* Gunther Kauer, *Art Direction* Ken Letvin, *Editor* Richard Greer, *Distribution* Sterling World Distributors.
Cast: Scott Peters (Tom Wright), Linda Connell (Sally Markham), Jason
  Johnson (Hauron), Katherine Victor (Nadja), Chuck Howard (General
  Hollister).
Black and White; 69 minutes; released 1960?
  I was unable to find a release date for the film. Many filmographies list 1960, but many others list 1961 and 1962. The trade journal *Boxoffice*, in its 1960 yearbook, *Boxoffice Barometer*, lists the film as 1960 but notes that it was in production.

Circus of Horrors (British)
Production Lynx Films, *Director* Sidney Hayers, *Producers* Julian Wintle and Leslie Parkyn, *Story and Screenplay* George Baxt, *Photography* Douglas Slocombe, *Music* Franz Reizenstein, *Art Direction* Jack Shampan, *Editor* Reginald Mills, *Distribution* American International Pictures.
Cast: Anton Diffring (Rossiter/Schuler), Erika Remberg (Elissa), Yvonne
  Monlaur (Nicole), Donald Pleasence (Vanet), Jane Hylton (Angela), Kenneth
  Griffith (Martin), Conrad Phillips (Inspector Arthur Ames), Jack Gwillim
  (Superintendent Andrews), Vanda Hudson (Magda).
SpectaColor by Eastman; 91 minutes; released May 1960.

The Colossus of New York
Production William Alland Productions, *Director* Eugene Lourié, *Producer* William Alland, *Screenplay* Thelma Schnee, *Story* Willis Goldbeck, *Photography* John F. Warren, *Special Photography* John P. Fulton, *Music* Van Cleave, *Art Direction* Hal Pereira and John Goodman, *Editor* Floyd Knudtson, *Distribution* Paramount Pictures.

CAST: John Baragrey (Dr. Henry Spensser), Mala Powers (Anne Spensser), Otto Kruger (Dr. William Spensser), Robert Hutton (Prof. John Carrington), Ross Martin (Dr. Jeremy Spensser), Charles Herbert (Billy Spensser), Ed Wolff (The Colossus).

Black and White; 70 minutes; released June 1958 on double bill with *The Space Children.*

Commando Cody, Sky Marshal of the Universe
Production Republic Pictures, *Directors* Fred C. Brannon, Harry Keller and Franklin Adreon, *Producer* Franklin Adreon, *Story and Screenplay* Ronald Davidson and Barry Shipman, *Photography* Bud Thackery, *Special Photography* Howard and Theodore Lydecker, *Art Direction* Frank Arrigo, *Editors* Cliff Bell and Harold Minter, *Distribution* Republic Pictures.

CAST: Judd Holdren (Commando Cody), Aline Towne (Joan), Gregory Gay (The Ruler).

Black and White; originally a television series but released to theatres in 1953; a serial in twelve chapters: (1) *Enemies of the Universe* (Davidson/Brannon), (2) *Atomic Peril* (Davidson/Brannon), (3) *Cosmic Vengeance* (Davidson/Brannon), (4) *Nightmare Typhoon* (Davidson/Brannon), (5) *War of the Space Giants* (Davidson/Adreon), (6) *Destroyers of the Sun* (Davidson/Keller), (7) *Robot Monster of Mars* (Davidson/Adreon), (8) *Hydrogen Hurricane* (Shipman/Keller), (9) *Solar Sky Riders* (Shipman/Keller), (10) *SOS Ice Age* (Shipman/Adreon), (11) *Lost in Outer Space* (Davidson/Keller), (12) *Captives of the Zero Hour* (Davidson/Keller).

The Cosmic Man
Production Futura Productions, *Director* Herbert Greene, *Producer* Robert A. Terry, *Story and Screenplay* Arthur C. Pierce, *Photography* John F. Warren, *Special Photography* Charles Duncan, *Music* Paul Sawtell and Bert Shefter, *Art Direction* No credits, *Editors* Richard C. Currier and Helene Turner, *Distribution* Allied Artists Pictures Corporation.

CAST: Bruce Bennett (Dr. Karl Sorenson), John Carradine (The Cosmic Man), Angela Greene (Kathy Grant), Paul Langton (Col. Matthews), Scotty Morrow (Ken Grant), Lyn Osborne (Sgt. Gray), Walter Maslow (Dr. Ritchie), Herbert Lytton (Gen. Knowland).

Black and White; 72 minutes; released February 1959 on double bill with *House on Haunted Hill.*

The Cosmic Monsters (British: *The Strange World of Planet X*)
Production Eros Films Ltd., *Director* Gilbert Gunn, *Producer* George Maynard, *Screenplay* Paul Ryder, *Story* [BBC television serial and novel] René Ray, *Photography* Joe Ambor, *Special Photography* Unavailable, *Music* Robert Sharples, *Art Direction* Bernard Sarron, *Editor* Francis Bieber, *Distribution* Distributors Corporation of America (DCA) [later Valiant Films].

CAST: Forrest Tucker (Gil Graham), Gaby Andre (Michelle Dupont), Martin Benson (Smith), Hugh Latimer (Jimmy Murray), Wyndham Goldie (Brigadier Cartwright), Alec Mango (Dr. Laird), Geoffrey Chater (Gerald Wilson), Patricia Sinclair (Helen Forsyth), Catherine Lancaster (Gillian Betts), Richard Warner (Inspector Burns), Neil Wilson (P. C. Tidy).

Black and White; 75 minutes; released in USA November 1958 on double bill with *The Crawling Eye.*

The Crawling Eye (British: *The Trollenberg Terror*)
Production Tempean Films, *Director* Quentin Lawrence, *Producers* Robert S. Baker and Monty Berman, *Screenplay* Jimmy Sangster, *Story* [BBC television serial] Peter Key, *Photography* Monty Berman, *Special Photography* Les Bowie, *Music* Stanley Black, *Art Direction* Duncan Sutherland, *Editor* Henry Richardson, *Distribution* Distributors Corporation of America (DCA) [later Valiant Films].
CAST: Forrest Tucker (Alan Brooks), Laurence Payne (Philip Truscott), Janet Munro (Anne Pilgrim), Jennifer Jayne (Sarah Pilgrim), Warren Mitchell (Crevett), Frederick Schiller (Klein), Stuart Sanders (Dewhurst), Andrew Foulds (Brett), Colin Douglas (Hans), Derek Sydney (Wilde).
Black and White; 85 minutes; released in USA November 1958 on double bill with *The Cosmic Monsters.*

Creature from the Black Lagoon
Production Universal, *Director* Jack Arnold, *Producer* William Alland, *Screenplay* Harry Essex and Arthur Ross, *Story* Maurice Zimm, *Photography* William E. Snyder, *Special Photography* James C. Havens, Charles S. Welbourne, and David S. Horsley, *Music Supervision* Joseph Gershenson, *Art Direction* Hilyard Brown and Bernard Herzbrun, *Editor* Ted J. Kent, *Distribution* Universal-International.
CAST: Richard Carlson (David Reed), Julia [later Julie] Adams, Richard Denning (Mark Williams), Antonio Moreno (Carl Maia), Nestor Paiva (Lucas), Whit Bissell (Edwin Thompson), Rodd Redwing (Luis), Ben Chapman and Ricou Browning (The Creature).
Black and White in 3-Dimension; 79 minutes; released March 1954.
   I have listed this film because of its title, but I do not consider it an alien invasion film since a scientific expedition, rather than the creature, is the invader.

Creature from the Haunted Sea
Production Filmgroup, *Producer-Director* Roger Corman, *Story and Screenplay* Charles B. Griffith, *Photography* Jacques Marquette, *Music* Fred Katz, *Editor* Angela Scellers, *Distribution* Filmgroup, no other credits available.
CAST: Antony Carbone (Renzo Capeto), Betsy Jones-Moreland (Mary-Belle), Edward Wain (Sparks Moran), Edmundo Rivera Alvarez (Col. Tostada), Robert Bean (Jack), Sonya Noemi (Mango).
Black and White; 60 minutes; released September 1960 on double bill with *The Devil's Partner.*

The Creature Walks among Us
Production Universal, *Director* John Sherwood, *Producer* William Alland, *Story and Screenplay* Arthur Ross, *Photography* Maury Gertsman, *Special Photography* Clifford Stine, *Music Supervision* Joseph Gershenson, *Art Direction* Alexander Golitzen and Robert E. Smith, *Editor* Edward Curtiss, *Distribution* Universal-International.
CAST: Jeff Morrow (Dr. William Barton), Rex Reason (Dr. Thomas Morgan), Leigh Snowden (Marcia Barton), Gregg Palmer (Jed Grant), Maurice Manson (Dr. Borg), James Rawley (Dr. Johnson), David McMahon (Capt. Stanley), Paul Fierro (Morteno), Don Megowan (The Creature).
Black and White; 78 minutes; released April 1956.

Creature with the Atom Brain
Production Clover Productions, *Director* Edward L. Cahn, *Producer* Sam Katzman [listed as "Executive Producer" in credits], *Story and Screenplay* Curt Siodmak, *Photography* Fred Jackman, Jr., *Special Photography* Jack Erickson, *Music Coordinator* Mischa Bakaleinikoff, *Art Direction* Paul Palmentola, *Editor* Aaron Stell, *Distribution* Columbia Pictures.

CAST: Richard Denning (Dr. Chet Walker), Angela Stevens (Joyce Walker), S. John Launer (Capt. Dave Harris), Michael Granger (Frank Buchanan), Gregory Gay (Prof. Steigg), Linda Bennett (Penny Walker), Tristram Coffin (District Attorney MacGraw).

Black and White; 69 minutes; released July 1955 on double bill with *It Came from Beneath the Sea*.

Screenwriter Curt Siodmak was responsible for most of the stories for Universal's horror classics of the late thirties and forties. In *The Wolf Man*, probably his best, Siodmak created the werewolf lore of silver bullets and "autumn moons full and bright." His work in the fifties was minor. He wrote and directed *Bride of the Gorilla* (1951), a lame voodoo story with Raymond Burr, Barbara Payton, and Lon Chaney, and then teamed with Ivan Tors for two science fiction films, *The Magnetic Monster* (q.v.) and *Riders to the Stars*. In the late fifties he wrote and directed *Curucu, Beast of the Amazon* and wrote, produced, and directed *Love Slaves of the Amazon*, neither of which come anywhere near the imagination and vitality of his work at Universal. Like those of the horror stars of the thirties and forties, Siodmak's contributions to the alien invasion film are negligible.

The Creeping Unknown (British: *The Quatermass Experiment*)
Production Hammer Films, *Director* Val Guest, *Producer* Anthony Hinds, *Screenplay* Richard Landau, *Story* [BBC television serial] Nigel Kneale, *Photography* Walter Harvey, *Special Photography* Les Bowie, *Music* James Bernard, *Art Direction* J. Elder Wills, *Editor* James Needs, *Distribution* United Artists.

CAST: Brian Donlevy (Prof. Quatermass), Jack Warner (Inspector Lomax), Margia Dean (Judith Carroon), Richard Wordsworth (Victor Carroon), David King Wood (Dr. Gordon Briscoe), Thora Hird (Rosie), Lionel Jeffries (Blake), Harold Lang (Christie), Maurice Kaufman (Marsh), Gordon Jackson (TV Announcer), Jane Asher (Little Girl).

Black and White; 78 minutes (British version: 82 minutes); released in USA June 1956 on double bill with *The Black Sleep*.

This film looks very much like a horror film (moody, gray tones for daylight and sharp chiaroscuro contrast for night) but is an alien invasion film in the strictest sense. An astronaut returns from space and slowly metamorphoses into a slimy, tentacled "thing." Apart from its photography, the real power of the film is in the performances of Brian Donlevy and Richard Wordsworth. Wordsworth, a British actor of considerable talent, portrays the astronaut, Victor Carroon, whose total being is slowly consumed by the thing. There are moments of genuine pathos as Carroon struggles to remain "himself," striking violently against the thing that has completely taken over his arm. This emotional dynamic is offset by Donlevy's Prof. Quatermass, a rocket scientist. Quatermass is similar to Peter Cushing's Frankenstein: arrogant, coldly logical, and totally amoral. In the hospital scene early in the film, Quatermass seems genuinely concerned about Carroon's condition, but we later learn that he is concerned only because he fears Carroon will die before he can report on the mission. Carroon's wife (Margia Dean) assails Quatermass for his lack of compassion, but he coldly responds, "There is no room for personal feelings in science."

The Curse of Frankenstein (British)
Production Hammer Films, *Director* Terence Fisher, *Producer* Anthony Hinds, *Screenplay* Jimmy Sangster, *Story* [novel] Mary Wollstonecraft Shelley, *Photography* Jack Asher, *Special Photography* No credits, *Music* James Bernard, *Art Direction* Bernard Robinson and Ted Marshall, *Editor* James Needs, *Distribution* Warner Brothers.

CAST: Peter Cushing (Victor Frankenstein), Hazel Court (Elizabeth), Robert Urquhart (Paul Krempe), Christopher Lee (The Creature), Valerie Gaunt (Justine), Noel Hood (Aunt Sophie), Paul Hardmuth (Prof. Bernstein), Melvyn Hayes (Victor as young man).

Color by WarnerColor [credits read: "Eastman Colour by Humphries Laboratories"]; 83 minutes; released in USA June 1957 on double bill with *X–The Unknown;* reissued in 1963 by Seven Arts Pictures on double bill with *Horror of Dracula.*

The Cyclops

Production AB & H, *Producer-Director* Bert I. Gordon, *Story and Screenplay* Bert I. Gordon, *Photography* Ira Morgan, *Special Photography* Bert I. Gordon and Flora M. Gordon, *Music* Albert Glasser, *Art Direction* No credits, *Editor* Carlo Lobato, *Distribution* Allied Artists Pictures Corporation.

CAST: Gloria Talbott (Susan Winter), James Craig (Russ Bradford), Lon Chaney (Melville), Tom Drake (Lee Brand), Duncan Parkin (The Cyclops).

Black and White; 75 minutes; released July 1957 on double bill with *The Daughter of Dr. Jekyll;* originally scheduled for release by RKO-Radio Pictures.

The Daughter of Dr. Jekyll

Production Film Ventures, *Director* Edgar G. Ulmer, *Producer* Jack Pollexfen, *Story and Screenplay* Jack Pollexfen, *Photography* John F. Warren, *Special Photography* Unavailable, *Music* Melvyn Lenard, *Art Direction* Mawbray Berkeley, *Editor* Holbrook N. Todd, *Distribution* Allied Artists Pictures Corporation.

CAST: John Agar (George Hastings), Gloria Talbott (Janet Smith), Arthur Shields (Dr. Lomas), John Dierkes (Jacob), Mollie McCart (Maggie), Martha Wentworth (Mrs. Merchant).

Black and White; 74 minutes; released July 1957 on double bill with *The Cyclops.*

One of several films produced by Jack Pollexfen, of whom little is known. In the early fifties he was associated with Aubrey Wisberg and together they wrote and produced several alien invasion films. Midway through the decade Pollexfen went out on his own and continued writing, producing, and directing. *The Man from Planet X* (q.v.) is probably his and Wisberg's best story.

The Day the Earth Stood Still

Production Twentieth Century-Fox, *Director* Robert Wise, *Producer* Julian Blaustein, *Screenplay* Edmund H. North, *Story* [short story, "Farewell to the Master"] Harry Bates, *Photography* Leo Tover, *Special Photography* Fred Sersen, *Music* Bernard Herrmann, *Art Direction* Lyle R. Wheeler and Addison Hehr, *Editor* William Reynolds, *Distribution* Twentieth Century-Fox.

CAST: Michael Rennie (Klaatu), Patricia Neal (Helen Benson), Hugh Marlowe (Tom Stevens), Billy Gray (Bobby Benson), Sam Jaffe (Prof. Barnhardt), Lock Martin (Gort), Frances Bavier (Mrs. Barley), Olan Soulé (Mr. Kurll), H. V. Kaltenborn, Drew Pearson, Elmer Davis, Gabriel Heatter (Themselves).

Black and White; 92 minutes; released September 1951.

The Day the World Ended

Production Golden State Productions, *Producer-Director* Roger Corman, *Story and Screenplay* Lou Rusoff, *Photography* Jock Feindel, *Special Photography* Paul Blaisdell, *Music* Ronald Stein, *Art Direction* No credits, *Editor* Ronald Sinclair, *Distribution* American Releasing Corporation [later American International Pictures].

CAST: Richard Denning (Rick), Lori Nelson (Louise Madison), Adele Jergens (Ruby), Touch [later Mike] Connors (Tony), Paul Birch (Madison), Raymond Hatton (Pete), Paul Dubov (Radek), Jonathan Haze (Contaminated Man), Paul Blaisdell (The Mutant).

Black and White in SuperScope; 79 minutes; released January 1956 on double bill with *The Phantom from 10,000 Leagues.*

The Deadly Mantis

Production Universal, *Director* Nathan Juran *Producer* William Alland, *Screenplay* Martin Berkeley, *Story* William Alland, *Photography* Ellis W. Carter, *Special Photography* Clifford Stine, *Music Supervision* Joseph Gershenson, *Art Direction* Alexander Golitzen and Robert Clatworthy, *Editor* Chester Schaeffer, *Distribution* Universal-International.

CAST: Craig Stevens (Col. Joe Parkman), Alix Talton (Marge Blaine), William Hopper (Dr. Nedrick Jackson), Donald Randolph (Gen. Mark Ford), Florenz Ames (Prof. Anton Gunther), Pat Conway (Sgt. Pete Allen), Phil Harvey (Lou), Paul Smith (Corporal).

Black and White; 79 minutes; released May 1957 as lower half of double bill with *The Girl in the Kremlin.*

Devil Girl from Mars (British)

Production The Danzigers, *Director* David MacDonald, *Producers* Edward J. and Harry Lee Danziger, *Screenplay* John C. Mather and James Eastwood, *Story* [play] John C. Mather and James Eastwood, *Photography* Jack Cox, *Special Photography* Jack Whitehead, *Music* Edwin Astley, *Art Direction* Norman Arnold, *Editor* Peter Taylor, *Distribution* Spartan.

CAST: Patricia Laffan (Nyah), Hugh McDermott (Michael Carter), Hazel Court (Ellen Prestwick), Adrienne Corri (Doris), Peter Reynolds (Albert), Joseph Tomelty (Prof. Hennessey), John Laurie (Jamieson).

Black and White; 77 minutes; released in USA April 1955.

Dinosaurus

Production Fairview Productions, *Director* Irvin S. Yeaworth, Jr., *Producer* Jack H. Harris, *Story and Screenplay* Jean Yeaworth and Dan E. Weisburd, *Photography* Stanley Cortez, *Special Photography* Tim Barr, Wah Chang, and Gene Warren, *Music* Ronald Stein, *Art Direction* Jack Senter, *Editor* John A. Bushelman, *Distribution* Universal-International.

CAST: Ward Ramsey (Bart Thompson), Kristina Hanson (Betty Piper), Paul Lukather (Chuck), Gregg Martell (The Neanderthal Man), Alan Roberts (Julio), Fred Engelberg (Mike Hacker), Wayne C. Tredway (Dumpy).

Color by DeLuxe in CinemaScope; 85 minutes; released July 1960.

Donovan's Brain

Production Dowling Productions, *Director* Felix Feist, *Producer* Tom Gries, *Screenplay* Felix Feist and Hugh Brooks, *Story* [novel] Curt Siodmak, *Photography* Joseph Biroc, *Special Photography* Harry Redmond, Jr., *Music* Eddie Dunstedter, *Art Direction* Boris Leven, *Editor* Herbert L. Strock, *Distribution* United Artists.

CAST: Lew Ayres (Dr. Patrick Cory), Nancy Davis (Janice Cory), Gene Evans (Dr. Frank Schratt), Steve Brodie (Herbie Yocum), Lisa K. Howard (Chloe Donovan).

Black and White; 83 minutes; released September 1953.

Earth vs. the Flying Saucers

Production Clover Productions, *Director* Fred F. Sears, *Producer* Charles H. Schneer, *Screenplay* George Worthing Yates and Raymond T. Marcus, *Story* Curt Siodmak [adapted from the book *Flying Saucers from Outer Space* by Donald E. Keyhoe], *Photography* Fred Jackman, Jr., *Special Photography* Ray Harryhausen, *Musical Direction* Mischa Bakaleinikoff, *Art Direction* Paul Palmentola, *Editor* Danny Landres, *Distribution* Columbia Pictures.

CAST: Hugh Marlowe (Dr. Russell Marvin), Joan Taylor (Carol Hanley Marvin), Donald Curtis (Maj. Huglin), Morris Ankrum (Gen. John Hanley), Thomas Browne Henry (Adm. Enright), John Zaremba (Prof. Kanter), Gran-

don Rhodes (Gen. Edmunds), Frank Wilcox (Alfred Cassidy), Harry Lauter (Cutting).
Black and White; 83 minutes; released July 1956 on double bill with *The Werewolf.*

Earth vs. the Spider
Production Santa Rosa Productions, *Producer-Director* Bert I. Gordon, *Screenplay* Laszlo Gorog and George Worthing Yates, *Story* Bert I. Gordon, *Photography* Jack Marta, *Special Photography* Bert I. Gordon and Flora M. Gordon, *Music* Albert Glasser, *Art Direction* No credits other than Set Decorations by Walter Keller, *Editor* Ronald Sinclair, *Distribution* James H. Nicholson and Samuel Z. Arkoff through American International Pictures.
CAST: Edward Kemmer (Mr. Kingman), June Kenney (Carol Flynn), Gene Persson (Mike Simpson), Gene Roth (Sheriff Cagle), Hal Torey (Mr. Simpson), June Jocelyn (Mrs. Flynn), Sally Fraser (Mrs. Kingman), Troy Patterson (Joe), Skip Young (Sam), Hank Patterson (Hugo).
Black and White; 72 minutes; released October 1958 on double bill with *The Brain Eaters;* film is advertised as *The Spider.*

The Electronic Monster (British: *Escapement* [1957])
Production Anglo-Amalgamated/Merton Park Studios, *Director* Montgomery Tully, *Producer* Alec C. Snowden, *Screenplay* Charles Eric Maine and J. Mac-Laren-Ross, *Story* [novel] Charles Eric Maine, *Photography* Bert Mason, *Special Photography* Teddy Catford, *Music* Soundrama and Richard Taylor, *Art Direction* Wilfred Arnold, *Editor* Geoffrey Muller, *Distribution* Columbia Pictures.
CAST: Rod Cameron (Jeff Kennan), Mary Murphy (Ruth), Meredith Edwards (Dr. Maxwell), Peter Illing (Zakon), Carl Jaffe (Dr. Erich Hoff), Kay Callard (Laura Maxwell).
Black and White; 72 minutes; (British version: 80 minutes); released in USA May 1960 on double bill with *13 Ghosts.*

Enemy from Space (British: *Quatermass II*)
Production Hammer Films, *Director* Val Guest, *Producer* Anthony Hinds, *Screenplay* Nigel Kneale and Val Guest, *Story* [BBC television serial] Nigel Kneale, *Photography* Gerald Gibbs, *Special Photography* Bill Warrenton, *Music* James Bernard, *Art Direction* Bernard Robinson, *Editor* James Needs, *Distribution* United Artists.
CAST: Brian Donlevy (Prof. Bernard Quatermass), John Longdon (Inspector Lomax), Vera Day (Sheila), William Franklyn (Tom Brand), Tom Chatto (Vincent Broadhead), Sidney James (Jimmy Hall), Bryan Forbes (Marsh), Percy Herbert (Paddy Gorman), Charles Lloyd Pack (Dawson), John Van Eyssen (The PRO), Michael Ripper (Ernie).
Black and White; 74 minutes; released in USA October 1957.

Fiend without a Face (British)
Production Amalgamated Productions, *Director* Arthur Crabtree, *Producer* John Croydon, *Screenplay* Herbert J. Leder, *Story* [short story, "The Thought Monster,"] Amelia Reynolds Long, *Photography* Lionel Banes, *Special Photography* Peter Nielsen, Ruppell & Nordhoff, *Music* Buxton Orr, *Art Direction* John Elphick, *Editor* R. Q. McNaughton, *Distribution* Metro-Goldwyn-Mayer.
CAST: Marshall Thompson (Maj. Jeff Cummings), Kynaston Reeves (Prof. R. E. Walgate), Kim Parker (Barbara Grisselle), Stanley Maxted (Col. Butler), Michael Balfour (Sgt. Kasper), Gil Winfield (Dr. Warren), Peter Madden (Dr. Bradley), James Dyrenforth (Mayor), Launce Maraschal (Melville).
Black and White; 74 minutes; released in USA August 1958 on double bill with *The Haunted Strangler.*

First Man into Space (British)
Production Amalgamated Productions, *Director* Robert Day, *Producers* John Croydon and Charles F. Vetter, Jr., *Screenplay* John C. Cooper and Lance Z. Hargraves, *Story* Wyott Ordung, *Photography* Geoffrey Faithfull, *Special Photography* Unavailable, *Music* Buxton Orr, *Art Direction* Denys Pavitt, *Editor* Peter Mayhew, *Distribution* Metro-Goldwyn-Mayer.
CAST: Marshall Thompson (Lt. Commander Chuck Prescott), Marla Landi (Tia Francesca), Bill Edwards (Dan Prescott), Robert Ayres (Ben Richards), Bill Nagy (Wilson), Carl Jaffe (Dr. von Nessen), Roger Delgado (Mexican Consul), John McLaren (State Department Official).
Black and White; 77 minutes; released in USA February 1959.
 Follows the theme set by *The Creeping Unknown:* An astronaut returns to earth as a monster. The theme is also found in Bernard L. Kowalski's *Night of the Blood Beast.*

The Flame Barrier
Production Gramercy Pictures, *Director* Paul Landres, *Producers* Arthur Gardner and Jules V. Levy, *Screenplay* Pat Fielder and George Worthing Yates, *Story* George Worthing Yates, *Photography* Jack McKenzie, *Special Photography* Westheimer Company, *Art Direction* James Vance, *Editor* Jerry Young, *Distribution* United Artists.
CAST: Arthur Franz (Dave Hollister), Kathleen Crowley (Carol Dahlman), Robert Brown (Matt Hollister), Vincent Padula (Julio), Rodd Redwing (Waumi), Kaz Oran (Tispe), Grace Mathews (Mexican Girl), Pilar Del Rey (Indian Girl), Larry Duran (Bearer), Bernie Grozier (Wounded Indian), Roberto Contreras (Village Indian).
Black and White; 70 minutes; released April 1958 on double bill with *The Return of Dracula.*
 Gramercy Pictures was a corporate name in the fifties for producers Jules V. Levy, Arthur Gardner, and Arnold Laven. They produced several genre pieces for United Artists, most of which were westerns and science fiction films. They also produced the TV series *The Rifleman* and *The Big Valley.*

The Fly
Production Twentieth Century-Fox, *Producer-Director* Kurt Neumann, *Screenplay* James Cavell, *Story* [short story] George Langelaan, *Photography* Karl Struss, *Special Photography* L. B. Abbott, *Music* Paul Sawtell, *Art Direction* Lyle R. Wheeler and Theobold Holsopple, *Editor* Merril G. White, *Distribution* Twentieth Century-Fox.
CAST: Al [later David] Hedison (Andre Delambre), Patricia Owens (Helene Delambre), Vincent Price (Francois Delambre), Herbert Marshall (Inspector Charas), Kathleen Freeman (Emma), Charles Herbert (Phillippe).
Color by DeLuxe in CinemaScope; 94 minutes; released June 1958 as top half of double bill with *Space Master X-7.*

The Flying Disc Man from Mars
Production Republic Pictures, *Director* Fred C. Brannon, *Producer* Franklin Adreon [listed as "Associate Producer"], *Story and Screenplay* Ronald Davidson, *Photography* Walter Strenge, *Special Photography* Howard and Theodore Lydecker, *Music* Stanley Wilson, *Art Direction* Fred Ritter, *Editors* Cliff Bell and Sam Starr, *Distribution* Republic Pictures.
CAST: Walter Reed (Kent Fowler), Lois Collier (Helen Hall), Gregory Gay (Mota), James Craven (Bryant), Harry Lauter (Drake), Richard Irving (Ryan), Sandy Sanders (Steve), Michael Carr (Trent), Dale Van Sickel (Watchman), Tom Steele (Taylor).
Black and White; released 1951; a serial in 12 chapters: (1) *Menace from Mars*, (2) *The Volcano's Secret*, (3) *Death Rides the Stratosphere*, (4) *Execution by Fire*,

(5) *The Living Projectile*, (6) *Perilous Mission*, (7) *Descending Doom*, (8) *Suicidal Sacrifice*, (10) *Weapons of Hate*, (11) *Disaster on the Highway*, (12) *Volcanic Vengeance;* feature version entitled *Missile Monsters* released May 1958 on double bill with *Satan's Satellites.*

The Flying Saucer
Production Colonial Productions, *Producer-Director* Mikel Conrad, *Screenplay* Mikel Conrad and Howard Irving Young, *Story* Mikel Conrad, *Photography* Philip Tannura, *Music* Darrell Calker, *Editor* Robert Crandall, *Distribution* Film Classics; no other credits available.

CAST: Mikel Conrad (Mike Trent), Pat Garrison (Vee Langley), Hantz von Teuffen (Hans), Lester Sharpe (Colonel Marikoff), Virginia Hewitt (Nanette), Russell Hicks (Hank Thorn).

Black and White; 69 minutes; released January 1950.

Not exactly an alien invasion film; I list it here because of its title. It is akin to such "red scare" films as R. G. Springsteen's *The Red Menace* (1949), George Sidney's *The Red Danube* (1949), and Robert Stevenson's *I Married a Communist* (1949) with John Agar, exploiting the red paranoia of the era by combining the "imagined" threat of outer space invasion with what the film terms the "real" threat of Soviet invasion. It is negligible that the saucer, by the film's end, is considered extraterrestrial. Another film often listed as science fiction that might be claimed as alien invasion is William Cameron Menzies's *The Whip Hand* (1951), which tells of Soviet agents experimenting with biological warfare in a small town.

Flying Saucer Daffy
Production Columbia Pictures, *Producer-Director* Jules White, *Story and Screenplay* Jack White, *Photography* Fred Jackman, Jr., *Art Direction* Cary Odell, *Editor* Saul A. Goodkind, *Distribution* Columbia Pictures.

CAST: Moe Howard (Moe), Larry Fine (Larry), Joe Besser (Joe), Gail Bonny (Moe and Larry's mother), Emil Sitka (Mr. Barton), Harriette Tarler, Bek Nelson, Diana Darrin (Girls at Party).

Black and White; 17 minutes; A Three Stooges Comedy Short; released October 1958.

Flying saucer scenes are from *Earth vs. the Flying Saucers.*

The Flying Saucer Mystery
Production/Distribution TeleNews.

Black and White; 10 minutes; released 1950. No other information available.

The 4-D Man
Production Fairview Productions, *Director* Irvin Shortess Yeaworth, Jr., *Producer* Jack H. Harris, *Screenplay* Theodore Simonson and Cy Chermak, *Story* Jack H. Harris, *Photography* Theodore J. Pahle, *Special Photography* Barton Sloane, *Music* Ralph Carmichael, *Art Direction* William Jersey, *Editor* William B. Murphy, *Distribution* Universal-International.

CAST: Robert Lansing (Dr. Scott Nelson), Lee Meriwether (Linda Davis), James Congdon (Tony Nelson), Robert Strauss (Roy Parker), Edgar Stehli (Carson), Patty Duke (Marjorie).

Color by DeLuxe; 85 minutes; released November 1959; reissued by Jack H. Harris in 1965 as *Master of Terror.*

Four-Sided Triangle (British)
Production Hammer Films, *Director* Terence Fisher, *Producer* Alexander Paal, *Screenplay* Paul Tabori and Terence Fisher, *Story* [novel] William F. Temple, *Photography* Reginald Wyer, *Music* Malcolm Arnold, *Art Direction* J. Elder Wills, *Editor* Maurice Rootes, *Distribution* Astor Pictures.

CAST: Barbara Payton (Lena and Helen), Stephen Murray (Bill), John Van Eyssen (Robin), Percy Marmount (Sir Walter), James Hayter (Dr. Harvey).

Black and White; 74 minutes (British version: 81 minutes); released in USA June 1953.

Frankenstein 1970

Production Allied Artists, *Director* Howard W. Koch, *Producer* Aubrey Schenk, *Screenplay* Richard Landau and George Worthing Yates, *Story* Aubrey Schenk and Charles A. Moses, *Photography* Carl Guthrie, *Music* Paul Dunlap, *Art Direction* Jack T. Collins, *Editor* John Bushelman, *Distribution* Allied Artists Pictures Corporation.

CAST: Boris Karloff (Baron Victor von Frankenstein), Tom Duggan (Mike Shaw), Donald Barry (Douglas Row), Jana Lund (Carolyn Hayes), Charlotte Austin (Judy Stevens), Irwin Berke (Inspector Raab), Rudolph Anders (Wilhelm Gottfried), John Dennis (Morgan Haley), Norbert Schiller (Shuter), Mike Lane (Hans).

Black and White in CinemaScope; 83 minutes; released June 1958 on double bill with *Queen of Outer Space*.

Frankenstein's Daughter

Production Layton Productions, *Director* Richard Cunha, *Producer* Marc Frederic, *Story and Screenplay* H. E. Barrie, *Photography* Meredith M. Nicholson, *Special Photography* Ira Anderson, *Music* Nicholas Carras, *Art Direction* No credits, *Editor* Everett Dodd, *Distribution* Astor Pictures.

CAST: John Ashley (Johnny Bruder), Sandra Knight (Trudy Morton), Donald Murphy (Oliver Frank), Sally Todd (Suzie), Harold Lloyd, Jr. (Don), Felix Lochner (Carter Morton), Wolfe Barzell (Elsu).

Black and White; 85 minutes; released December 1958 on double bill with *Missile to the Moon*.

From Hell It Came

Production Milner Brothers, *Director* Dan Milner, *Producer* Jack Milner, *Screenplay* Richard Bernstein, *Story* Richard Bernstein, Dan Milner, and Jack Milner, *Photography* Brydon Baker, *Special Photography* Paul Blaisdell and James H. Donnelly, *Art Direction* Rudi Feld, *Editor* Jack Milner, *Distribution* Allied Artists Pictures Corporation.

CAST: Tod Andrews (Dr. William Arnold), Tina Carver (Dr. Terry Mason), Suzanne Ridgway (Korey), Gregg Palmer (Kimo), Robert Swan (Tano), Baynes Barron (Chief Maranka), Linda Watkins (Mrs. Kilgore), John McNamara (Prof. Clark).

Black and White; 73 minutes; released August 1957 on double bill with *The Disembodied*.

Similar to *Blood of the Vampire* in that it mixes the supernatural (voodoo curses) with scientific experimentation. In this film, however, it is a mere coincidence that atomic radiation is fulfilling an ancient tribal legend and curse.

The Gamma People (British)

Production Warwick Film Productions, *Director* John Gilling, *Producer* John Gossage, *Screenplay* John Gilling and John Gossage, *Story* Louis Pollack, *Photography* Ted Moore, *Special Photography* Tom Howard, *Music* George Melachrino, *Art Direction* John Box, *Editors* Alan Osbitson and Jack Slade, *Distribution* Columbia Pictures.

CAST: Paul Douglas (Mike Wilson), Eva Bartok (Paula Wendt), Leslie Phillips (Howard Meade), Walter Rilla (Boronski), Philip Leaver (Koerner), Martin Miller (Lochner), Michael Caridia (Hugo Wendt), Paul Hardtmuth (Hans).

Black and White; 76 minutes; (British version: 79 minutes); released in USA December 1956 on double bill with *1984*.

The Giant Behemoth (British: *Behemoth, The Sea Monster*)

Production Eros Films/Artistes Alliance/David Diamond, *Director* Eugene Lourié, *Producer* Ted Lloyd, *Screenplay* Eugene Lourié, *Story* Robert Abel and

Allen Adler, *Photography* Ken Hodges, *Special Photography* Jack Rabin, Irving Block, Louis DeWitt, Willis H. O'Brien, Pete Petersen, *Music* Edwin Astley, *Art Direction* Harry White, *Editor* Lee Doig, *Distribution* Allied Artists Pictures Corporation.

CAST: Gene Evans (Dr. Steven Karnes), Andre Morell (Professor Bickford), John Turner (Ian Duncan), Leigh Madison (Jean MacDougall), Jack McGowan (Dr. Sampson), Maurice Kaufman (Submarine Commander).

Black and White; 80 minutes; released in USA March 1959 on double bill with *Arson for Hire;* British version credits direction to Lourié and Douglas Hickox.

The Giant Claw
Production Clover Productions, *Director* Fred F. Sears, *Producer* Sam Katzman, *Story and Screenplay* Samuel Newman and Paul Gangelin, *Photography* Benjamin H. Kline, *Special Photography* Ralph Hammeras and George Teague, *Musical Director* Mischa Bakaleinikoff, *Art Direction* Paul Palmentola, *Editors* Saul A. Goodkind and Tony DiMarco, *Distribution* Columbia Pictures.

CAST: Jeff Morrow (Mitch MacAfee), Mara Corday (Sally Caldwell), Morris Ankrum (Gen. Edward Lewis), Edgar Barrier (Dr. Noyman), Louis D. Merrill (Pierre Broussard), Robert Shayne (Gen. Ben Penner), Clark Howat (Major Sperling), Morgan Jones (Lieutenant).

Black and White; 75 minutes; released June 1957 on double bill with *The Night the World Exploded.*

The Giant from the Unknown
Production Screencraft Enterprises, *Director* Richard E. Cunha, *Producer* Arthur A. Jacobs, *Story and Screenplay* Frank Hart Taussig and Ralph Brooke, *Photography* Dick Cunha, *Special Photography* Harold Banks, *Music* Albert Glasser, *Art Direction* No credits, *Editor* Screencraft Enterprises, *Distribution* Astor Pictures.

CAST: Edward Kemmer (Wayne Brooks), Sally Fraser (Janet Cleveland), Buddy Baer (Vargas, the Giant), Morris Ankrum (Professor Cleveland), Bob Steele (Sheriff Parker), Joline Brand (Ann Brown).

Black and White; 77 minutes; released March 1958 on double bill with *She Demons.*

The Giant Gila Monster
Production McLendon Radio Pictures, *Director* Ray Kellog, *Producer* Ken Curtis, *Story and Screenplay* Jay Simms and Ray Kellogg, *Photography* Wilfrid Cline, *Special Photography* Ralph Hammeras and Wee Risser, *Music* Jack Marshall, *Art Direction* Louis Caldwell, *Editor* Aaron Stell, *Distribution* McLendon Radio Pictures.

CAST: Don Sullivan (Chace Winstead), Lisa Simone (Lisa), Shug Fisher (Mr. Harris), Jerry Cortwright (Bob), Beverly Thurman (Gay), Don Flourney (Gordy), Clarke Browne (Chuck), Pat Simmons (Sherry), Pat Reaves (Rick), Fred Graham (Sheriff), Ann Sonka (Whila), Bob Thompson (Wheeler), Cecil Hunt (Compton).

Black and White; 74 minutes; released November 1957 on double bill with *The Killer Shrews.*

McLendon Radio Pictures was a production and distribution company owned by Gordon McLendon, the head of a chain of radio stations and theatres in Texas.

The Giant Leeches
Advertised title for *Attack of the Giant Leeches* (q.v.).

Gigantis, the Fire Monster (Japanese: Gojira no Gyakushyu [1955])
Production Toho Company Ltd., *Director* Motoyoshi Odo, *Producer* Tomoyuki Tanaka, *Screenplay* Takeo Murata and Sigeaki Hidaka, *Story* Shigeru Kayama, *Photography* Selichi Endo, *Special Photography* Eiji Tsuburaya,

Akira Watanabe, Hiroshi Mukoyama, Masso Shirota, *Music* Masaru Sato, *Art Direction* Takeo Kita, *Editor* Hugo Grimaldi, *Distribution* Paul Schreibman through Warner Brothers.

CAST: Hiroshi Koizumi (Tsukioka), Setsuko Wakayama (Hedemi), Mindru Chiaki (Kobayashi).

Black and White; 78 minutes (Japanese version: 82 minutes); released in USA June 1959 on double bill with *Teenagers from Outer Space*.

This film is actually the first sequel to *Godzilla*, but since Warner Brothers did not own the rights to the Godzilla name, Godzilla became Gigantis.

Godzilla, King of the Monsters (Japanese: *Gojira*)

Production Toho Company Ltd., *Director* Inoshiro Honda, *Producer* Tomoyuki Tanaka, *Screenplay* Takeo Murata and Inoshiro Honda, *Story* Sigeru Kayama, *Photography* Masao Tamai, *Special Photography* Eiji Tsuburaya, Akira Watanabe, Hiroshi Mukouyama, Kuichiro Chuko, *Music* Akira Ifukube, *Art Direction* Satoshi Chuko, *Editor* Terry O. Morse, *English Version* Terry O. Morse, *Distribution* Trans World Films.

CAST: Raymond Burr (Steve Martin), Akira Takarada (Ogato), Takashi Shimura (Professor Yamane), Momoko Kochi (Emilo Yamane).

Black and White; 81 minutes (Japanese version: 98 minutes); released in USA April 1956.

Almost all the Japanese science fiction films were products of Toho Company, a large firm which also produced many of Akira Kurosawa's samurai films. The science fiction films were usually the work of producer Tomoyuki Tanaka, director Inoshiro Honda, and special effects director Eiji Tsuburaya, whose films are distinctly marked by scenes of mass destruction. Toho, incidentally, was responsible for developing the first Japanese anamorphic lens, Tohoscope, which Tanaka-Honda-Tsuburaya used to great effect in their spectacles of destruction.

Gog

Production Ivan Tors Productions, *Director* Herbert L. Strock, *Producer* Ivan Tors, *Screenplay* Tom Taggart and Richard G. Taylor, *Story* Ivan Tors, *Photography* Lothrop Worth, *Special Photography* Harry Redmond, Jr., *Music* Harry Sukman, *Art Direction* William Ferrari, *Editor* Herbert L. Strock, *Distribution* United Artists.

CAST: Richard Egan (David Sheppard), Constance Dowling (Joanna Merritt), Herbert Marshall (Dr. Van Ness), John Wengraf (Dr. Seitman), Philip Van Zandt (Dr. Elzevir), Michael Fox (Dr. Hubertus), William Schallert (Engle), Aline Towne (Dr. Kirby).

Filmed in 3-Dimension and Color; 82 minutes; released June 1954.

Most sources say that the original 3-D color version is not in existence; only a black and white copy is said to exist.

Goons from the Moon

Production Terrytoons, *Director* Connie Rasinski, *Producer* Paul Terry, *Distribution* Twentieth Century-Fox; no other credits available.

Color by DeLuxe; 7 minutes; A Mighty Mouse Terrytoon Cartoon; released April 1951.

Gorgo (British)

Production King Brothers, *Director* Eugene Lourié, *Producer* Wilfred Eades, *Screenplay* John Loring and Daniel Hyatt, *Story* Eugene Lourié and Daniel Hyatt, *Photography* F. A. Young, *Special Photography* Tom Howard, *Music* Francesco Lavagnino, *Art Direction* Elliott Scott, *Editor* Eric Boyd-Perkins, *Distribution* Metro-Goldwyn-Mayer.

CAST: Bill Travers (Joe Ryan), William Sylvester (Sam Slade), Vincent Winter (Sean), Bruce Seton (Flaherty), Joseph O'Connor (Prof. Hendricks), Martin Benson (Dorkin), Barry Keegan (First Mate), Dervis Ward (Bo'sun), Christopher Rhodes (McCartin), Basil Dignam (Admiral Brooks), Maurice Kaufman (Radio Announcer), Thomas Duggan (Naval Officer), Howard Lang (Colonel). Color by Technicolor; 78 minutes; released in USA February 1961.

The H-Man (Japanese: *Bijo To Ekitai-Ningen*)
Production Toho Company Ltd., *Director* Inoshiro Honda, *Producer* Tomoyki Tanaka, *Screenplay* Takeshi Kimura, *Story* Hideo Kaijo, *Photography* Hajime Koizumi, *Special Photography* Eiji Tsuburaya, *Music* Masaru Sato, *Art Direction* Takeo Kita, *Editor* Unavailable, *Distribution* Columbia Pictures.
CAST: Kenji Sahara (The Detective), Yumi Shirakawa (The Girl), Akihiko Hirata (The Scientist).
Filmed in Eastman Color and Tohoscope; 79 minutes (Japanese version: 87 minutes); released in USA June 1959 on double bill with *The Woman Eater*.

The Hideous Sun Demon
Production Clarke-King Productions, *Producer-Director* Robert Clarke, *Screenplay* E. S. Seeley, Jr., and Doane Hoag, *Story* Robert Clarke and Phil Hiner, *Photography* John Morrill, Vilis Lapenieks, Jr., Stan Follis, *Special Photography* Gianbatista Cassarrino, *Music* John Seeley, *Art Direction* Gianbatista Cassarrino and Tom Miller, *Editor* Thomas Boutross, *Distribution* Pacific International Pictures.
CAST: Robert Clarke (Dr. Gilbert McKenna), Patricia Manning (Ann Russell), Nan Peterson (Trudy Osborne), Patrick Whyte (Dr. Frederick Buckell), Fred LaPorta (Dr. Jacob Hoffman), Bill Hampton (Police Lieutenant), Donna Conkling (Mother), Sandra Conkling (Little Girl), Del Courtney (Radio Announcer).
Black and White; 74 minutes; released December 1959.

I Married a Monster from Outer Space
Production Paramount Pictures, *Producer-Director* Gene Fowler, Jr., *Story and Screenplay* Louis Vittes, *Photography* Haskell Boggs, *Special Photography* John P. Fulton, *Music* Unavailable, *Art Direction* Hal Pereira and Henry Bumstead, *Editor* George Tomasini, *Distribution* Paramount Pictures.
CAST: Tom Tryon (Bill Farrell), Gloria Talbott (Marge Farrell), Ken Lynch (Dr. Wayne), John Eldredge (Collins), Valerie Allen (Francine), Maxie Rosenbloom (Grady), Alan Dexter (Sam Benson), Jean Carson (Helen).
Black and White; 78 minutes; released October 1958 on double bill with *The Blob*.

I Was a Teenage Frankenstein
Production Santa Rosa Productions, *Director* Herbert L. Strock, *Producer* Herman Cohen, *Story and Screenplay* Kenneth Langtry, *Photography* Lothrop Worth, *Music* Paul Dunlap, *Art Direction* Leslie Thomas, *Editor* Jerry Young, *Distribution* James H. Nicholson and Samuel Z. Arkoff through American International Pictures.
CAST: Whit Bissell (Prof. Frankenstein), Phyllis Coates (Margaret), Gary Conway (Teenage Monster), Robert Burton (Dr. Carlton), George Lynn (Sgt. Burns), John Cliff (Sgt. McAfee), Marshall Bradford (Dr. Randolph).
Black and White with final sequence in Color; 74 minutes; released November 1957 on double bill with *The Blood of Dracula*.

One of several fifties films that incorporate color footage into an otherwise black and white film. At the end of the film, when the teenage monster falls against the electronic panel, color is used for the pyrotechnics and blood. Two other American International films use the gimmick: *How to Make a Monster* (1958), with its fiery finale, and *War of the Colossal Beast* (1958), with the electrical destruction of the colossal beast. Interestingly, AIP advertising prominently displays the word *color;* upon closer examination, one finds such words as "See *Frankenstein's monster* in color. Non-AIP films using the gimmick include *Monster from Green Hell, The Return of Dracula,* and *The Tingler.* See also *Them!*

I Was a Teenage Werewolf
Production Sunset Productions, *Director* Gene Fowler, Jr., *Producer* Herman Cohen, *Story and Screenplay* Ralph Thornton, *Photography* Joseph LaShelle, *Music* Paul Dunlap, *Art Direction* Leslie Thomas, *Editor* George Gittens, *Distribution* James H. Nicholson and Samuel Z. Arkoff through American International Pictures.
CAST: Michael Landon (Tony Rivers), Yvonne Lime (Arlene), Whit Bissell (Dr. Alfred Brandon), Tony Marshall (Jimmy), Dawn Richard (Theresa), Barney Phillips (Detective Donovan), Malcolm Atterbury (Charles Rivers), Vladamir Sokoloff (Pepi), Guy Williams (Officer Stanley).
Black and White; 76 minutes; released June 1957 on double bill with *Invasion of the Saucer Men.*

The Indestructible Man
Production C. G. K. Productions, *Producer-Director* Jack Pollexfen, *Story and Screenplay* Vy Russell and Sue Bradford, *Photography* John Russell, *Music* Albert Glasser, *Art Direction* Theobold Holsopple, *Editor* Fred Feitshans, Jr., *Distribution* Allied Artists Pictures Corporation.
CAST: Lon Chaney (The Butcher), Casey Adams [later Max Showalter] (Chasen), Marian Carr (Eva Martin), Ross Elliott (Paul Lowe), Robert Shayne (Professor Bradshaw), Stuart Randall (Police Chief), Kenneth Terrell (Joe Marcella).
Black and White; 70 minutes; released March 1956 on double bill with *World Without End.*

Invaders from Mars
Production National Pictures, *Director* William Cameron Menzies, *Producer* Edward L. Alperson, *Story and Screenplay* Richard Blake, *Photography* John F. Seitz, *Special Photography* Jack Cosgrove, *Music* Raoul Kraushar, *Art Direction* William Cameron Menzies, *Editor* Arthur Roberts, *Distribution* Twentieth Century-Fox.
CAST: Arthur Franz (Prof. Stuart Kelston), Helena Carter (Dr. Patricia Blake), Jimmy Hunt (David McLean), Leif Erickson (George McLean), Hillary Brooke (Mary McLean), Morris Ankrum (Col. Fielding), Max Wagner (Sgt. Rinaldi), Milburn Stone (Capt. Roth), Bert Freed (Police Chief), Robert Shayne (Dr. Wilson), Janine Perreau (Kathy Wilson), Walter Sande (Desk Sergeant), Bill Phipps (Major Cleary), Douglas Kennedy (Officer Jackson), Charles Kane (Officer Blaine), Barbara Billingsley (Kelston's Secretary).
Photographed in Color; 78 minutes; released May 1953.
  Although no one seems to know for certain, many sources claim *Invaders from Mars* was shot in a 3-Dimension process. Interior evidence—the number of z-axis tracking shots and the cluttered foreground mise-en-scène—lends support to the claim.

Invasion of the Body Snatchers
Production Walter Wanger Pictures, *Director* Don Siegel, *Producer* Walter Wanger, *Screenplay* Daniel Mainwaring, *Story* [novel] Jack Finney, *Photography* Ellsworth Fredericks, *Special Photography* Milt Rice, *Music* Carmen Dragon, *Art Direction* Edward Haworth, *Editor* Robert S. Eisen, *Distribution* Allied Artists Pictures Corporation.
CAST: Kevin McCarthy (Dr. Miles Bennell), Dana Wynter (Becky Driscoll), King Donovan (Jack Belicac), Carolyn Jones ("Teddy" Belicac), Larry Gates (Dr. Daniel Kaufman), Jean Willes (Sally Withers), Virginia Christine (Wil-

ma Lentz), Richard Deacon (Dr. Harvey Bassett), Whit Bissell (Dr. Hill). Black and White in SuperScope; 80 minutes; released February 1956 on double bill with *The Atomic Man.*

Invasion of the Saucer Men
Production Malibu Productions, *Director* Edward L. Cahn, *Producers* James H. Nicholson and Robert Gurney, Jr., *Screenplay* Robert Gurney, Jr., and Al Martin, *Story* Paul Fairman [credits read: "A true story of a Flying Saucer"], *Photography* Frederick E. West, *Special Photography* Howard A. Anderson, Alex Weldon, and Paul Blaisdell, *Music* Ronald Stein, *Art Direction* Don Ament, *Editors* Ronald Sinclair and Charles Goss, *Distribution* James H. Nicholson and Samuel Z. Arkoff through American International Pictures.
CAST: Steve Terrell (Johnny Carter), Gloria Castillo (Joan), Lyn Osborne (Artie), Frank Gorshin (Joe), Raymond Hatton (Larkin), Russ Bender (Doctor), Douglas Henderson (Lt. Wilkins), Sam Buffington (Colonel), Jason Johnson (Detective), Kelly Thordson (Sgt. Bruce).
Black and White; 69 minutes; released June 1957 on double bill with *I Was a Teenage Werewolf.*

Unique among alien invasion films: a comedy, and the comedy actually works. One would never know it, however, by examining the advertising posters: huge bug-eyed monsters carrying off scantily clad women and a throng of saucers destroying a major city. In the film, the saucer men are dwarfs; the narrative concentrates on the threat of just one saucer, which remains grounded for most of the film's 69 minutes; and there is no assault on a major city. And no, there are no scantily clad women carried off by the saucer men. Such graphic, lurid images are typical of American International's advertising art; often the ads are better than the films.

Invasion USA
Production Albert Zugsmith/Robert Smith Productions, *Director* Alfred E. Green, *Producers* Albert Zugsmith and Robert Smith, *Screenplay* Robert Smith, *Story* Robert Smith and Franz Spencer, *Photography* John L. Russell, Jr., *Music* Albert Glasser, *Art Direction* James Sullivan, *Editor* W. Don Hayes, *Distribution* Columbia Pictures.
CAST: Gerald Mohr (Vince), Peggie Castle (Carla), Dan O'Herlihy (Mr. Ohman), Robert Bice (George Sylvester), Erik Blythe (Ed Mulfory), Wade Crosby (Congressman), Phyllis Coates (Mrs. Mulfory), Tom Kennedy (Bartender), Knox Manning (TV Reporter).
Black and White; 73 minutes; released December 1953.

The Invisible Boy
Production Pan Productions, *Director* Herman Hoffman, *Producer* Nicholas Nayfack, *Screenplay* Cyril Hume, *Story* [short story] Edmund Cooper, *Photography* Harold Wellman, *Special Photography* Jack Rabin, Irving Block, and Louis DeWitt, *Music* Les Baxter, *Art Direction* Merrill Pye, *Editor* John Faure, *Distribution* Metro-Goldwyn-Mayer.
CAST: Richard Eyer (Timmy Merrinoe), Philip Abbott (Dr. Merrinoe), Diane Brewster (Mary Merrinoe), Harold J. Stone (Gen. Swayne), Robert H. Harris (Prof. Allerton), Robby the Robot (Himself).
Black and White; 90 minutes; released October 1957.

Invisible Invaders
Production Premium Pictures, *Director* Edward L. Cahn, *Producer* Robert E. Kent, *Story and Screenplay* Samuel Newman, *Photography* Maury Gertsman, *Art Direction* William Glasgow, *Editor* Grant Whytock, *Distribution* United Artists.
CAST: John Agar (Maj. Bruce Jay), Jean Byron (Phyllis Penner), Robert Hutton (Dr. John Lemont), Philip Tonge (Dr. Adam Penner), John Carradine (Dr. Karol Noyman).

Black and White; 67 minutes; released May 1959 on double bill with *The Four Skulls of Jonathan Drake*.

One of several exploitative double bills and second features produced for United Artists under the various corporate names (Premium Pictures, Vogue Pictures, Imperial Pictures) of producer Edward Small's organization. Impressive about Small's group is the sheer mass of films produced; between October 1958 and September 1960, for example, no fewer than sixteen features with such titles as *Guns, Girls, and Gangsters, Inside the Mafia, Riot in Juvenile Prison, Noose for a Gunman, Timbuktu,* and *Vice Raid* were released as second features for double bills. All were produced by Robert E. Kent and all but one were directed by Edward L. Cahn.

It Came from Beneath the Sea

Production Clover Productions, *Director* Robert Gordon, *Producer* Charles H. Schneer, *Screenplay* George Worthing Yates and Hal Smith, *Story* George Worthing Yates, *Photography* Henry Freulich, *Special Photography* Ray Harryhausen, *Music Conductor* Mischa Bakaleinikoff, *Art Direction* Paul Palmentola, *Editor* Jerome Thoms, *Distribution* Columbia Pictures.

CAST: Kenneth Tobey (Commander Pete Matthews), Faith Domergue (Dr. Leslie Joyce), Donald Curtis (Dr. John Carter), Ian Keith (Admiral Burns), Dean Maddox, Jr. (Admiral Norman), Lt. C. Griffiths, USN ("Griff"), Harry Lauter (Bill Nash).

Black and White; 77 minutes; released July 1955 on double bill with *The Creature with the Atom Brain*.

It Came from Outer Space

Production Universal, *Director* Jack Arnold, *Producer* William Alland, *Screenplay* Harry Essex, *Story* Ray Bradbury, *Photography* Clifford Stine, *Special Photography* David S. Horsley, *Music Supervision* Joseph Gershenson, *Art Direction* Bernard Herzbrun and Robert Boyle, *Editor* Paul Weatherwax, *Distribution* Universal-International.

CAST: Richard Carlson (John Putnam), Barbara Rush (Ellen Fields), Charles Drake (Sheriff Matt Warren), Joe Sawyer (Frank Daylon), Russell Johnson (George), Alan Dexter (Dave Loring), Dave Willock (Pete Davis), George Eldredge (Dr. Snell), Kathleen Hughes (Jane), Brad Jackson (Dr. Snell's Assistant), William Pullen (Deputy Reed), Robert S. Carson (Dugan), Warren McGregor (Toby), Virginia Mullen (Mrs. Daylon), George Selk (Tom), Edgar Dearing (Sam).

Black and White in 3-Dimension; 81 minutes; released June 1953.

It Conquered the World

Production Sunset Productions, *Producer-Director* Roger Corman, *Story and Screenplay* Lou Rusoff, *Photography* Frederick West, *Special Photography* Paul Blaisdell, *Music* Ronald Stein, *Editor* Charles Goss, *Distribution* James H. Nicholson and Samuel Z. Arkoff through American International Pictures.

CAST: Peter Graves (Dr. Paul Nelson), Beverly Garland (Claire Anderson), Lee Van Cleef (Dr. Tom Anderson), Sally Fraser (Joan Nelson), Russ Bender (Gen. Pattick), Jonathan Haze (Pvt. Ordiz), Dick Miller (Sgt. Neill), Charles B. Griffith (Pete Shelton), Paul Blaisdell (The Monster).

Black and White; 71 minutes; released July 1956 on double bill with *The She Creature*.

It! The Terror from Beyond Space

Production Vogue Pictures, *Director* Edward L. Cahn, *Producer* Robert E. Kent, *Story and Screenplay* Jerome Bixby, *Photography* Kenneth Peach, *Special Photography* Paul Blaisdell, *Music* Paul Sawtell and Bert Shefter, *Art Direction* William Glasgow, *Editor* Grant Whytock, *Distribution* United Artists.

CAST: Marshall Thompson (Col. Carruthers), Shawn Smith (Ann Anderson), Kim Spalding (Col. Van Heusen), Ann Doran (Mary Royce), Dabbs Greer

(Eric Royce), Paul Langton (Calder), Robert Bice (Purdue), Richard Benedict (Bob Finelli), Richard Hervey (Gino Finelli), Thom Carney (Keinholz), Ray Corrigan (The Monster).
Black and White; 69 minutes; released August 1958 on double bill with *The Curse of the Faceless Man*.

Paul Blaisdell, a former cover artist for science fiction pulp magazines, was responsible for the design and construction of monster costumes for several films, notably the It in this film, the Mutant in Corman's *Day the World Ended*, and the quintessential bug-eyed Martians in Cahn's *Invasion of the Saucer Men*, which is certainly Blaisdell's best effort. In *The Ghost of Dragstrip Hollow* (AIP 1959), an odd mixture of comedy, teenage monsters, and music, the ghost wears an altered design of Blaisdell's She Creature costume from Cahn's *The She Creature* (AIP 1956); at the end of the film, the ghost is revealed to be Blaisdell, "an out of work monster actor." Ray Corrigan is the cowboy actor Ray "Crash" Corrigan.

The Killer Shrews
Production McLendon Radio Pictures, *Director* Ray Kellog, *Producer* Ken Curtis, *Story and Screenplay* Jay Simms, *Photography* Wilfred Cline, *Music* Harry Bluestone and Emil Cadkin, *Art Direction* Louis Caldwell, *Editor* Aaron Stell, *Distribution* McLendon Radio Pictures.
Cast: James Best (Thorne Sherman), Ingrid Goude (Ann Draigis), Baruch Lumet (Dr. Draigis), Ken Curtis (Jerry Farrell), Gordon McLendon (Radford Baines), Alfredo DeSoto (Mario), J. H. Dupree (Rook).
Black and White; 69 minutes; released November 1959 on double bill with *The Giant Gila Monster*.

Killers from Space
Production Planet Filmplays Inc., *Producer-Director* W. Lee Wilder, *Screenplay* Bill Raynor, *Story* Myles Wilder, *Photography* William H. Clothier, *Special Photography* Consolidated Film Industries, *Music* Manuel Compinsky, *Editor* William Farris, *Distribution* RKO-Radio Pictures.
Cast: Peter Graves (Doug Martin), James Seay (Col. Banks), Steve Pendleton (Briggs), Barbara Bestar (Ellen Martin), Frank Gerstle (Dr. Kruger), John Merrick (Deneb-Tala).
Black and White; 71 minutes; released January 1954.

W. Lee Wilder, of whom little is known, is reportedly Billy Wilder's brother.

Kronos
Production Regal Films Inc., *Producer-Director* Kurt Neumann, *Screenplay* Lawrence Louis Goldman, *Story* Irving Block, *Photography* Karl Struss, *Special Photography* Jack Rabin, Irving Block, Louis DeWitt, Meinrad von Mullidorfer, William Reinhold, and Gene Warren, *Music* Paul Sawtell and Bert Shefter, *Art Direction* Theobold Holsopple, *Editor* Jodie Copeland, *Distribution* Twentieth Century-Fox.
Cast: Jeff Morrow (Dr. Leslie Gaskell), Barbara Lawrence (Vera Hunter), John Emery (Dr. Hubbell Eliot), George O'Hanlon (Dr. Arnold Culver), Morris Ankrum (Dr. Albert Stern), John Parish (Gen. Perry), José Gonzalez Gonzalez (Manuel Ramirez).
Black and White in Regalscope; 78 minutes; released April 1957 on double bill with *She Devil*.

The Leech Woman
Production Universal, *Director* Edward Dein, *Producer* Joseph Gershenson, *Screenplay* David Duncan, *Story* Ben Pivar and Francis Rosenwald, *Photography* Ellis W. Carter, *Music* Irving Gertz, *Art Direction* Alexander Golitzen and Robert Clatworthy, *Editor* Milton Carruth, *Distribution* Universal-International.

Cast: Coleen Gray (June Talbot), Philip Terry (Dr. Paul Talbot), Grant Williams (Neil Foster), Gloria Talbott (Sally), John Van Dreelen (Bertram Garvey), Estelle Hemsley (Old Malla), Kim Hamilton (Young Malla), Chester Jones (Ladu), Arthur Batanides (Jerry).

Black and White; 77 minutes; released June 1960 on double bill with *The Brides of Dracula*.

The Little Shop of Horrors

Production Filmgroup, *Producer-Director* Roger Corman, *Story and Screenplay* Charles B. Griffith, *Photography* Archie Dalzell, *Music* Fred Katz, *Art Direction* Daniel Haller, *Editor* Marshall Neilan, Jr., *Distribution* Filmgroup.

Cast: Jonathan Haze (Seymour Krelboing), Jackie Joseph (Audrey), Mel Welles (Mr. Gravis Mushnik), Dick Miller (Detective), Jack Nicholson (Masochist in Dentist's Office).

Black and White; 70 minutes; released August 1960 on double bill with *The Last Woman on Earth*.

The Lost Missile

Production William Berke Productions, *Director* Lester William Berke, *Producer* Lee Gordon, *Screenplay* John McPartland and Jerome Bixby, *Story* Lester William Berke, *Photography* Kenneth Peach, *Special Photography* Jack R. Glass, *Music* Gerald Fried, *Art Direction* William Farrari, *Editor* Ed Sutherland, *Distribution* United Artists.

Cast: Robert Loggia (David Loring), Ellen Parker (Joan Woods), Larry Kerr (Gen. Barr), Philip Pine (Joe Freed), Marilee Earle (Ella Freed), Selmer Jackson (Secretary of State).

Black and White; 70 minutes; released December 1958.

Little has been written about this film, and I have not seen it, but its storyline sounds much like the storyline of an alien invasion film: "All western hemisphere defenses go on the alert as a giant missile from outer space appears, cutting an incinerating path of destruction around the world until blown to bits minutes before it reaches New York" (*Boxoffice Barometer*, February 29, 1960, p. 127).

The Lost Planet

Production Clover Productions, *Director* Spencer G. Bennet, *Producer* Sam Katzman, *Story and Screenplay* George H. Plympton and Arthur Hoerl, *Photography* William Whitley, *Special Photography* Jack Erickson, *Music Director* Mischa Bakaleinikoff, *Editor* Earl Turner, *Distribution* Columbia Pictures.

Cast: Judd Holdren (Rex Barrow), Vivian Mason (Ella Dorn), Ted Thorpe (Tim Johnson), Forrest Taylor (Professor Dorn), Michael Fox (Dr. Grood), Gene Roth (Reckov), Karl Davis (Karlo), Leonard Penn (Ken Wolper), John Cason (Hopper), Pierre Watkin (Ned Hilton).

Black and White; released 1953; a serial in 15 chapters: (1) *Mystery of the Guided Missile*, (2) *Trapped by the Axial Propeller*, (3) *Blasted by the Thermic Disintegrator*, (4) *The Mind Control Machine*, (5) *The Atomic Plane*, (6) *Disaster in the Stratosphere*, (7) *Snared by Prysmic Catapult*, (8) *Astray in Space*, (9) *The Hypnotic Ray Machine*, (10) *To Free the Planet People*, (11) *Dr. Grood Defies Gravity*, (12) *Trapped in a Cosmo Jet*, (13) *The Invisible Enemy*, (14) *In the Grip of the De-Thermo Ray*, (15) *Sentenced to Space*.

The Magnetic Monster

Production A-Men Productions, *Director* Curt Siodmak, *Producer* Ivan Tors, *Story and Screenplay* Curt Siodmak and Ivan Tors, *Photography* Charles Van Enger, *Special Photography* Jack R. Glass, *Music* Blaine Sanford, *Art Direction* George Van Marter, *Editor* Herbert L. Strock, *Distribution* United Artists.

Cast: Richard Carlson (Jeffrey Stewart), King Donovan (Dan Forbes), Jean Byron (Connie Stewart), Harry Ellerbe (Dr. Allard), Leo Britt (Dr. Benton),

Leonard Mudie (Howard Denker), Byron Foulger (Mr. Simon), Michael Fox (Dr. Serney), John Zaremba (Chief Watson).
Black and White; 76 minutes; released February 1953.

This is one, and probably the best, of Ivan Tors's scientifically accurate productions, or at least as accurate as the narrative would allow. Tors was also responsible for two television series "extrapolated from known scientific fact": Ziv's *Science Fiction Theatre* and NBC's *Man and the Challenge*.

The Man from Planet X

Production Mid-Century Films, *Director* Edgar G. Ulmer, *Producers* Jack Pollexfen and Aubrey Wisberg, *Story and Screenplay* Jack Pollexfen and Aubrey Wisberg, *Photography* John L. Russell, *Special Photography* Jack Rabin, Andy Anderson, and Howard Weeks, *Music* Charles Roff, *Art Direction* Angelo Scibetti, *Editor* Fred R. Feitshans, Jr., *Distribution* United Artists.

CAST: Robert Clarke (John Lawrence), Margaret Field [later Maggie Mahoney] (Enid Elliott), William Schallert (Dr. Mears), Raymond Bond (Professor Elliott), Roy Engel (Constable), Charles Davis (Geordie), David Ormont (Inspector Porter), Gilbert Fallman (Doctor Blaine).
Black and White; 70 minutes; released April 1951.

The Man Who Could Cheat Death

Production Hammer Films, *Director* Terence Fisher, *Producer* Anthony Hinds, *Screenplay* Jimmy Sangster, *Story* [play] Barré Lyndon, *Photography* Jack Asher, *Music* Richard Rodney Bennett, *Art Direction* Bernard Robinson, *Editor* James Needs, *Distribution* Paramount Pictures.

CAST: Anton Diffring (Dr. Georges Bonner), Hazel Court (Janine), Christopher Lee (Pierre), Arnold Marle (Ludwig), Delphi Lawrence (Margo), Francis DeWolff (Legris).
Color by Technicolor; 83 minutes; released June 1959; some sources say the film was released on a double bill with *Tarzan's Greatest Adventure*.

The Man Who Turned to Stone

Production Clover Productions, *Director* Leslie Kardos, *Producer* Sam Katzman, *Story and Screenplay* Raymond T. Marcus, *Photography* Benjamin H. Kline, *Music Conductor* Mischa Bakaleinikoff, *Art Direction* Paul Palmentola, *Editor* Charles Nelson, *Distribution* Columbia Pictures.

CAST: Victor Jory (Dr. Murdock), Charlotte Austin (Carol Adams), William [later John] Hudson (Dr. Jess Rogers), Frederick Ledebur (Eric), Jean Willes (Tracy), Ann Doran (Mrs. Ford), Paul Cavanagh (Cooper).
Black and White; 71 minutes; released March 1957 on double bill with *Zombies of Mora Tau*.

Screenwriter Raymond T. Marcus was a pseudonym, or "front" in this case, for blacklisted writer Bernard Gordon. He also used the name John T. Williams. The name Marcus is also credited to Katzman's horror film *Zombies of Mora Tau* and the alien invasion film *Earth vs. the Flying Saucers*.

Missile Monsters

Feature version of the serial *Flying Disc Man from Mars* (q.v.), released May 1958 on double bill with *Satan's Satellites*.

The Monolith Monsters

Production Universal, *Director* John Sherwood, *Producer* Howard Christie, *Screenplay* Norman Jolley and Robert M. Fresco, *Story* Jack Arnold and Robert M. Fresco, *Photography* Ellis W. Carter, *Special Photography* Clifford Stine, *Music Supervision* Joseph Gershenson, *Art Direction* Alexander Golitzen and Robert E. Smith, *Editor* Patrick McCormack, *Distribution* Universal-International.

CAST: Grant Williams (Dave Miller), Lola Albright (Cathy Barrett), Les Tre-

mayne (Martin Cochrane), Trevor Bardette (Prof. Arthur Flanders), Phil Harvey (Ben Gilbert), Steve Darrell (Joe Higgins).
Black and White; 77 minutes; released December 1957.

Monster from Green Hell
Production Gross/Krasne, *Director* Kenneth G. Crane, *Producer* Al Zimbalist, *Story and Screenplay* Louis Vittes and Endre Bohem, *Photography* Ray Flin, *Special Photography* Jess Davison, Jack Rabin, and Louis DeWitt, *Music* Albert Glasser, *Art Direction* Ernst Fegté, *Editor* Kenneth G. Crane, *Distribution* Distributors Corporation of America (DCA).
Cast: Jim Davis (Quentin Brady), Robert E. Griffin (Dan Morgan), Barbara Turner (Lorna), Eduardo Ciannelli (Mahri), Vladamir Sokoloff (Dr. Lorentz), Joel Fluellen (Arobi).
Black and White with final sequence in Color; 71 minutes; released July 1958 on double bill with *Half-Human.*

Monster from the Ocean Floor
Production Palo Alto Productions, *Director* Wyatt Ordung, *Producer* Roger Corman, *Story and Screenplay* William Danch, *Photography* Floyd Crosby, *Special Photography* Bob Baker, *Music* Andre Brumer, *Art Direction* Ben Hayne, *Editor* Ed Sampson, *Distribution* Lippert Pictures.
Cast: Stuart Wade (Steve Dunning), Dick Pinner (Dr. Baldwin), Anne Kimball (Julie Blair), Wyatt Ordung (Pablo), Inez Palange (Tula).
Black and White; 65 minutes; released May 1954.

Monster of Piedras Blancas
Production Vanwick Productions, *Director* Irwin Berwick, *Producer* Jack Kevan, *Story and Screenplay* Haile Chace, *Photography* Philip Lathrop, *Editor* George Gittens, *Distribution* Filmservice Corporation; no other credits available.
Cast: Jeanne Carmen (The Girl), Don Sullivan (The Biologist), Les Tremayne (The Doctor), John Harmon (The Lighthouse Keeper), Frank Arvidson (The Storekeeper), Wayne Berwick (Little Jimmy), Pete Dunn (Eddie), Joseph LaCava (Mike).
Black and White; 71 minutes; released June 1959 on double bill with *Okefenokee.*

Monster on the Campus
Production Universal, *Director* Jack Arnold, *Producer* Joseph Gershenson, *Story and Screenplay* David Duncan, *Photography* Russell Metty, *Special Photography* Clifford Stine, *Music Supervision* Joseph Gershenson, *Art Direction* Alexander Golitzen, *Editor* Ted J. Kent, *Distribution* Universal-International.
Cast: Arthur Franz (Prof. Donald Blake), Joanna Moore (Madeline Howard), Troy Donahue (Jimmy Flanders), Judson Pratt (Mike Stevens), Whit Bissell (Dr. Cole), Helen Westcott (Molly Riordan), Nancy Walters (Sylvia Lockwood), Phil Harvey (Sgt. Powell), Ross Elliott (Eddie Daniels), Hank Patterson (Mr. Townsend).
Black and White; 76 minutes; released October 1958 on double bill with *Blood of the Vampire.*

The Monster That Challenged the World
Production Gramercy Pictures, *Director* Arnold Laven, *Producers* Jules V. Levy and Arthur Gardner, *Screenplay* Pat Fielder, *Story* David Duncan, *Photography* Lester White, *Special Photography* Augie Lohman, *Music* Heinz Roemheld, *Art Direction* James Vance, *Editor* John Faure, *Distribution* United Artists.
Cast: Tim Holt (Lt. Commander John Twillinger), Audrey Dalton (Gail McKenzie), Hans Conried (Dr. Jess Rogers), Harlan Warde (Lt. Bob Clemens), Casey Adams [later Max Showalter] (Tad Johns), Mimi Gibson

(Sandy McKenzie), Gordon Jones (Josh Peters), Ralph Moody (Gatekeeper). Black and White; 83 minutes; released June 1957 on double bill with *The Vampire.*

The Mysterians (Japanese: *Chikyu Boeigun*)
Production Toho Company Ltd., *Director* Inoshiro Honda, *Producer* Tomoyuki Tanaka, *Screenplay* S. Kayama and Takeshi Kimura, *Story* Jojio Okami, *Photography* Hajime Koizuma, *Special Photography* Eiji Tsuburaya, *Music* Akira Ifukube, *Art Direction* Teruaki Abe, *Editor* Hiochi Iwashita, *English Version* Peter Rietof, Carlos Montalban, Jay Bonafield, *Distribution* Metro-Goldwyn-Mayer.
CAST: Kenji Sahara (Joji Atumi), Yumi Shirakawa (Etsuko Shiraishi), Momoko Kochi (Hiroko), Akihiko Hirata (Ryoichi Shiraishi), Takashi Shirmura (Dr. Adachi).
Filmed in Eastman Color and Tohoscope; 89 minutes; released in USA June 1959; originally scheduled for release by RKO-Radio Pictures.

The Neanderthal Man
Production Global Productions, *Director* E. A. Dupont, *Producers* Jack Pollexfen and Aubrey Wisberg, *Story and Screenplay* Jack Pollexfen and Aubrey Wisberg, *Photography* Stanley Cortez, *Special Photography* Jack Rabin and Irving Block, *Music* Albert Glasser, *Art Direction* Walter Koestler, *Editor* Fred Feitshans, Jr., *Distribution* United Artists.
CAST: Robert Shayne (Professor Groves), Richard Crane (Dr. Ross Harkness), Doris Merrick (Ruth Marshall), Joyce Terry (Jan), Robert Long (Jim Oakes), Dick Rich (Sheriff Andrews), Jean Quinn (Celia).
Black and White; 77 minutes; released June 1953.
    E. A. Dupont also directed *Variety* (1926). The evocative light and shadow style associated with Dupont is evident in *The Neanderthal Man* but diluted to a point of insignificance.

Night of the Blood Beast
Production Balboa Productions, *Director* Bernard Kowalski, *Producer* Gene Corman, *Screenplay* Martin Varno, *Story* Gene Corman, *Photography* John M. Nicholaus, Jr., *Special Photography* Unavailable, *Music* Alexander Laszlo, *Art Direction* Daniel Haller, *Editor* Dick Currier, *Distribution* American International Pictures.
CAST: Michael Emmet (Major John Corcoran), Angela Greene (Dr. Julie Benson), John Baer (Steve Dunlap), Ed Nelson (Dave Randall), Tyler McVey (Dr. Alex Wyman), Georgiana Carter (Donna Bixby), Ross Sturlin (The Beast).
Black and White; 65 minutes; released November 1958 on double bill with *She Gods of Shark Reef.*

Not of This Earth
Production Los Altos Productions, *Producer-Director* Roger Corman, *Story and Screenplay* Charles B. Griffith and Mark Hanna, *Photography* John Mescall, *Special Photography* Paul Blaisdell, *Music* Ronald Stein, *Art Direction* No credits, *Editor* Charles Goss, *Distribution* Allied Artists Pictures Corporation.
CAST: Paul Birch (Paul Johnson), Beverly Garland (Nadine Storey), Morgan Jones (Harry Sherbourne), Jonathan Haze (Jeremy Perrin), Dick Miller (Joe Piper), William Roerick (Dr. Frederick Rochelle).
Black and White; 67 minutes; released March 1957 on double bill with *Attack of the Crab Monsters.*

Outer Space Visitor
Production Terrytoons, *Director* Dave Tendlar, *Producer* Paul Terry, *Distribution* Twentieth Century-Fox; no other credits available.

Color by DeLuxe in CinemaScope; 7 minutes; A Mighty Mouse Terrytoons Cartoon; released November 1959.

Panther Girl of the Kongo

Production Republic Pictures, *Producer-Director* Franklin Adreon, *Story and Screenplay* Ronald Davidson, *Photography* Bud Thackery, *Special Photography* Howard and Theodore Lydecker, *Music* R. Dale Butts, *Art Direction* Frank Hotaling, *Editor* Cliff Bell, *Distribution* Republic Pictures.

CAST: Phyllis Coates (Jean Evans), Myron Healey (Larry Sanders), Arthur Space (Morgan), John Daheim (Cass), Mike Ragan (Rand), Morris Buchanan (Tembu), Roy Glenn (Danka), Archie Savage (Ituri), Ramsay Hill (Stanton).

Black and White; released 1954; a serial in 12 chapters: (1) *The Claw Monster*, (2) *Jungle Ambush*, (3) *The Killer Beast*, (4) *Sands of Doom*, (5) *Test of Terror*, (6) *High Peril*, (7) *Timber Trap*, (8) *Crater of Flame*, (9) *River of Death*, (10) *Blasted Evidence*, (11) *Double Danger*, (12) *House of Doom*.

The Perfect Woman (British)

Production Two Cities Productions, *Director* Bernard Knowles, *Producers* George and Alfred Black, *Screenplay* George Black and Bernard Knowles, *Story* [play] Wallace Geoffrey and Basil John Mitchell, *Photography* Jack Hildyard, *Music* Arthur Wilkinson, *Art Direction* J. Elder Wills, *Editor* Peter Graham-Scott, *Distribution* Eagle-Lion Films.

CAST: Patricia Roc (Penelope), Nigel Patrick (Roger), Miles Malleson (Professor Belmond), Stanley Holloway (Ramshead), Irene Handl (Mrs. Butler), Pamela Devis (Olga, the Robotix).

Black and White; 89 minutes; released in USA April 1950.

Phantom from Space

Production Planet Filmplays Inc., *Producer-Director* W. Lee Wilder, *Screenplay* Bill Raynor and Myles Wilder, *Story* Myles Wilder, *Photography* William H. Clothier, *Special Photography* Alex Weldon and Howard A. Anderson, *Music* William Lava, *Editor* George Gale, *Distribution* United Artists.

CAST: Ted Cooper (Lt. Hazen), Rudolph Anders (Dr. Wyatt), Noreen Nash (Barbara), James Seay (Major Andrews), Dick Sands (The Phantom).

Black and White; 72 minutes; released May 1953.

The Phantom from 10,000 Leagues

Production Milner Brothers, *Director* Dan Milner, *Producers* Jack Milner and Dan Milner, *Screenplay* Lou Rusoff, *Story* Dorys Lukather, *Photography* Brydon Baker, *Special Photography* Jack Milner, *Music* Ronald Stein, *Art Direction* Earl Harper, *Editors* Dan Milner and Jack Milner, *Distribution* American Releasing Corporation [later American International Pictures].

CAST: Kent Taylor (Dr. Ted Stevens), Cathy Downs (Lois King), Michael Walen (Professor King), Philip Pine (George Thomas), Vivi Janiss (Ethel Hall).

Black and White; 81 minutes; released January 1956 on double bill with *The Day the World Ended*.

Plan 9 from Outer Space

Production J. Edward Reynolds, *Producer-Director* Edward D. Wood, Jr., *Story and Screenplay* Edward D. Wood, Jr., *Photography* William C. Thompson, *Special Photography* Charles Duncan, *Music* Gordon Zahler, *Art Direction* Harry Reif, *Editor* Edward D. Wood, Jr., *Distribution* Distributors Corporation of America (DCA).

CAST: Bela Lugosi (The Ghoul Man), Vampira (The Ghoul Woman), Lyle Talbot (Gen. Roberts), Gregory Walcott (Jeff Trent), Mona McKinnon (Paula Trent), Duke Moore (Lt. Harper), Tor Johnson (Inspector Clay), Tom Keene (Col. Edwards), Dudley Manlove (Eros), John Breckinridge (The Ruler), Joanne Lee (Tanna).

Black and White; 79 minutes; released July 1958.

So much time and effort have been spent by the "worst movie" cultists berating this film that one wonders if it doesn't have some kind of merit. Improvised airplane cockpits, cardboard tombstones, and embarrassing histrionics are only a portion of its crudity, but the film nonetheless is not as bad as the "trash collectors" contend. It is extremely low budget; but many good films have been produced on microcosmic budgets. It is actually no worse than many other inexpensive films, including some of Roger Corman's "quickies." Its narrative is adept, but its form is crude. Its content is typical of the extraterrestrial invasion myth, its theme similar to *It Came from Outer Space*. But its formal qualities are so far removed from usual production standards (even for its time) that these formal shortcomings make the film an easy target. At another level, we can accept the film's ridiculousness as its own estrangement from our ego-inflated world and let it take us to the visionary world of dreams.

Port Sinister

Production American Pictures, *Director* Harold Daniels, *Producers* Jack Pollexfen and Aubrey Wisberg, *Story and Screenplay* Jack Pollexfen and Aubrey Wisberg, *Photography* William Bradford, *Special Photography* Jack Rabin and Rocky Bradford, *Music* Albert Glasser, *Art Direction* Theobold Holsopple, *Editor* Fred R. Feitshans, Jr., *Distribution* RKO-Radio Pictures.

CAST: James Warren (Tony Ferris), Lynne Roberts (Jean Hunter), Paul Cavanagh (John Kolvac), William Schallert (Collins), House Peters, Jr. (Jim Gerry), Anne Kimball (Nurse), Robert Bice (Burt), Ken Terrell (Hollis).

Black and White; 65 minutes; released April 1953; reissued in 1957 as *Beast of Paradise Island*.

Another film I have not seen (prints seem to be nonexistent) but include here because of narrative descriptions by various sources.

Radar Men from the Moon

Production Republic Pictures, *Director* Fred C. Brannon, *Producer* Franklin Adreon [listed in credits as "Associate Producer"], *Story and Screenplay* Ronald Davidson, *Photography* John MacBurnie, *Special Photography* Howard and Theodore Lydecker, *Music* Stanley Wilson, *Art Direction* Fred Ritter, *Editor* Cliff Bell, *Distribution* Republic Pictures.

CAST: George Wallace (Commando Cody), Aline Towne (Joan Gilbert), Roy Barcroft (Retik), William Bakewell (Ted Richards), Clayton Moore (Graber), Peter Brocco (Krog), Bob Stevenson (Daly), Don Walters (Henderson), Tom Steele (Zerg), Dale Van Sickel (Alon), Wilson Wood (Hank).

Black and White; released 1951; a serial in 12 chapters: (1) *Moon Rocket*, (2) *Molten Terror*, (3) *Bridge of Death*, (4) *Flight to Destruction*, (5) *Murder Car*, (6) *Hills of Death*, (7) *Human Targets*, (8) *The Enemy Planet*, (9) *Battle in the Stratosphere*, (10) *Mass Execution*, (11) *Planned Pursuit*, (12) *Death of the Moon Man*.

This serial opened each chapter with the credit line: "Republic Pictures introduces a new character, Commando Cody." It is the predecessor to *Commando Cody, Sky Marshal of the Universe* (q.v.).

The Return of the Fly

Production Associated Producers, *Director* Edward L. Bernds, *Producer* Bernard Glasser, *Story and Screenplay* Edward L. Bernds, *Photography* Brydon Baker, *Music* Paul Sawtell and Bert Shefter, *Art Direction* Lyle R. Wheeler and John Mansbridge, *Editor* Richard C. Meyer, *Distribution* Twentieth Century-Fox.

CAST: Vincent Price (Francois Delambre), Brett Halsey (Philippe Delambre), David Frankham (Alan Hinds), John Sutton (Inspector Beauchamp), Dan Seymour (Max Berthold), Danielle DeMetz (Cecile Bonnard).

Black and White in CinemaScope; 78 minutes; released August 1959 on double bill with *The Alligator People*.

The Revenge of Frankenstein
Production Hammer Films, *Director* Terence Fisher, *Producer* Anthony Hinds, *Story and Screenplay* Jimmy Sangster, *Photography* Jack Asher, *Music* Leonard Salzedo, *Art Direction* Bernard Robinson, *Editor* James Needs, *Distribution* Columbia Pictures.

CAST: Peter Cushing (Baron Frankenstein), Francis Matthews (Dr. Hans Kleve), Eunice Gayson (Margaret), Lionel Jeffries (Fritz), Michael Gwynn (Karl), John Welsh (Bergman), Oscar Quitak (Dwarf), Richard Wordsworth (Patient).

Color by Technicolor; 91 minutes; released July 1958 on double bill with *The Curse of the Demon*.

Revenge of the Creature
Production Universal, *Director* Jack Arnold, *Producer* William Alland, *Screenplay* Martin Berkeley, *Story* William Alland, *Photography* Charles S. Welbourne, *Special Photography* Clifford Stine, *Music Supervision* Joseph Gershenson, *Art Direction* Alexander Golitzen and Alfred Sweeney, *Editor* Paul Weatherwax, *Distribution* Universal-International.

CAST: John Agar (Prof. Clete Ferguson), Lori Nelson (Helen Dobson), John Bromfield (Joe Hayes), Nestor Paiva (Lucas), Grandon Rhodes (Jackson Foster), Dave Willock (Lou Gibson), Robert B. Williams (George Johnson), Charles Cane (Police Captain), Clint Eastwood (Jennings), Brett Halsey (Pete).

Black and White in 3-Dimension; 82 minutes; released May 1955.

Robot Monster
Production Three-Dimensional Pictures, *Producer-Director* Phil Tucker, *Story and Screenplay* Wyatt Ordung, *Photography* Jack Greenhalgh, *Special Photography* Jack Rabin and David Commons, *Music* Elmer Bernstein, *Editor* Bruce Schoengarth, *Distribution* Astor Pictures.

CAST: George Nader (Roy), Claudia Barrett (Alice), John Mylong (The Professor), George Barrows (Ro-Man), Gregory Moffett (Johnny).

Black and White in 3-Dimension; 62 minutes; released June 1953.

Robot Rabbit
Production Warner Brothers, *Director* Friz Freleng, *Producer* Leon Schlesinger, *Distribution* Warner Brothers. No other credits available.

Color by Technicolor; 7 minutes; a Bugs Bunny Cartoon; released December 1953.

The Rocket Man
Production Panoramic Productions, *Director* Oscar Rudolph, *Producer* Leonard Goldstein, *Screenplay* Lenny Bruce and Jack Henley, *Story* George W. George and George F. Slavin, *Photography* John F. Seitz, *Music* Lionel Newman, *Art Direction* George Patrick, *Editor* Paul Weatherwax, *Distribution* Twentieth Century-Fox.

CAST: George Winslow (Timmy), Anne Francis (June Brown), John Agar (Tom Baxter), Spring Byington (Justice Amelia Brown), Charles Coburn (Mayor Johnson), Stanley Clements (Bob), Emory Parnell (Big Bill Watkins).

Color by DeLuxe; 79 minutes; released April 1954.

Rodan, the Flying Monster (Japanese: *Radon*)
Production Toho Company Ltd., *Director* Inoshiro Honda, *Producer* Tomoyuki Tanaka, *Screenplay* Takishi Kimura and Takeo Murata, *Story* Takashi Kuronuma, *Photography* Isamu Ashida, *Special Photography* Eiji Tsuburaya, *Music* Tadashi Yamauchi, *Art Direction* Tatsuo Kita, *Editor* Robert S. Eisen, *English*

Dialogue David Duncan, *Distribution* King Brothers through Distributors Corporation of America (DCA).
CAST: Kenji Sahara (Shigeru), Yumi Shirakawa (Kyo), Akihiko Hirata (Dr. Kashiwagi), Akio Kobori (Nashimura).
Filmed in Eastman Color; 79 minutes; released in USA August 1957.

Satan's Satellites
Feature version of serial *Zombies of the Stratosphere* (q.v.), released May 1958 on double bill with *Missile Monsters*.

Sex Kittens Go to College (Television release title: *Beauty and the Robot*)
Production Photoplay Associates, *Producer-Director* Albert Zugsmith, *Screenplay* Robert Hill, *Story* Albert Zugsmith, *Photography* Ellis W. Carter, *Special Photography* Augie Lohman, *Music* Dean Elliott, *Art Direction* David Milton, *Editor* William Austin, *Distribution* Allied Artists Pictures Corporation.
CAST: Mamie Van Doren (Dr. Mathilda West), Tuesday Weld (Jody), Mijanou Bardot (Suzanne), Mickey Shaughnessy (Boomie), Louis Nye (Dr. Zorch), Pamela Mason (Dr. Myrtle Carter), Martin Milner (George Barton), Conway Twitty (Himself), Jackie Coogan (Wildcat MacPherson), John Carradine (Professor Watts), Vampira (Etta Toodie), Norman Grabowski (Woo Woo).
Black and White; 93 minutes; released August 1960.

She Demons
Production Screencraft Enterprises, *Director* Richard E. Cunha, *Producer* Arthur A. Jacobs, *Story and Screenplay* Richard Cunha and H. E. Barrie, *Photography* Meredith M. Nicholson, *Special Photography* David Koehler, *Music* Nicholas Carras, *Art Direction* Harold Banks, *Editor* William Shea, *Distribution* Astor Pictures.
CAST: Irish McCalla (Jerrie Turner), Tod Griffin (Fred Maklin), Victor Sen Yung (Sammy Ching), Rudolph Anders (Herr Osler), Gene Roth (Egore), Leni Tana (Mona), Charlie Opuni (Kris Kamara).
Black and White; 77 minutes; released March 1958 on double bill with *Giant from the Unknown*.

She Devil
Production Regal Films Inc., *Producer-Director* Kurt Neumann, *Story and Screenplay* Carroll Young and Kurt Neumann, *Photography* Karl Struss, *Music* Paul Sawtell and Bert Shefter, *Art Direction* Theobold Holsopple, *Editor* Carl Pierson, *Distribution* Twentieth Century-Fox.
CAST: Mari Blanchard (Kyra Zelas), Jack Kelly (Dr. Daniel Scott), Albert Dekker (Dr. Bach), John Archer (Kendall), Fay Baker (Mrs. Kendall), Blossom Rock (Hannah), Paul Cavanagh (Sugar Daddy).
Black and White in Regalscope; 77 minutes; released April 1957 on double bill with *Kronos*.

The Snow Creature
Production Planet Filmplays Inc., *Producer-Director* W. Lee Wilder, *Story and Screenplay* Myles Wilder, *Photography* Floyd Crosby, *Special Photography* Lee Zavitz, *Music* Manuel Compinsky, *Editor* Jodie Copeland, *Distribution* United Artists.
CAST: Paul Langton (Frank Parish), Leslie Denison (Peter Wells), Teru Shimada (Subra), Darlene Fields (Joyce Parish), Robert Bice (Fleet), Rudolph Anders (Dr. Dupont), Bill Phipps (Lt. Dunbar), Jack Daley (Edwards), Rollin Moriyama (Leva), Robert Kino (Inspector Karma).
Black and White; 71 minutes; released November 1954.

Son of Dr. Jekyll
Production Columbia Pictures, *Director* Seymour Friedman, *Producer* No credits, *Screenplay* No credits, *Story* Mortimer Braus and Jack Pollexfen, *Photogra-*

phy Henry Freulich, *Music* Paul Sawtell, *Art Direction* Walter Holscher, *Editor* Gene Havlick, *Distribution* Columbia Pictures.

CAST: Louis Hayward (Edward Jekyll), Jody Lawrence (Lynn), Alexander Knox (Curtis Lanyon), Lester Matthews (John Utterson), Gavin Muir (Richard Daniels), Paul Cavanagh (Inspector Stoddard), Rhys Williams (Michaels).

Black and White; 78 minutes; released November 1951.

On the prints I have seen only the story is given credit. Many sources claim that the screenplay was written by Edward Huebsch, who was blacklisted after refusing to testify before the House Un-American Activities Committee. I have found nothing to substantiate this. The lack of a producer's credit is also a mystery.

The Space Children

Production William Alland Productions, *Director* Jack Arnold, *Producer* William Alland, *Screenplay* Bernard C. Schoenfeld, *Story* Tom Filer, *Photography* Ernest Laszlo, *Special Photography* John P. Fulton, *Music* Van Cleave, *Art Direction* Hal Pereira and Roland Anderson, *Editor* Terry Morse, *Distribution* Paramount Pictures.

CAST: Adam Williams (Dave Brewster), Peggy Webber (Ann Brewster), Michel Ray (Burt Brewster), John Crawford (Ken Brewster), Jackie Coogan (Hank Johnson), Sandy Descher (Edie Johnson), Richard Shannon (Lt. Col. Manley), John Washbrook (Tim Gamble), Russell Johnson (Joe Gamble), Raymond Bailey (Dr. Wahrman).

Black and White; 69 minutes; released June 1958 on double bill with *The Colossus of New York.*

Space Master X-7

Production Regal Films Inc., *Director* Edward Bernds, *Producer* Bernard Glasser, *Story and Screenplay* George Worthing Yates and Daniel Mainwaring, *Photography* Brydon Baker, *Special Photography* Unavailable, *Music* Josef Zimanich, *Art Direction* Edward Shiells, *Editor* John F. Link, *Distribution* Twentieth Century-Fox.

CAST: Bill Williams (John Hand), Lyn Thomas (Laura Greeling), Robert Ellis (Joe Rattigan), Paul Frees (Dr. Charles Pommer), Joan Barry (Miss Meyers), Thomas B. Henry (Professor West), Fred Sherman (Morse), Jesse Kirkpatrick (Captain), Moe Howard (Cab Driver).

Black and White in Regalscope; 71 minutes; released June 1958 as lower half of double bill with *The Fly.*

The Spider

Advertised title for *Earth vs. the Spider* (q.v.).

Superman and the Mole Men

Production National Periodicals through Robert J. Maxwell and Bernard Luber, *Director* Lee Sholem, *Producer* Barney A. Sarecky, *Story and Screenplay* Richard Fielding, *Photography* Clark Ramsey, *Special Photography* Ray Mercer, *Music* Darrell Calker, *Art Direction* Ernst Fegté, *Editor* Al Joseph, *Distribution* Lippert Pictures.

CAST: George Reeves (Clark Kent/Superman), Phyllis Coates (Lois Lane), Jeff Corey (Luke Benson), Walter Reed (Bill Corrigan), J. Farrell MacDonald (Pop Sherman), Stanley Andrews (The Sheriff).

Black and White; 67 minutes; released November 1951.

Tarantula

Production Universal, *Director* Jack Arnold, *Producer* William Alland, *Screenplay* Martin Berkeley and Robert M. Fresco, *Story* Jack Arnold and Robert M. Fresco, *Photography* George Robinson, *Special Photography* Clifford Stine,

Music Supervision Joseph Gershenson, *Art Direction* Alexander Golitzen and Alfred Sweeney, *Editor* William Morgan, *Distribution* Universal-International.

CAST: John Agar (Dr. Matt Hastings), Mara Corday (Stephanie "Steve" Clayton), Leo G. Carroll (Prof. Gerald Deemer), Nestor Paiva (Sheriff Jack Andrews), Ross Elliott (Joe Burch), Ed Rand (Lt. John Nolan), Raymond Bailey (Prof. Townsend), Hank Patterson (Josh), Steve Darrell (Andy Anderson), Bert Holland (Barney Russell), Clint Eastwood (First Pilot).

Black and White; 80 minutes; released December 1955.

Target Earth

Production Abtcon Pictures, *Director* Sherman A. Rose, *Producer* Herman Cohen, *Screenplay* William Raynor, *Story* [novel] Paul W. Fairman, *Photography* Guy Roe, *Special Photography* Dave Koehler, *Music* Paul Dunlap, *Art Direction* James Sullivan, *Editor* Sherman A. Rose, *Distribution* Allied Artists Pictures Corporation.

CAST: Richard Denning (Frank Brooks), Kathleen Crowley (Nora King), Richard Reeves (Jim Wilson), Virginia Grey (Vicki Harris), Robert Roark (Davis), Whit Bissell (The Scientist), Arthur Space (The General).

Black and White; 75 minutes; released November 1954.

Teenage Monster

Production Marquette Productions, *Producer-Director* Jacques Marquette, *Story and Screenplay* Ray Buffum, *Photography* Taylor Byers, *Special Photography* Unavailable, *Music* Walter Greene, *Art Direction* No credits, *Editor* Irving Schoenberg, *Distribution* Howco International Pictures.

CAST: Anne Gwynne (Ruth Cannon), Gloria Castillo (Kathy North), Stuart Wade (Sheriff Bob), Gilbert Perkins (Charles Cannon), Stephen Parker (Charles Cannon as Boy), Charles Courtney (Marv Howell), Norman Leavitt (Deputy Ed), Jim McCullough (Jim Cannon), Gaybe Mooradian (Fred Fox), Arthur Berkeley (Man with Burro), Frank Davis (Man on Street).

Black and White; 65 minutes; released December 1957 on double bill with *The Brain from Planet Arous.*

The title is deceptive, since Gilbert Perkins, the monster, is no teenager. Many sources say the original title was *Meteor Monster* (its TV title) but it was altered to *Teenage Monster* to capitalize on the popular teenage films (*Rebel without a Cause, I was a Teenage Werewolf, Diary of a High School Bride,* etc.) of the late fifties.

Teenagers from Outer Space

Production Topor Corporation, *Produced, Directed, Written, Photographed and Edited by* Tom Graeff; *also Special Photography and Music by* Mr. Graeff, *Distribution* Warner Brothers.

CAST: David Love [also Mr. Graeff] (Derek), Dawn Anderson (Betty Morgan), Harvey B. Dunn (Grandpa Morgan), Bryan Grant (Thor), Tom Lockyear (Joe Rogers), King Moody (Captain), Helen Sage (Miss Morse), Frederic Welch (Dr. Brandt), Sonia Torgesson (Swimmer).

Black and White; 85 minutes; released June 1959 on double bill with *Gigantis, the Fire Monster.*

Termites from Mars

Production Walter Lantz Productions, *Director* Paul J. Smith, *Producer* Walter Lantz, *Distribution* Universal-International, no other credits available.

Color by Technicolor; 7 minutes; a Woody Woodpecker cartoon; released December 1952.

Terror from the Year 5000

Production La Jolla Productions, *Producer-Director* Robert J. Gurney, *Story and Screenplay* Robert J. Gurney, *Photography* Arthur Florman, *Special Pho-*

tography Unavailable, *Music* Unavailable, *Art Direction* Beatrice Gurney and
William Hoffman, *Editor* Dede Allen, *Distribution* James H. Nicholson and
Samuel Z. Arkoff through American International Pictures.

CAST: Ward Costello (Robert Hedges), Joyce Holden (Claire Erling), John
Stratton (Victor), Frederick Downs (Prof. Howard Erling), Fred Herrick
(Angelo), Salome Jens (The Woman from A.D. 5000).

Black and White; 74 minutes; released October 1958 on double bill with *The
Screaming Skull*.

This seldom seen film offers a variation on the alien invasion theme by
having the invader come to earth from the future.

Terror Is a Man

Production Lynn-Romero Productions, *Director* Gerry de Leon, *Producers* Ken
Lynn and Eddie Romero, *Story and Screenplay* Harry Paul Harber, *Photography* Emmanual I. Rojos, *Special Photography* Unavailable, *Music* Ariston Au-
erlino, *Art Direction* Vincente Bonus, *Editor* Gerry de Leon, *Distribution* Val-
iant Films (formerly Distributors Corporation of America).

CAST: Francis Lederer (Dr. Girard), Greta Thyssen (Frances Girard), Richard
Derr (Fitzgerald), Oscar Keesee (Walter).

Black and White; 89 minutes; released December 1959.

Them!

Production Warner Brothers, *Director* Gordon Douglas, *Producer* David Weis-
bart, *Screenplay* Ted Sherdeman, *Story* George Worthing Yates, *Photography*
Sid Hickox, *Special Photography* Ralph Ayers, *Music* Bronislau Kaper, *Art
Direction* Stanley Fleisher, *Editor* Thomas Reilly, *Distribution* Warner Brothers.

CAST: James Whitmore (Sgt. Ben Petersen), James Arness (Robert Graham),
Edmund Gwenn (Prof. Harold Medford), Joan Weldon (Dr. Patricia Med-
ford), Onslow Stevens (Gen. O'Brien), Sean McClory (Major Kibbee), Sandy
Descher (Little Girl).

Black and White with Color titles; 93 minutes; released June 1954.

Bill Warren claims in *Keep Watching the Skies* that the titles were filmed
in color. As far as I can tell he is the only one to declare this. I support his
claim because as a youthful movie-brat attending the Majestic theatre in
Dallas, Oregon, I distinctly recall seeing the word "Them!" in bright red
against the desert background. Every screening I've seen since, however, has
used black and white titles.

The Thing from Another World

Production Winchester Pictures, *Director* Christian Nyby, *Producer* Howard
Hawks, *Screenplay* Charles Lederer, *Story* [novella: "Who Goes There?"] Don
A. Stuart, *Photography* Russell Harlan, *Special Photography* Linwood Dunn
and Donald Stewart, *Music* Dimitri Tiomkin, *Art Direction* Albert S. D'Agosti-
no and John J. Hughes, *Editor* Roland Cross, *Distribution* RKO-Radio Pictures.

CAST: Kenneth Tobey (Capt. Patrick Hendry), Margaret Sheridan (Nikki
Nicholson), Robert Cornthwaite (Professor Carrington), Douglas Spencer
(Ned "Scotty" Scott), Dewey Martin (Bob), Robert Nichols (Lt. Ken "Mac"
MacPherson), William Self (Sgt. Barnes), John Dierkes (Dr. Chapman),
Eduard Franz (Dr. Stern), Paul Frees (Dr. Voorhees), George Fenneman (Dr.
Redding), Norbert Schiller (Dr. Laurenz), James Arness (The Thing).

Black and White; 86 minutes; released April 1951; reissued by RKO June
1954.

The Thirty Foot Bride of Candy Rock

Production D. R. B. Productions, *Director* Sidney Miller, *Producer* Lewis J.
Rachmil, *Screenplay* Rowland Barber and Arthur Ross, *Story* Lawrence L.

Goldman, Jack Rabin and Irving Block, *Photography* Frank G. Carson, *Special Photography* Jack Rabin, Irving Block, and Louis DeWitt, *Music* Raoul Kraushaar, *Art Direction* William Flannery, *Editor* Al Clark, *Distribution* Columbia Pictures.

CAST: Lou Costello (Artie Pinsetter), Dorothy Provine (Emmy Lou Raven), Gale Gordon (Raven Rossiter), Jimmy Conlin (Magruder), Charles Lane (Stanford Bates), Robert Burton (First General), Will Wright (Pentagon General), Lenny Kent (Sergeant), Ruth Perrott (Aunt May), Peter Leeds (Bill Burton), Robert Nichols (Bank Manager), Veola Vonn (Jackie Delaney), Jack Straw (Pilot).

Black and White; posters advertise "Amazoscope"; 75 minutes; released August 1959.

This Island Earth
Production Universal, *Director* Joseph Newman, *Producer* William Alland, *Screenplay* Franklin Coen and Edward G. O'Callaghan, *Story* [novel] Raymond F. Jones, *Photography* Clifford Stine, *Special Photography* Clifford Stine, David S. Horsley, and Roswell A. Hoffman, *Music Supervision* Joseph Gershenson, *Art Direction* Alexander Golitzen and Richard H. Riedel, *Editor* Virgil Vogel, *Distribution* Universal-International.

CAST: Jeff Morrow (Exeter), Rex Reason (Prof. Cal Meacham), Faith Domergue (Dr. Ruth Adams), Lance Fuller (Brak), Russell Johnson (Steve Carlson), Robert Nichols (Joe Wilson), Douglas Spencer (The Monitor), Karl Lindt (Dr. Adolph Engelborg).

Color by Technicolor; 86 minutes; released June 1955.

Science fiction fans have an insatiable appetite for finding "hidden truths" about their favorite films and filmmakers. In this instance, many sources report (and seemingly are confirmed by Universal's own catalog of nontheatrical films) that Jack Arnold directed the Metaluna sequences in the second half of the film.

The Tingler
Production William Castle/Robb White Productions, *Producer-Director* William Castle, *Story and Screenplay* Robb White, *Photography* Wilfred M. Cline, *Music* Von Dexter, *Art Direction* Phil Bennett, *Editor* Chester Schaeffer, *Distribution* Columbia Pictures.

CAST: Vincent Price (Dr. Warren Chapin), Judith Evelyn (Mrs. Higgins), Darryl Hickman (David Morris), Patricia Cutts (Isabel Chapin), Philip Coolidge (Ollie Higgins), Pamela Lincoln (Lucy Stevens).

Black and White with Color sequence in middle; 82 minutes; released October 1959.

Robb White's story for *The Tingler*, like Jimmy Sangster's story for *X–The Unknown* described in the main text, is wonderfully absurd. In the language of scientism, the story theorizes that humans die of fright because fear allows a creature to grow unchecked inside the spine. If the victim fails to scream, the "tingler" grows out of control and eventually causes death. To prove the theory, a deaf woman frightened at the sight of blood is scared to death by such ordinary household objects as faucets dripping blood and a bathtub full of blood. The tingler grows so unstable that it is removed from the body by pathologist Vincent Price and accidentally let loose inside a movie theatre. The tingler is caught and returned to the body of the deaf woman; she then returns to life and kills her husband, who had rigged all the household items to drip blood and thereby scare her to death.

Tobor the Great
Production Dudley Pictures, *Director* Lee Sholem, *Producer* Richard Goldstone, *Screenplay* Philip MacDonald, *Story* Carl Dudley, *Photography* John L.

Russell, *Special Photography* Howard and Theodore Lydecker, *Music* Howard Jackson, *Art Direction* Gabriel Scognamillo, *Editor* Basil Wrangell, *Distribution* Republic Pictures.

CAST: Charles Drake (Dr. Ralph Harrison), Karin Booth (Janice Robertson), Billy Chapin (Gadge Robertson), Taylor Holmes (Dr. Nordstrom), Lew Smith (Tobor), Peter Brocco (Dr. Gustav), Henry Kulky (Paul), Hal Baylor (Max).

Black and White; 77 minutes; released September 1954.

Twenty Million Miles to Earth

Production Morningside Productions, *Director* Nathan Juran, *Producer* Charles H. Schneer, *Screenplay* Bob Williams and Christopher Knopf, *Story* Charlotte Knight, *Photography* Irving Lippman and Carlos Ventigmilla, *Special Photography* Ray Harryhausen, *Music Director* Mischa Bakaleinikoff, *Art Direction* Cary Odell, *Editor* Edwin Bryant, *Distribution* Columbia Pictures.

CAST: William Hopper (Col. Bob Calder), Joan Taylor (Marisa), Frank Puglia (Dr. Leonardo), John Zaremba (Dr. Judson Uhl), Thomas Browne Henry (Gen. A. D. MacIntosh), Jan Arvan (Signor Contino), Arthur Space (Dr. Sharman).

Black and White; 84 minutes; released July 1957 on double bill with *The 27th Day*.

The 27th Day

Production Romson Productions, *Director* William Asher, *Producer* Helen Ainsworth, *Story and Screenplay* John Mantley, *Photography* Henry Freulich, *Music Director* Mischa Bakaleinikoff, *Art Direction* Ross Bellah, *Editor* Jerome Thoms, *Distribution* Columbia Pictures.

CAST: Gene Barry (Jonathan Clark), Valerie French (Eve Wingate), George Voskovec (Prof. Klaus Bechner), Azenath Janti (Ivan Godofsky), Marie Tsien (Su Tan), Stefan Schnabel (The Leader), Arnold Moss (The Alien), Frederick Ledebur (Dr. Karl Neuhaus).

Black and White; 74 minutes; released July 1957 on double bill with *Twenty Million Miles to Earth*.

The Twonky

Production Arch Oboler Productions, *Producer-Director* Arch Oboler, *Screenplay* Arch Oboler, *Story* [short story] Lewis Padgett, *Photography* Joseph Biroc, *Music* Jack Meakin, *Editor* Betty Steinberg, *Distribution* United Artists.

CAST: Hans Conried (Kerry West), Gloria Blondell (Eloise), Janet Warren (Caroline West), Billy Lynn (Coach Trout), Ed Max (Ed), Norman Field (Doctor), Steve Roberts (Government Agent).

Black and White; 72 minutes; released June 1953.

The Unearthly

Production AB-PT, *Producer-Director* Brooke L. Peters, *Screenplay* Geoffrey Davis and Jane Mann, *Story* Jane Mann, *Photography* Merle Connell, *Music* Henry Vars and Michael Terr, *Art Direction* Dan Hall, *Editor* Richard Currier, *Distribution* Republic Pictures.

CAST: John Carradine (Prof. Charles Conway), Allison Hayes (Grace Thomas), Myron Healy (Mark Houston), Sally Todd (Natalie), Tor Johnson (Lobo).

Black and White; 73 minutes; released June 1957 on double bill with *The Beginning of the End*.

Unidentified Flying Objects

Production Ivan Tors Films, *Director* No credits, *Producer* Clarence Greene, *Story and Screenplay* Francis Martin, *Photography* Howard Anderson, Ed Fitzgerald, and Bert Spielvogel, *Music* Ernest Gold, *Editor* Chester Schaeffer, *Distribution* United Artists.

CAST: Tom Powers as Albert M. Chop/Narrator.

Black and White with Color sequences; 92 minutes; released April 1956.

An interesting documentary from Ivan Tors on the many UFO sightings in the fifties. The film contains purportedly real footage of UFOs taken by various professional and amateur photographers. The scenes with Powers as reporter Al Chop are dramatized, and the final sequence involving Air Force jets chasing UFOs is quite suspenseful. There is no director's credit, but many sources credit Winston Jones.

The Unknown Terror

Production Emirau Productions and Regal Films Inc., *Director* Charles Marquis Warren, *Producer* Robert Stabler, *Story and Screenplay* Kenneth Higgins, *Photography* Joseph Biroc, *Music* Raoul Kraushaar, *Art Direction* James Sullivan, *Editor* Fred W. Berger, *Distribution* Twentieth Century-Fox.

CAST: John Howard (Dan Mathews), Mala Powers (Gina Mathews), Paul Richards (Pete Morgan), Gerald Milton (Dr. Ramsey), May Wynn (Concha), Martin Garralaga (Old Indian).

Black and White in Regalscope; 76 minutes; released September 1957 on double bill with *Back from the Dead.*

The Vampire

Production Gramercy Pictures, *Director* Paul Landres, *Producers* Arthur Gardner and Jules V. Levy, *Story and Screenplay* Pat Fielder, *Photography* Jack MacKenzie, *Music* Gerald Fried, *Art Direction* James Vance, *Editor* John Faure, *Distribution* United Artists.

CAST: John Beal (Dr. Paul Beecher), Coleen Gray (Carol Butler), Kenneth Tobey (Detective Buck Donnelly), Lydia Reed (Betsy Beecher), Dabbs Greer (Dr. Will Beaumont), Herb Vigran (George Ryan), James Griffith (Henry Winston).

Black and White; 75 minutes; released June 1957 on double bill with *The Monster That Challenged the World.*

Village of the Damned (British)

Production MGM, *Director* Wolf Rilla, *Producer* Ronald Kinnoch, *Screenplay* Sterling Silliphant, Wolf Rilla, and George Barclay, *Story* [novel, *The Midwich Cuckoos]* John Wyndham, *Photography* Geoffrey Faithfull, *Special Photography* Tom Howard, *Music* Ron Goodwin, *Art Direction* Ivan King, *Editor* Gordon Hales, *Distribution* Metro-Goldwyn-Mayer.

CAST: George Sanders (Gordon Zellaby), Barbara Shelley (Anthea Zellaby), Michael Gwynn (Maj. Alan Bernard), Martin Stephans (David), Laurence Naismith (Dr. Willers), John Phillips (General Leighton), Richard Vernon (Sir Edgar Hargraves), Jenny Laird (Mrs. Harrington), Richard Warner (Mr. Harrington), Thomas Heathcote (James Pawle).

Black and White; 78 minutes; released December 1960.

Visit to a Small Planet

Production Hal Wallis Productions, *Director* Norman Taurog, *Producer* Hal B. Wallis, *Screenplay* Edmund Beloin and Henry Garson, *Story* [television play] Gore Vidal, *Photography* Loyal Griggs, *Special Photography* John P. Fulton, *Music* Leigh Harline, *Art Direction* Hal Pereira and Walter Tyler, *Editor* Frank Bracht, *Distribution* Paramount Pictures.

CAST: Jerry Lewis (Kreton), Joan Blackman (Ellen Spelding), Earl Holliman (Conrad), Fred Clark (Roger Putnam Spelding), Lee Patrick (Rheba Spelding), Gale Gordon (Bob Mayberry), Jerome Cowan (George Abercrombie), John Williams (Delton), Barbara Lawson (Beatnik Dancer).

Black and White; 85 minutes; released April 1960.

War of the Colossal Beast
Production Carmel Productions, *Producer-Director* Bert I. Gordon, *Screenplay* George Worthing Yates, *Story* Bert I. Gordon, *Photography* Jack Marta, *Special Photography* Bert I. Gordon and Flora M. Gordon, *Music* Albert Glasser, *Art Direction* Walter Keller, *Editor* Ronald Sinclair, *Distribution* James H. Nicholson and Samuel Z. Arkoff through American International Pictures.
Cast: Sally Fraser (Joyce Manning), Dean Parkin (Col. Glenn Manning), Roger Pace (Major Baird), Russ Bender (Dr. Carmichael), Charles Stewart (Captain Harris), George Becwar (Swanson), Robert Hernandez (Miguel).
Black and White with final scene in Color; 68 minutes; released August 1958 on double bill with *Attack of the Puppet People*.

War of the Satellites
Production Santa Cruz Productions, *Producer-Director* Roger Corman, *Screenplay* Lawrence Louis Goldman, *Story* Jack Rabin and Irving Block, *Photography* Floyd Crosby, *Special Photography* Jack Rabin, Irving Block, and Louis DeWitt, *Music* Walter Greene, *Art Direction* Daniel Haller, *Editor* Irene Morra, *Distribution* Allied Artists Pictures Corporation.
Cast: Susan Cabot (Sybil Carrington), Dick Miller (Dave Boyer), Richard Devon (Dr. Van Ponder), Robert Shayne (Hodkiss), Jerry Barclay (John), Eric Sinclair (Dr. Lazar), Michael Fox (Akad), Jay Sayer (Jay), Mitzi McCall (Mitzi).
Black and White; 66 minutes; released May 1958 on double bill with *Attack of the Fifty Foot Woman*.

War of the Worlds
Production Paramount, *Director* Byron Haskin, *Producer* George Pal, *Screenplay* Barré Lyndon, *Story* [novel] H. G. Wells, *Photography* George Barnes, *Special Photography* Gordon Jennings, Wallace Kelley, Chester Pate, Bob Springfield, Paul K. Lerpae, Jack Caldwell, *Music* Leith Stevens, *Art Direction* Hal Pereira and Albert Nozaki, *Editor* Everett Douglas, *Distribution* Paramount Pictures.
Cast: Gene Barry (Dr. Clayton Forrester), Ann Robinson (Sylvia Van Buren), Les Tremayne (General Mann), Lewis Martin (Pastor Matthew Collins), Robert Cornthwaite (Dr. Pryor), Sandro Giglio (Dr. Bilderbeck).
Color by Technicolor; 85 minutes; released October 1953.

The Wasp Woman
Production Santa Clara Productions, *Producer-Director* Roger Corman, *Screenplay* Leo Gordon, *Story* Kinta Zertuche, *Photography* Harry Newman, *Music* Fred Katz, *Art Direction* Daniel Haller, *Editor* Carlo Lodato, *Distribution* Filmgroup.
Cast: Susan Cabot (Janice Starlin), Fred [later Anthony] Eisley (Bill), Barboura Morris (Mary), Michael Marks (Dr. Zinthrop), William Roerick (Cooper), Frank Gerstle (Hellman).
Black and White; 66 minutes; released October 1959 on double bill with *Beast from Haunted Cave*.

The Werewolf
Production Clover Productions, *Director* Fred F. Sears, *Producer* Sam Katzman, *Story and Screenplay* Robert E. Kent and James B. Gordon, *Photography* Edwin Linden, *Music Director* Mischa Bakaleinikoff, *Art Direction* Paul Palmentola, *Editor* Harold White, *Distribution* Columbia Pictures.
Cast: Don Megowan (Sheriff Jack Haines), Joyce Holden (Amy Standish), Steven Ritch (Duncan Marsh), S. John Launer (Dr. Emery Forrest), George M. Lynn (Dr. Morgan Chambers), Harry Lauter (Clovey).
Black and White; 79 minutes; released July 1956 on double bill with *Earth vs. the Flying Saucers*.

Woodpecker from Mars
Production Walter Lantz Productions, *Director* Paul J. Smith, *Producer* Walter Lantz, *Distribution* Universal-International; no other credits available.
Color by Technicolor; 7 minutes; a Woody Woodpecker cartoon; released July 1956.

X–The Unknown (British)
Production Hammer Films, *Director* Leslie Norman, *Producer* Anthony Hinds, *Story and Screenplay* Jimmy Sangster, *Photography* Gerald Gibbs, *Special Photography* Bowie/Margutti Ltd., *Music* James Bernard, *Art Direction* Bernard Robinson, *Editor* James Needs, *Distribution* Sol Lesser Productions through Warner Brothers.
CAST: Dean Jagger (Dr. Adam Royston), Leo McKern (McGill), Edward Chapman (John Elliott), William Lucas (Peter Elliott), John Harvey (Maj. Cartwright), Anthony Newley (Cpl. Webb), Ian MacNaughton (Haggit), Peter Hammond (Lt. Bannerman), Michael Ripper (Sgt. Grimsdyke), Marianne Brauns (Zena).
Black and White; 78 minutes; released in USA July 1957 on double bill with *The Curse of Frankenstein*.

Zombies of the Stratosphere
Production Republic Pictures, *Director* Fred C. Brannon, *Producer* Franklin Adreon [listed in credits as "Associate Producer"], *Story and Screenplay* Ronald Davidson, *Photography* John MacBurnie, *Special Photography* Howard and Theodore Lydecker, *Music* Stanley Wilson, *Art Direction* Fred Ritter, *Editor* Cliff Bell, *Distribution* Republic Pictures.
CAST: Judd Holdren (Larry Martin), Aline Towne (Sue Davis), Wilson Wood (Bob Wilson), Lane Bradford (Marex), Stanley Waxman (Harding), John Crawford (Roth), Craig Kelly (Steele), Leonard Nimoy (Narab).
Black and White; released 1952; a serial in twelve chapters: (1) *The Zombie Vanguard*, (2) *Battle of the Rockets*, (3) *Undersea Agents*, (4) *Contraband Cargo*, (5) *The Iron Executioner*, (6) *Murder Mine*, (7) *Death on the Waterfront*, (8) *Hostage for Murder*, (9) *The Human Torpedo*, (10) *Flying Gas Chamber*, (11) *Man vs. Monster*, (12) *Tomb of the Traitors;* feature version entitled *Satan's Satellites* released May 1958 on double bill with *Missile Monsters*.

Index

EDITOR: Kenneth Goodall
BOOK DESIGNER: Matt Williamson
JACKET DESIGNER: Matt Williamson
PRODUCTION COORDINATOR: Harriet Curry
TYPEFACE: Aster with Korinna
TYPESETTER: Kachina Typesetting, Inc.
PRINTER: Thomson-Shore, Inc.
PAPER: 60 lb. Warren's old style
BINDER: John H. Dekker and Sons, Inc.

PATRICK LUCANIO has served as visiting instructor of film history at the University of Oregon. His areas of interest include genre studies and the history of Hollywood film.